SACRED ADVENTURE

Beginning Theological Study

William C. Graham

With Contributions by:

Avery Dulles, SJ, Michael P. Horan, Dominic Colonna,
Mark McVann, FSC, Alan Revering, Andrew Krivak,
Curtiss S. DeMars Johnson, Molly K. Stein, Julia Upton, RSM,
G. Penny Nixon, Martin Carney, Johann Vento, Lee Stuart,
Stephen Maret, Rose Zuzworsky, et al.

University Press of America,® Inc.
Lanham · New York · Oxford

Copyright © 1999 by
University Press of America,® Inc.
4720 Boston Way
Lanham, Maryland 20706

12 Hid's Copse Rd.
Cumnor Hill, Oxford OX2 9JJ

Library of Congress Cataloging-in-Publication Data

Graham, William C.
Sacred adventure : beginning theological study / William C. Graham;
with contributions by Avery Dulles. . . (et al.).
p.   cm
Includes bibliographical references and index.
1. Catholic Church—Doctrines. 2. Theology, Doctrinal Introduction.
I. Dulles, Avery Robert. II. Title.
BX1751.2.G694   1999   230'.071'1—dc21   99-34527 CIP

ISBN 0-7618-1445-0 (pbk. : alk. ppr.)

Dedicated to

Sister Maura Campbell, OP

whose love of learning

has inspired generations

of students and colleagues

What has been is what will be,
and what has been done is what will be done;
and there is nothing new under the sun.
-Ecclesiastes 1:9

And the One who sat upon the throne said,
'Behold, I make all things new.'
-Revelation 21:5

Say ye: 'We believe
In God, and the revelation
Given to us, and to Abraham
Isma'il, Isaac, Jacob,
And all the Tribes, and that given
To Moses and Jesus, and that given
To (all) Prophets from their Lord:
We make no difference
Between one and another of them:
And we bow to God (in Islam).'
-Qur'an 2:136

*The shell must break
before the bird can fly.*
-Alfred, Lord Tennyson (1809-1892)

*The greatest discovery of my generation
is that a human being can alter his life
by altering his attitudes of mind.*
-William James (1842-1910)

*The real voyage of discovery
consists not in seeking new landscapes,
but in having new eyes.*
-Marcel Proust (1871-1922)

*there is so much to touch,
but it is inches from reach.*
-Robert Louis Marsh, Jr.
Caldwell College graduate, 1995

A Scholar's Prayer

God of all creation,
we come before you
perceiving that we have little time
for all that needs to be done.
We ask you to help us develop a sense of priorities.
Help us use our daily gift of time
to do all the things that need to be done.
Give us patience and strength
to adjust to when unexpected people and
events demand our time.
Grant us a wider perspective on our days.
Give us the vision to see these times
as working toward a purposeful end
and as times of possibility for those you love.
Into your hands, we commit our bodies and our spirits.
Lead us to purposeful days and restful nights.
Grant us your Spirit
and help us to recognize and fulfill your will
in all the demands of our lives.
Amen.

–An anonymous prayer
rewritten by Joseph Simplicio, Ph.D.
Caldwell College

Prayer of St. Thomas Aquinas

Grant, O merciful God,
that I may ardently desire,
prudently examine,
truthfully acknowledge,
and perfectly accomplish
what is pleasing to you
for the praise and glory
of your name.

Amen.

Prayer: Discussion Questions

1.) What is asked for in the Scholar's Prayer? Why?
2.) Why might St. Thomas's prayer be uttered by any person of prayer, any place and any time?

Contents

Faith, Religion, Theology, and Biblical Studies

Christianity

Continuing Concerns

Ten Tips for Beginning College Well

How very exciting it is to be a college freshman, preparing to begin classes and a new life. Each faculty member that you will meet, and all who wrote for you in this book, have been before where you are today. Faculty members bring what we have learned from those who have taught us. We bring also our unique heritage, our gifts, our stories, our traditions. Imagine the years of study and travel and opportunity represented in any college faculty. We Doctors, then, are not pediatricians, or orthodontists or veterinarians, but we are the very first doctors, those first to hold the title flowing from its Latin root, *docere*, to teach.

Here is the faculty's task: to invite, to teach, to spread before you wisdom's table, that you might eat and drink of what holy wisdom has prepared for you. Being a college student is very, very different from being a student in a technical institute. We will not teach you to weld or to sew. We will not put stuff into your heads so much as we will challenge you to read and reach and stretch and grow and think and judge. We will take great delight and count it an enormous privilege to spread the table before you. But you must come freely, to eat and drink of what holy wisdom offers if you are to be strong, loving and wise. Here is the secret of wisdom's table: it never ends. It goes on forever, and you are never filled. You will know that you are at the table if it brings life. If it brings death or destruction, you are eating at the wrong table.

If you choose to be strong, loving and wise, if you will succeed as a college student, there are **Ten Paths** that you must follow. As you read about them, keep count of how many you are prepared to follow. Those who say, "Yes, that's me!" ten times are already on the road to graduation with honors. Those who say, "Yes, here I am!" nine times are sure to find themselves on the Dean's List. A score of eight is still excellent, and seven quite good. If you are prepared to follow fewer than six of these suggestions, have a stern talk with yourself right away today to be sure that your priorities are in order for a successful and happy college experience. Remember, we can only offer and suggest. You get to choose.

Path One: Believe in yourself. You can be a successful college student. If you couldn't do it, you would not have been admitted into college. Already, any number of people have expressed plenty of confidence in your abilities. You must be as well. There are students who choose not to succeed; don't be one of them.

Two: Introduce your posterior to the library chairs. Learn to sit there for long stretches. A college degree is no proof that one is brilliant. What a true student does have is a butt made out of cast iron. Sit. Study. Then you will succeed.

Three: Treat study as your job and your duty. Make a study schedule and stick to it. Many students divide their time between studying, and worrying that they are not studying. Don't fall into that trap. Study first, play when study is complete. You have heard it before: one hour in class requires two in preparation. If you are taking 15 credits, you have more than the equivalent of a full time job.

Four: Don't forget to play. Remember that the people you meet in college are very likely to be your friends and associates all the days of your life. Cherish them. Delight in those late night conversations when you know that you have found your soul-mates. Know and appreciate every day that you are standing on holy ground. And do not ever be bored. Even the smallest campuses have libraries through which you have access to every great and worthwhile thought ever recorded. Know and appreciate that fact.

Five: Don't believe that some quick swigs of Mad Dog 20/20 will make history or philosophy more exciting. Marijuana will not make you an artist. Crack and cocaine will not make you more sophisticated. Alcohol and drug abuse will scuttle your college career. If you see your friends enter this dark world, you must not sit quietly and let it happen. Be smart. And, remember that the weekend does not begin on Thursday.

Six: Know that what happens at your College is important for your salvation, and for the salvation of all the world. The leisure that is ours to study and think, to exchange ideas freely is a great privilege. If we who have the leisure to study and to think cannot be at peace, sharing residence halls and parking lots and dining rooms, if we cannot live and model peace, then there will be no peace. There will be no peace at the College or in our cities, and there will be no peace on earth. In our diversity, we must go beyond tolerance. Beyond multiculturalism. Go for shalom, the recognition of God within. Tolerance simply means putting up with someone or something–and that is hardly a standard from which life can spring.

Seven: Know when to look for help. It is the rare human who will not occasionally need a sympathetic ear and some sense of direction. There are times you need to have a listener who is not a member of your peer group. Before even you need the folks who are available to you in Campus Ministry and in the Counseling Office. Stop to see a favorite professor, and ask if you can sit to chat. The wise will know when it is time to share difficult moments. None of us can do it alone. You cannot be strong, loving or wise without knowing how, where and when to ask for help.

Eight: Visit with your professors. If you were not here, neither would we be here. We want to know you. Stop into our offices. Most professors in most places want to meet and know you. If you want to know if a certain department or class might fit you, stop in, say hello, ask. Do not be timid. Walk right up.

Nine: Do not abandon your traditions. We who are Jews and Christians and Muslims are people of the Book, relying on God's promise. All of us, with our Buddhist and Hindu friends, with all who seek God or seek truth with sincere hearts, must remain faithful, seeking new ways to live ancient truths. Don't wander far from what is so very precious. Our heritage is to seek the truth. You cannot do this while watching television. Go, or go back, to the synagogue, church, mosque or temple.

Ten: Come with eager joy to wisdom's table. Auntie Mame, in that great Broadway extravaganza, had wonderful insight. Maybe you saw the movie in which Lucille Ball played Auntie Mame. "Life's a banquet," said she, "but most poor suckers are starving to death." You can excuse her crude language, I hope, even while you appreciate her sense of urgency. Do not starve. Come, share in the feast which has been prepared for you!

Acknowledgements

For the reprinting of material in this volume that is not in the public domain or within the fair-use practice, the editor and the publisher of *Sacred Adventure: Beginning Theological Study* are grateful to the copyright holders of the titles cities below for the permission received.

A Time for Resurrection first appeared in the April/May 1987 issue of *Today's Parish*, Vol. 19, No. 4.

The Key to Prayer is from *More Urgent Than Usual: The Final Homilies of Mark Hollenhorst*, edited by William C. Graham (Collegeville, MN: The Liturgical Press, 1995).

What We Dare to Say! first appeared in *Celebration* (February 1999).

The Welcoming Spirit was originally published in *Outlook*, The newspaper for the diocese of Duluth in Minnesota.

The Basic Teaching of Vatican II was originally published as Chapter 2 or *The Reshaping of Catholicism: Current Challenges in the Theology of Church*, by Avery Dulles, SJ (San Francisco: Harper&Row Publishers, 1988).

Spike and the Diminished Body of Christ first appeared in the November 23, 1996, Volume 175, No. 16 issue of *America.*

The Sadness of a City first appeared in the July 5-12, 1997, Volume 177, No. 1, issue of *America.*

From *An Aquinas Reader*, edited, with an introduction by Mary T. Clark (Garden City, NY: Doubleday, 1972).

I am grateful to all who, in any way and many ways, have contributed to getting this work into print:

The authors, as well as the copyright holders of the previously published articles, stories, hymns and poems;

Caldwell College in Caldwell, New Jersey, which provided space and resources;

Br. Mark McVann of Lewis University who offered many valuable additional suggestions;

A Caldwell scholar, Orsolya Pandi, who assisted in the preparation of the final manuscript; and,

Finally and especially, my students at Caldwell College who, by their perceptive questions and comments, helped shape this discussion.

To all who assisted, I am happy to offer thanks. However, any shortcomings in this text are my responsibility alone.

William C. Graham
Saturday of Lent Three
Caldwell, NJ
13 March 1999

Sacred Adventure: An Introduction

"Adventure. Sure," snorts the student. Already, she or he has logged at least twelve years of study, and knows that the kind of vicarious adventure to be found in a textbook is not that of gliding down a crystal path on cross country skis, jumping the silver wake on a slalom, or pursuing the quarterback down a field bounded by loud and happy fans. Can theology's thrill be the equivalent of white water rafting? A late night stroll down the great Broadway?

Yes. With richer reward. And greater danger as well.

Annie Dillard, an author who is impressively attentive to the holy which surrounds us, suggests that worshippers are not, in her view, very sensible. She asks, "Does anyone have the foggiest idea what sort of power we so blithely invoke?" No more velvet hats in church, writes she. Rather, crash helmets ought to be the order of the day. And "Ushers should issue life preservers and signal flares; they should lash us to our pews." Such is the power of the God we invoke who "may draw us out to where we can never return."

This study on which you embark is a beginning consideration of Christianity, a tradition which seeks to hear God's voice. Sometimes clearly and distinctly. Sometimes as if it is dark night.

God calls, and humanity is to pick up the phone. The authors of this text invite you to begin with them the study of call and response. This study is an adventure because religion's task is to contemplate the unknown. Guides have gone before us, but we do not know entirely or see completely what faith assures is so. Humankind, alone and together, considers the invitation and embarks on the trek. Or, one can stay home to watch sit-com reruns.

Here are issues of life, of mercy, of wickedness and repentance, of Love which knows no bounds. The brave will enter, the thoughtful will encounter the mystery, the sensitive will be touched and formed, the inquisitive will be challenged.

This study is not one more catechism class. The point is not to convert or indoctrinate. This pursuit is academic. However, most theologians are people of faith. In fact, St. Anselm of Canterbury wrote in the eleventh century that theology is faith seeking understanding. A consideration of the discipline of theology is an important part of a liberal education. It is possible to make this study either as a person of faith, or as an inquirer, as a curious person, even as an outsider looking in. Actually, no one practices all three of the major monotheistic religions. Anyone who reads this text, whether a person of one or another faith, will be an outsider looking in at how other groups pray, practice, and theologize. The hope is that the student will see both the interconnectedness and the distinct features of all religions in hearing and responding to God's call.

The real adventure, then, is twofold: one can either make the encounter with the holy or consider vicariously the adventures of those who have done so.

The authors represented here are among the clearest of theological thinkers. Their special skill is not just understanding theology, but presenting it in an understandable way. The typical reader of this text will have completed high school, and is now beginning college. Many students assert that they have encountered a vast number of boring teachers. Whether or not that is the case, all of us who have been students remember, or ought to, what it feels like to be overwhelmed by new material, or to be uninterested in a topic because of the manner of presentation. Because I have spent long hours in classrooms where the promise of the moment was not immediately evident to me, my firm resolution as a teacher has been to present the matter under consideration in as lively a manner as possible. To that end, I have invited scholars who have intrigued me both with their insights as well as with their style to be part of this book. If these writers fail to intrigue and challenge, then perhaps that task cannot be accomplished.

Consider these insights, embark on this adventure confident that you will encounter not magic but mystery, not rote answers but inviting questions. Here is the stuff of which dreams are made and worlds redeemed. Enter this study carefully because if you feel impelled and drawn, you will emerge new and different, closer to being both whole and holy.

William C. Graham

Faith, Religion, Theology: Coming to Terms with Being Human

Michael P. Horan

Introduction

My students have taught me a great deal about faith, religion and theology. In turn I've taught them something about the relationship among these terms, and together we have explored the concepts beneath the words. In what follows we will consider the insights and assumptions which students often bring to the academic study of theology, or formal reflection on Christian faith. We will do this by "coming to terms" with the terms themselves. In doing so we will consider how faith, religion and theology respond to human needs. The needs which arise from being human are the need to trust, the need to connect with others, and the need to make sense of our experience. Faith relates to the human need to trust. Religion arises from the human need to connect with others. Theology grows out of our human drive toward intelligibility or understanding, our need to "make sense" of faith.

Models of Faith: Starting with Human Beings

When asked to identify people who make Christian faith worth believing today, university students frequently name their parents or grandparents, as well as teachers or coaches from their youth who took an interest in them. These people are the ones whom students in college often recognize as those who "planted seeds" without forcing growth. What is striking about the students' recollections is that, in the course of their analysis, they generally include a practical distinction between religion and faith, or sometimes between religion and spirituality. My students are not so certain that religion is a good thing, but they clearly are attracted to models of faith or models of spirituality. That is, the students know when they have met a "person of faith." But what exactly is faith? Students seem less clear about that. With this question in mind, let us turn to an examination of the term itself, with a view to its use in Christian tradition.

Faith in Christian Tradition:
Being Human Means Trusting and Believing

Faith as Trust

The term *faith* is used in two senses in the Christian tradition. On the one hand, faith refers to the action of trusting, that free gift of God which is inside the human heart and which allows us to trust anyone or anything outside ourselves. In its barest sense, we trust all the time. We trust that the building in which our class is held will not fall down as we study. When we apply the brake pedal in the car, we trust that the brakes will work for the safety of all. In fact, buildings do fall during earthquakes and car brakes *do* fail at times. Yet our basic attitude of trust remains intact. That is, after all, a healthy response to reality. Were we to try to anticipate every accident, we could not have any real relationship with the world. We would need to sit at home in the dark, under house arrest by fear of the outside world, frightened that our home might catch fire even as we sit stunned by the potential world of accidents.

Healthy people trust the essential goodness of reality, allowing us in turn to be in relationship with the world. Healthy people also trust other persons. Sometimes that trust is violated, and we are disappointed and hurt by friends. Yet we continue to trust that most people are trustworthy most of the time. If we were unable to trust in others, we would have no friendships in our lives.

Faith, as that openness to trust God, is both different from and similar to the experience of trusting reality and other people. It is different because, at least in the beginning of the journey of faith, it appears that trusting God is more difficult than trusting reality or people. After all, with events and people, we get signals that encourage us to go forward in trust, or warnings that caution us. With God, invisible and mysterious, there are fewer external signals which either validate or challenge our initial trust.

But our experience of trusting God is similar to trusting reality or persons because trust is a requirement for getting to know God. It is the necessary ingredient for the start of any relationship. We know that this is true of friendships with people. Somehow we generally forget that when we consider the faith relationship. Our desire motivates us to trust other persons. In the same way, Christians throughout the ages have understood faith as that posture or attitude of trusting that allows for the possibility of a relationship in the first place. And it seems that "people of faith," at least those whom college students identify as such, possess that trust. They know that there is more to reality than meets the eye, and they do not sit at home until they are sure that the world is accident free, devoid of risk. On the contrary, they recognize that life would be very dull if they took no risks at all. And they seem to be open to relationships which really grow through trust. And still these people often tell others that their trust in God is validated with "signals" that God hears them and is in relationship with them.

Faith as Belief

There is a second sense in which Christians use the term "faith," and this second sense relates to the first sense, that of faith as trust. For if we trust, our trust has some object. People often say to each other: "I trust you," or "I believe in you." Christians often speak about faith as the content or the object of trust. This content refers to the truth or the teachings that have been "revealed," or made manifest in the experience of being human and the experience of reflecting on the story of Jesus Christ as lived out in the community. In this sense, the terms "faith" and "belief" are similar. Christian faith has a unique content; that content is distinct from the content of other religious faiths because it is centered on Christ. In his particular time and place, Jesus' life revealed the deep truth about God's intention from all eternity to be in relationship with humans through our humanity, not in spite of it.

Religion: Being Human Means Connecting

So far we have discussed the need to trust in order for relationship to occur in the human situation, even if that relationship is one between humans and God. But why religion? After all, as my students have pointed out very persuasively, religion has been associated with violence and wars, internal strife, financial and sexual misconduct by religious leaders, and it has been the cause of numerous arguments in homes throughout the world. So is it worthwhile, and do we need it? To these questions disciples in the steady stream of Christian history reply:

"By all means we need religion because we need each other." If the Christian revelation were a private and individual one, then it could not be shared, but the interesting thing about the tradition is its fundamentally communal character.

The term "religion" means "to bind together in relationship" or "to betroth," as lovers commit themselves to each other. It connotes the human quest for meaning which is never done in isolation. Humans need to verify assumptions, to discuss feelings, to raise questions to more hearers than their own consciences, and to act on their convictions so that their world is in turn formed and reformed by beliefs about what really matters in life. If all the world's religions were to go "out of business" tomorrow, others would develop to take their place. The human need for community is the fuel that helps to carry the individual spiritual experiences of human beings to others. In turn, community is the medium through which life's meaning and values are communicated to the religious community's newcomers. Institutions grow up from these needs. Sometimes institutions, comprised as they are of people who make mistakes, do not faithfully reflect their own best founding values. Yet the need for institutions does not recede as long as people gather to share their experiences. Organizations try to respond to the needs of their members. In falling short of the mark, they remind all of us of the truth that none of us is perfect.

Theology: Being Human Means Questioning

Is faith blind? Or is faith supposed to have sight? If being human means trusting (and thus faith) and connecting (therefore the need for religions), then being human also means thinking, questioning, and probing for meaning and understanding about what life is telling us. In the case of faith, particularly the religious faith of the Christian community, there is a natural need for making sense of religious experience. Theology is the activity that pursues and helps to fulfill that need.

In current society one of the sources of suspicion of religion appears to be the groups of Christians as well as others who insist that one does not have faith unless it means surrender of the mind. Phrases like "blind faith" arise from this assumption. Unfortunately this approach does not respect the full humanity of human beings, since the capacity to think is respected by Christians as a gift from God. Therefore to reject that gift in favor of blind faith respects neither humanity nor Christianity.

Christian theologians describe theology with the classic phrase "faith seeking understanding." This phrase comes from the writing of St. Anselm of Canterbury (d. 1109), who made faith intelligible to his students nearly a millennium ago. Even then Anselm wanted people to understand that faith statements, or beliefs, cry out to be illumined with reason and imagination, both faculties of the mind. For without the activity of the intellect faith claims are merely words which carry little capacity for meaning in the life of the human being. In recent times theologies of liberation have challenged that earlier definition from Anselm, and invite the Christian community to understand theology as "critical reflection upon action." Liberation theologies, frequently called "contextual theologies," engage people about the ways in which God discloses truth: God does so in concert with us, by means of human experience and action on behalf of the gospel. Since action often includes work for the justice and dignity of all people as children of God, the task pursued in liberation theologies has to do with making sense of the gospel in a world of human suffering, for it must be good news for everyone, or else it is good news for no one. Those who have suffered are the very ones whom Jesus counted as friends: the poor, victims of racism like the Samaritans, women everywhere. Hence theologies of economic liberation from Latin America, along with theologies done in the African American, Caribbean, African and Asian contexts, as well as feminist theologies of many kinds can be found among the most recent theological texts which grace libraries and challenge the minds of their readers. New theologies often challenge the assumptions made by the theologians of an earlier time. This is true for contextual theologies, for they invite their participants to search out the untold stories in the Bible and Christian tradition, and to acknowledge the cultural bias which to date has allowed theologians to ignore altogether or to whisper cautiously the truth that Jesus brought a new understanding of the reign of God. The Lord's vision of the reign freed captives of the society of his day, and it remains liberating news for those who currently uncover, recover, or discover for the first time the power of the gospel to change hearts, to erase prejudice, and to weed out injustice.

Theologies of liberation also function as a healthy reminder of the ways in which Christian theology first began, at a time when dedicated disciples gathered in homes around eucharistic tables; there they made sense of their experience of suffering and mourning at the death of the Lord, and derived hope and consolation from reflections on the promise that the Lord's reign was hardly over at his execution; indeed, it had hardly begun. The good news of the gospel was and remains that death, suffering and oppression do not have the final word.

Theology: A Generalized and a Specialized Pursuit

People theologize whether they know it or not. Whenever Christians gather to reflect on the meaning of their faith, they are doing theology in an informal sense. The human quest for meaning is endless and essential to human history. While this kind of theology may properly be termed informal or implicit theology, there is also another kind of theology.

The Christian tradition contains a rich heritage of peoples' formal efforts to do theology. The quest for deeper insight into the gospel causes professional theologians to study ancient languages in order to understand the intentions of the writers of scripture. This same need propels people to step back from the language of communal faith statements, known as creeds, and to make sense of Christian belief in fresh language. This effort, known as systematic theology, uses philosophy, among other disciplines, in order to express and enhance the understanding of the tradition for a contemporary generation. Moral theology engages the human questioner about the impact that Christian faith can have on the formation of society and individual character (personal ethics) as well as on the actions of the world and its people (social ethics). These are only some of the branches of theology, signaling some of the ways in which theology attempts to give expression to peoples' search for meaning and value in the world today.

The Role of Theology in the University

Specifically within the Catholic Christian tradition, theology has played a major role in the life of the faith community. In our own time, Catholic colleges and universities attest to the Catholic commitment to the intellectual life and its relationship to religious faith by encouraging, often requiring, students to study theology. Frequently these courses open up the possibility for students to question the teachings to which they were exposed as children. The difference between theology and religious education (sometimes called catechesis or faith formation) is considerable. The proper task of religious education is exposure to the values and beliefs of a particular community. Religious education aims at welcoming members who practice the community's faith expression (through worship, behavior, and commitment to the community's health and future). The task of theology, however, includes *critical reflection* on the activity of faith in order to come to a deeper understanding of the community's values and beliefs. Theologians do not engage in critical reflection in order to criticize, but rather to analyze. It is the proper task of theology to know the tradition and to ask the formal questions: What does this mean in itself? What does this mean for the community of faith today? How does it reflect the dream of Jesus the Christ who lived and ministered and died for the kingdom of God, and whose death is not the final word of his life or our own? Big questions, for certain, yet the task of theology in the university often serves the needs of people who have not had previous opportunity to engage in this kind of thinking, reading, and analysis of the faith tradition of the community.

The search for an adequate theology frequently serves not only to formalize our own thoughts and to challenge previously formed (or poorly formed) assumptions. It can also serve the development of one's personal faith by providing an adult perspective on a previously presented but not fully explored story. After all, the story of being human is an unfinished epic, and the human desire for trusting, connecting and finding meaning in life is as ancient as the species and as fresh as this morning's best hopes.

Faith: Discussion Questions

1.) What people do you consider to be effective examples of Christian faith today?
2.) Do you know these people personally?
3.) Have these people spoken with you directly about their religious faith?
4.) If yes, what did they say that impressed you?
5.) If no, then what have you experienced in them that causes you to identify them as effective examples?
6.) Some people claim that the tradition of Christianity has emphasized "faith as belief" more than "faith as trust." Do you agree or disagree? What has been your experience of Christian teaching about faith?
7.) Do you think that the ability to trust is a requirement for healthy human relationships? For religious faith? Explain your response by offering some examples.
8.) Does "religion" deserve the reputation it seems to have in the minds of many searching people? What could organized Christian religions do to help the reputation of "religion" as we know it?

9.) Do you think that the distinction between theology and religious education helps to explain some of the disagreements which frequently go on between theologians and church officials?

10.) What insight did you gain from this reading which you think is most important for you? Why?

11.) Read the following two reflections, *A Time for Resurrection* and *Speaking Gently of Our Hope.* Consider how they offer examples of faith for contemporary life. Write your own story.

Faith: For Further Reading

Dermot Lane, The Experience of God: *An Invitation to Do Theology* (New York: Paulist, 1983) provides the serious student a fine introduction to the theology of revelation and grace which form the foundation for many contemporary theologies. Lane is especially helpful in furnishing the categories for a discussion of these topics in the heritage of the second Vatican council.

Elizabeth Johnson, *Consider Jesus: Waves of Renewal in Christology* (New York: Crossroad, 1990) offers an engaging and clear presentation of themes treated in this essay, including Christology, theologies of liberation, feminist theologies and theological method.

A Time for Resurrection

William C. Graham

I went to an estate sale recently. I've done this only a few times, and now I've figured out why. It's alarming to realize that the mementos of a lifetime are spread out for strangers to view strangers who most often did not know or care about the one who has died, strangers who are looking for a bargain and for whom these mementos hold no memories.

Actually, we weren't all strangers at this particular sale. There were several old and frail ladies who were obviously not in the market for any keepsakes, but who knew the dead owner. These ancients took great delight in poking around parts of the house where they had never been, observing that "Ethel used wheat germ, too, but she bought the great big jars."

There was a bottle of Pepto-Bismol for sale. Like the wheat germ, it was the large, economy size. I wondered why someone old and frail would buy the large size. It seemed to me that the odds were not in favor of the owner living long enough to take all the medicine in that very large bottle. Did she not know that death was coming? Was she not prepared to greet the angel of death? Did she think that buying the large, economy size would ward off death until she, at her leisure, had soothed minor ailments with the pink liquid?

This estate sale was part of my meditation throughout Lent, and I brought it to the weeks of Easter. Easter is the promise that death will visit each of us. More, it is the assurance that death does not complete life, but changes it. Easter prompts us to recall, from the darkest of grief to life's smallest trials, how God comforts us and gives us the courage to persevere.

Our Easter faith encourages us to ask the proper questions and to leave unasked those which have no answers. If we ask, "How can God allow suffering and tragedy?" or "why is there evil in the world?" we will find no answers. Pursuing such questions, we may only find bitterness and anger; the questions will remain unanswered.

Faith reminds us, in all disappointments and especially in grief, to thank God for love, affection, compassion and all good gifts. Faith demands that we remember the goodness enjoyed in years that are sometimes too short and too few, but can also be too long and pan-filled. Faith instructs us to accept our lives as the most precious gift of all.

The promise of Easter is the promise of resurrection, that from death will come new life. Easter faith prompts us to recall yesterday with gratitude, look toward tomorrow with courage and hope, and each day celebrate the moments that are ours.

Speaking Gently of Our Hope

William C. Graham

There were two kinds of wishes at our home in Proctor when we five kids were growing up. And only one of those ways of wishful thinking was encouraged. We might say, for example, that we would like to flap our arms and fly to the moon. That flight of fancy would be encouraged. We might be asked by the adults in the extended family to provide details, to expand the idea into a more complete story. These other lives within a story were encouraged particularly by our father who, on those nights when he put us to bed, would gather us into one of the big beds and continue the never ending story of the rabbit family whom he invented based on the story of Peter Rabbit. We kept Peter and Mr. McGregor the farmer, but working with Dad, invented the rest of the rabbit family and creatures of the forest and continued night by night to weave the intricate tales of the rabbits and their adventures. This kind of fanciful, wishful thinking became a sacred, peaceful activity. They were delicious, holy moments.

Another kind of wishful thinking was not encouraged. "I wish my arithmetic were done and I could watch television," for example. The child who said that to a parent or aunt or uncle would expect to see upturned eyeballs and hear the adult say, "I wish I were lying down." That was an inside, family joke. We talked in a code sometimes, and that one sentence reminded us of an antique incident we considered quite funny in a pathetic sort of way, but a story that also reminded us to do what needed to be done.

Grandma Graham, who died before my parents were married, is said to have told of a woman in bed, propped up on pillows. "I wish I were lying down," the woman said. We were told about this woman and her extraordinarily lazy wish on countless occasions. "Why didn't she just lie down then?" we would always ask. Aunt June would laugh, sigh, "Oh, honey!" and caress the child's cheek, but never answer the question. Mother, however, might patiently attempt to explain what was really very obvious.

I have never forgotten about this woman propped up on pillows who wished she were lying down. I have always been able to imaging the woman and even the bed and the pillows, and an open book on her lap and a box of chocolates to one side. And she wished she were lying down. I don't know if this woman ever lived and was a friend or acquaintance of Grandma's. Somehow, that didn't matter. She has always been as real to me as any other inhabitant of the village of Proctor.

Still today, any wish that shouldn't be a wish but should instead be a call to action is met by an understanding but unsympathetic look and the simple statement, "I wish I were lying down." That reminder is given freely across generational lines: to the sister who wishes that the company car could be a Blazer and not an Escort, to the cousin who would like to be a doctor but can't quite seem to finish the first year of college, to the priest who wishes that all the summer weddings could be performed in one huge ceremony so that the summer evenings could be freed up for other, less noble activities.

I have only recently understood that gentle voices of adult authority are, in fact, the voice of the Holy Spirit. The Spirit moves among us to cure us. The Spirit, too, helps us to rejoice, quickening us with hope. We are advised in the First Letter of Peter: "Should anyone ask you the reason for this hope of yours, be ever ready to reply, but speak gently and respectfully." Our hope is in Jesus who promises us this Spirit. I am glad when I recognize his presence.

I brought all of these reflections to a graveside on a recent Saturday afternoon when we buried my 22 year old cousin. Jonathan was named for his Uncle John, who was my father. We buried Jonathan in a grave at Forest Lawn near Grandma Graham, who first told the story that will never die of the woman who wished she were lying down. Jonathan's hopes have been left unfulfilled. His family left in shock and in grief. His wishes, whatever they were, will not be met on this earth.

We who live still must examine our own wishes. We must search for the difference between fantasy and possibility. What we wish to do and what can be done, we must work to accomplish. It is in this that we build up our human community and give glory to God. God blesses this honest activity of ours. We who love Jesus will be about our duties in love, speaking gently of our hope.

Adeline Schonhardt
and the Existence of God

William C. Graham

Curt Schonhardt came to see me one day because Adeline, his mother, sent him with a question that she had deflected. "Go ask the priest," she had said. And so Curt, dutiful son and curious, if not mischievous, Christian, did just that.

"Prove to me that God exists," he demanded with a sly grin, both hoping and believing that he had dealt me an impossible task and that he could watch his high school religion teacher and associate pastor twist in the discomfiting wind that blows when lack of certainty causes one to lose balance.

"Sit down, Curt," I invited him. And for just a moment, he thought, I think, that there was indeed proof and that Adeline and I and all believers had been holding out on him. "Let me tell you a story, and ask you a question or three, and see if together we can figure it out," I offered.

"This is one of those deals where you answer a question with a question, isn't it?" he asked.

"Is that what it sounds like?" I queried.

"Let's imagine that tonight, after school and after football practice," I continued, "you and big brothers Mike and Jeff all take the bus downtown where, surprisingly, you all meet your father, Harold, and younger brother Kevin. You all get on the next bus, the Woodland Windjammer, and settle down for the long ride quickened in hope with visions of Adeline's victuals waiting at home.

"When you get off the bus and trudge up the hill, all five of you enter the kitchen door and are greeted by the sweet smells that delight the nose and promise to tickle the tummy. You are prepared for a feast which no one else's mom could duplicate. Harold, thin but hearty, always wants two meats for dinner, and Adeline always obliges. Tonight is no exception. A pork roast and a beef roast had simmered slowly and were now sliced and on the table. Two gravies, smashed potatoes, string beans in a mushroom soup sauce, Wonder Bread and margarine, and a salad of orange Jell-O on a lettuce leaf with a dab of Hellman's mayonnaise.

"Harold and you four boys wash up and go quickly to the table. Preparing to recite a hasty grace, you notice that there is no Adeline.

"Mom," you holler impatiently. No answer.

"Mom," you holler again. No answer.

"Where is she?" Kevin wonders.

"The food'll get cold," Mike worries.

"We better look around," Harold suggests.

"I'll check the bathroom," Jeff offers.

You all fan out to find her so the meal can commence.

She's not in the bathroom, nor in the laundry room. Not gone early to bed. Didn't slip out to the garage. You look in every room. There is no Adeline to be found.

There seems to be no Adeline at all. Perhaps there was no cook!

"Of course there's a cook. Adeline cooked it. She must have gone to a meeting at church and forgot to leave us a note," Curt asserted.

"What's your evidence?" I asked.

"Perhaps, in mom's absence, there was a big bang in the kitchen, and a dinner resulted which now waits on the table," I offered.

"Maybe the beef and pork got tired of being in the fridge and cooked themselves, encouraging the other foods to do the same," I suggested.

"Maybe there is no Adeline, and Harold just made her up as one answer for your many questions," I challenged.

"No. Adeline made the dinner. I just know she did," he insisted.

"You have no proof," I parried, "only evidence."

"Hmpfh," Curt snorted. But the lights in the attic went on. Curt understood that sometimes we see something that speaks to us of that which we do not see. He began to understand analogy, considering the seen and the known and looking toward the unseen and the unknown. Analogies are imperfect, but they help us to begin to comprehend that which otherwise would be incomprehensible.

St. Thomas Aquinas developed five theories which suggest evidence that there actually is a prime mover, or first force, that people call God. Thomas, an Italian Dominican priest, theologian and philosopher in the thirteenth century, wrote a Summa, or Summary, of Theology. His fine mind was one of the best ever to assist human efforts to see the face of God. Writing in the 13th century, he interpreted what he saw and could reason, and offered clear teaching to those who, with him, would ponder the incomprehensibility of God.

Read Thomas's five proofs, and then compare them to Curt's assertions that the unseen Adeline was the cook, and that beef does not cook itself.

The Five Ways Philosophers Have Proven God's Existence

From Thomas Aquinas's **Summa of Theology** I, q. 2, a. 3

God's existence can be proven in five ways. First and most obvious is the way that begins with "change." It is obvious that some things in the world are undoubtedly in the process of changing. But anything undergoing change is being changed by something else. This is the case with anything in the process of changing, because it does not yet possess the perfection toward which it is changing, although it is capable of it; whereas anything causing change must already have the perfection it is causing, for to cause a change is to bring into existence what previously was capable of existing, and only something that already exists can do this (just as fire as actually hot, and in this way, causes the wood to change). Now, the same thing cannot be simultaneously both actually and potentially x; but it can be actually x and potentially y (the actually hot cannot be simultaneously potentially hot, although it can be potentially cold). Therefore, whatever is in the process of changing cannot cause its own changing; it cannot change itself. Anything in the process of changing is, therefore, being changed by something else. Moreover, if this something else is in the process of changing, it itself is being changed by another thing, and this by another. Now, the changing has to stop somewhere (i.e. there must be something unchanging) or else there will be not first cause of the changing and, consequently, no subsequent causes; for only when acted upon by the first cause do intermediate causes produce any change (if the stick is not moved by the hand, nothing else is moved by the stick). And so we have to come to some first cause of changing that is not itself changed by anything else, and this is what everyone understands by God.

The second way is derived from the nature of causation. In the sensible world we find causes in an order of succession; we never see, not could we, anything causing itself, for then it would have to pre-exist itself, and this is impossible. Any such succession of causes must begin somewhere, for in it a primary cause influences an intermediate, and the intermediate a last (whether the intermediate be one or many). Now, if you eliminate a cause, you also eliminate its effects, so that you cannot have a last cause or an intermediate one without having a first cause. Without an origin to the series of causes, and hence no primary cause, no intermediate causes would function and, therefore, no last effect, but the facts seem to contradict this (the effects are present). We must, therefore, suppose a First Cause, which all call "God."

The third way is drawn from the existence of the unnecessary and the necessary, and proceeds as follows. Our experience includes things certainly capable of existing but apparently unnecessary, since they come and go, coming to birth or dying. But if it is unnecessary for a thing to exist, it did not exist once upon a time, and yet everything cannot be like this, for if everything is unnecessary, there was once nothing. But if such were the case, there would now be nothing, because a nonexistent can only be brought into existence by something already existing. So that if ever there was nothing, not a thing could be brought into existence, and there would be nothing now, which contradicts the facts. And so not everything can be an unnecessary kind of being; there must exist some being that necessarily exists. But a thing that necessarily exists may or may not have this necessity from something else. But just as we must begin somewhere in a succession of causes, the case is the same with any succession of things that necessarily exist and receive this necessity from others. Hence we are compelled to suppose something that exists necessarily, having this necessity only from itself; in fact, it itself is the cause why other things exist.

The fourth way is supported by the gradation noticed in things. There are some things that are more good, more true, more noble, and so forth, and other things less so. But such comparisons denote different degrees of approach to a superlative; for instance, things are hotter and hotter the closer they approach what is hottest. There is, therefore, a truest and best and most noble thing, and so most fully existing. Now *when many things share some property, whatever possesses it most fully causes it in others*: "Fire," to use Aristotle's example, the hottest of all things, causes all other things to be hot. There is, therefore, something that causes in all other things their being, their goodness, and any other perfection they possess. And this we call "God."

The fifth way is taken from the ordered tendencies of nature. A direction of actions to an end is detected in all bodies following natural laws even when they are without awareness, for their action scarcely ever varies and nearly always succeeds; this indicates that they do tend toward a goal, not merely succeeding by accident. Anything, however, without awareness, tends to a goal only under the guidance of someone who is aware and knows; the arrow, for instance, needs an archer. Everything is nature, consequently, is guided to its goal by someone with knowledge, and this one we call "God."

God: Discussion Questions

1.) Explain that those things which are changed cannot change themselves. How tall were you in grade six? How tall are you today? How did you arrange that? Or was a force in charge that is beyond your control?

2.) What is a prime mover or an unchanged changer?

3.) Can a nonexistent thing be brought into existence by something that does not exist? Explain succession of causes, and what this succession has to do with God.

4.) St. Thomas's last proof is about signs of intelligent planning in parts of nature that we do not consider capable of such intelligence. Can you think of examples of what he is getting at? How do these examples point to the existence of God?

5.) Some theologians and preachers assert that arguments about God's existence are finally pointless because God's existence cannot be demonstrated or proved. Can God's existence be known as fact, or is it always an object of faith? What do you think?

God: For Further Reading

A History of God: The 4,000-Year Quest of Judaism, Christianity and Islam, by Karen Armstrong (New York: Ballantine Books, 1993).

"Can We Still Believe?" in *Do You Believe in God?* by Karl Rahner (New York: Newman, 1969).

Many valuable selections, including the Rahner citation above, will be found in *Foundations of Theological Study: A Sourcebook*, by Mark Massa and Richard Viladesau (New York: Paulist, 1991).

The Mystery of God and Our Own

Michael P. Horan

A Word from the Author

I am a middle-aged Catholic Christian. I was born into a Catholic family that lived in the suburbs of a major U.S. city in 1956. At that time Dwight Eisenhower was the nation's president. Elvis Presley was just getting started in the music business. Cars were the size of boats. My older brother and sister played early rock and roll music on ancient instruments called phonographs or record players; their records had different speeds, or RPMs (16, 33, 45 and 78 revolutions per minute). When I was in kindergarten I used to love to sneak into their record collection while the older kids were still in school and play records at the wrong speeds!

In my Catholic elementary school in the early 1960s, the teachers and priests tried to explain various aspects of religion to us children as we prepared for our first communion. Often their explanations of the Trinity or Jesus Christ's humanity-divinity, or heaven or hell, left us confused. Sometimes our teachers would end their explanation with this phrase: "It's a mystery." (If you don't believe my story about these old days in Catholicism, ask your parents!)

A lot has happened since those days. The changes in our society have affected not only cars and music. The Catholic approach to "mystery" also has undergone revision. Catholic theologians and teachers are less likely to try to separate each item of Catholic faith or spirituality and call each "a mystery." Today they are likely to speak less about "a mystery" and more about "God's Mystery" in a more whole and integrated way. What is the difference? I believe the distinction can be located and appreciated once one realizes the shift in thinking which has occurred in Catholic theology. The shift involves the starting point for the journey toward deeper spirituality. The generation that taught me tried to begin theological explanations by right away considering God. The current generation of theologians and teachers is more likely to start with a reflection on what it means to be a human being.

From the human starting point, we must admit that there are no hard and fast proofs that God exists, but reflecting on what it means to be human can help us on the journey to encounter Mystery, to encounter the Deeper Truth, to know God. In the encounter, we are able to become aware of our connections with God more as partners in a gracious dance than as detectives in an investigation. In that dance let us explore what we can know of the mystery of God.

First, we will consider the experience of the mystery of being human and imagine what that experience can tell us about our approach to God. Second, let us explore the dimensions of the mystery of God by considering where and how God "lives," with treatment of the Christian belief in Jesus Christ's humanity-divinity.

1. How God is Known: The Experience of Being Human

One of the most famous and important of the Catholic theologians of the twentieth century was a Jesuit priest named Karl Rahner (pronounced RONer). Rahner's name is frequently mentioned by those historians of Catholic theology who narrate the sea change in thought about grace and revelation in recent decades. Rahner's writings are challenging to the novice theologian, but his insights are valuable because they address the human condition and the quest for God in a way which seems applicable to religious searchers. Rahner described God as the horizon of human experience. Let us consider what he meant by that image.

When one looks at a beautiful sunset, a cityscape or mountaintop view, one can only see the foreground because there is a background, a field of vision which gives definition to the scene. If there were no horizon, it would be impossible for anyone to experience the scene. Whether one is conscious of the horizon is not nearly as crucial as the fact that the horizon is always there. The human eye perceives reality against some reference point, such as a horizon. Rahner understood that phenomenon in human experience and he proffered that God is the horizon of the human experience of knowing and being free. We cannot act freely, or know that we are free human agents, were it not for the horizon whom we call God. But questions arise: How do we ever consciously experience God as God? What of people who do not believe in God, or who have never heard of God? How do we even come to know ourselves as human, let alone know God as God?

Signs of Graced Humanity:
Questioning, Loving and Hoping

Rahner suggests that there are at least three signals that aid us to know more clearly that experience of being human. These are the phenomena of questioning, loving and hoping. In each case, we transcend ourselves, that is, we move beyond ourselves in ways which are as natural to humans as breathing, yet distinctive about us humans (as opposed to other creatures) in the family of creation. Let us consider each of these phenomena, as they help us to reflect upon the truth of our humanity and our graced connection with the divine.

(a) Questioning: The Quest for Meaning

Consider the case of the college student who must choose a major. "What do I want to study?" she asks. At the base of the question however, are larger ones: What do I want to BE? How will I make a living in the world? And how will I craft not just a living, but a LIFE? What will fulfill me and bring meaning and purpose to my life? As a university professor I have met hundreds of young people who make these decisions. The students who concern themselves only with making a large salary or with following their parents' advice (against their own impulses) often regret their decision a year or two after their graduation. Only then do these students engage the deeper questions. The students who are willing to live with these deeper questions during their college years generally learn more about themselves than courses and credits can provide. In the long run, they make more informed choices.

We humans construct the meaning of our lives and yet we are also aware, however subtly, of our fear of a lack of meaning, our limits before the questions which haunt us about life decisions. The curious thing about all this is that the questions do not cease. No matter our age or experience, we humans continue to wonder, to imagine, to dream and even to worry. According to our knowledge, the other animals in creation do not reflect on the present in light of future hopes. We humans wonder because we also have the ability to transcend, to go out of ourselves in love and concern toward our own existence and toward the life of another. The deepest question in our lives is the question of our own identity; "Who am I" is the preamble to questions about ultimate reality, what exists beyond me, what is ultimately real and lasting. The encounter with these questions leads into the search which is a life-long one. Whatever our tentative answers to these ultimate questions may be at any time in our lives, there is a certain recognition that we share these questions with others, and indeed we are connected at some deep level with all other human beings, themselves questioners. Recognizing our connections leads us to discuss the second signal of God's mystery communicated through God's life in us. A second way to take note of the horizon is to reflect on our ability to love.

(b) Falling in Love:
The Experience of the Divine Spark Within Us

The experience of falling in love is like no other. Most of us know or hope for that experience, and when we try to describe what we know or long for, we fall short of the right words. Why? If this is a universal experience, shared by all people, then why do words come so slow and hard? And why, even when we speak the words, are we dissatisfied with their power to "capture" the experience? Perhaps the experience of falling in love serves as a window into our viewing the mystery of God, Who is Love. The first letter of John in the New Testament makes clear how the earliest followers of Jesus encountered the God of Mystery: God is Love, and they who abide in love abide in God, and God abides in them. Love consists not in our loving God but in God loving us, and in showing us that ultimate love through Jesus the Christ (1 Jn. 4:9-12).

That experience of falling in love, of knowing that I am loved and that I can love another, is the beginning of recognizing the power of mystery in my life. This power is awesome and yet it is a bit frightening, because I do not know whence it comes. It is not something that I learn like ice skating or speaking French. It is more like an innate talent, an ability that lies waiting to be used, but which is not known until it is discovered, unfolded by the circumstances of life rather than by my willing it.

Perhaps that part of the experience of human mystery helps us to know something of the Mystery of God, the Mystery to which we are deeply connected. Nowhere in human experience is there a more profound spiritual adventure than loving and being loved. It is experienced, but it is not fully understood by anyone. Interestingly, my conversations with happily married couples convince me that the meaning and value of love as mystery grows in proportion to their willingness to "enter into the mystery" without full understanding. The experience is not poorer for its lack of clarity, or for the lovers' inability to capture it in words. Indeed, the richness of the love expands as the partners let go and recognize that they are being grasped by something greater than the human mind can analyze.

And here is the paradox: The "letting go" must precede the "being grasped." This paradox was well known by the mystics of the sixteenth century in Spain. St. Teresa of Avila and St. John of the Cross each described their spiritual journey toward God's deep mystery using metaphors about romantic love. They understood that God as mystery can be considered in theory, but that God as mystery can be met only in the letting go, in the mutual trust that creates and sustains a healthy marriage.

(c) Hoping: The Gift of Imagining a Future

The third characteristic of the human being that opens us up to the mystery of God is our ability, our need, our impulse to HOPE. Again, in the writings of Karl Rahner we find evidence that this gift of hoping is essential to, and distinctive about, the human condition. No matter our disappointments, we lean into the future. We make plans for the weekend, for the summer, for next year. We budget our time and manage our financial resources because we assume that there is more time. Perhaps that is why death is so shocking to all of us, but especially to young persons. If the life of a friend should end suddenly, it is hard to handle because we miss the person, we are saddened and confused, and we wonder if there is a purpose in life or death. But our tendency toward hope also provides some of the grief, as we had imagined that life would go on forever, or at least for a long time. We assume the future, we account for the future in our plans, we imagine it. The capacity to hope is part of being human. This third sign is, in the Christian view, one more indication of the Mystery to which we are related because we are created in the image of God (Genesis 1:26). As such we humans have the capacity to transcend ourselves by searching for meaning, caring for others, and hoping into the creation of future time.

Humans: Directed Toward Transcendence

Whenever we question or love or hope, we are staring into the more, the beyond, the future. We may not notice the horizon, but should we stop to reflect on the very act of staring, of seeing, we would readily admit that these capacities are related to the horizon, the reference point of all human acts of questioning, loving and hoping. Perhaps then, in the split second of our awareness, we are most ready to encounter God as Mystery. This encounter, however fleeting or tentative, shapes us as we continue to create ourselves by deeper questions, greater love, and fresh hope. The horizon is there even if we do not take note of it. Without the horizon we cannot take in the scene, we cannot put the elements in any perspective, we cannot have a coherent and clear picture. We benefit from the horizon although we may not consciously study it. Whenever we question or love or hope, we do so against the backdrop of the divine spark within us, that capacity which distinguishes us from the other animals in the kingdom. The capacity for transcendence readies us, if we choose, to come to fuller awareness of the presence of the One to Whom we are deeply related, and through Whom all creatures in creation are intrinsically connected.

2. Where Does God Live:
The Notions of Transcendence and Immanence,
and the Christian Belief in Jesus the Christ

In classical theology Christians have described God's mystery in two ways. God is both transcendent and immanent. By transcendence Christians mean that notion of God as wholly other, as utterly beyond us, possessing a wholeness and a holiness that cast a pale reflection on the wholeness and holiness which we know in human beings. Jews, Christians and Muslims refer to the God of creation, Lord of heaven and earth, and in that phrase they intend God's transcendence. They understand that transcendence as God's moving out of God's very self, breaking into the world and humanity from beyond our world and our human condition.

But there is another experience of God in these traditions as well. This is the experience of God's residing within creation and humanity, offering the source of divine life within the human heart and soul. This is God's immanence, or God's indwelling presence. By immanence Christians mean the life of God within the world and the human being, though not confined and certainly not determined by the world or humanity. The activity of the Holy Spirit as both outside and beyond all imagining, yet residing within creation and persons, may be a helpful metaphor for grasping the Christian idea of God's transcendence and immanence.

These two notions of God are essential to understanding the doctrine of the humanity-divinity of Jesus the Christ which is at the core of Christian belief about the Mystery of God made manifest in the world.

In calling Jesus the Christ, Christians affirm both God's transcendence and immanence. On the one hand Christians affirm that God is utterly outside the realm of human experience and chooses to become involved in the world. On the other hand, Christians also claim that God is within each human being, whether one acknowledges (or ignores or denies) that claim.

The first followers of Jesus questioned, loved, and hoped. They questioned the meaning of Jesus' teachings, and wondered whether the way of life which he espoused was practical, worthwhile or real. The synoptic gospels are filled with accounts of arguments between Jesus and his friends about who is the greatest in the reign of God, how children and women and Sadducees should be treated, about how to serve and therefore be first in God's kingdom. Their questions only led them deeper into the mystery of God and the ways in which that mystery was revealed in the life and death and self-giving of Jesus.

The gospel accounts demonstrate that the death of the human Jesus revealed his full humanity. Jesus was utterly faithful to the processes of questioning, loving and hoping. He questioned his Father's will for him, wondering about the meaning and purpose of his life. According to two of the synoptic gospels, on the cross, he prayed Psalm 22, which begins with the human question: Why? (Mt. 27:46; Mk. 15:35).

Jesus made choices. Had Jesus not been faithful to the human call to loving, he would not have been executed. The civil and religious authorities would not have found him threatening to their programs were it not for the transformation of the people who were healed by his compassion, challenged by his parables, or changed by his reaching out in friendship.

Following the death of Jesus, the writers of the gospels were not shy about telling stories on themselves. They did not really understand the divinity of the Christ among them because they did not understand Jesus' full humanity. They had tried to be less than human. They attempted to avoid the hard moments that accompany acts of questioning, loving, and hoping. They tried to keep the crowds of needy people away from their leader. They argued about who is the greatest in the kingdom of God, and they did not like Jesus' response that the greatest must serve the needs of the rest, that in losing life one finds life, that in the kingdom of God the last shall be first. According to their own words, the disciples resisted Jesus' fully human insight that the kingdom belongs to the very ones who don't count for much in polite society's eyes: Prostitutes, tax collectors, children who had no legal powers in the empire, widows without income, lepers left uncured and disrespected.

Through the gospels' resurrection accounts the disciples tell us that transformation is possible. The risen Christ appears to them in the form of a stranger on the road to Emmaus (Lk. 24:13), a gardener near an empty tomb (Jn. 20:15), a fisherman frying the catch (Jn. 21:10). When they respond in their full humanity, imitating their rabbi and Lord, the disciples encounter the truth that the fully human one is also the divine

Son, the firstborn of many brothers and sisters (Rom. 8:29). These followers come to know that their friend who questioned, loved and hoped was so fully human that he revealed God in Himself. In acts of self-transcendence the mystery of Jesus' humanity displayed for the disciples and for successive generations the truth that the starting point for encountering the Mystery of God is living a life like the one Jesus lived. In Jesus' free choice to be faithful to his life commitments and to faith in God, he died and into God's embrace and was raised by God. From both his life and his death the disciples finally learned faithfulness of the most excellent kind. And so the Christian movement was forged by a small band of faithful Jews. Because of them, we have the gospel, the good news that Jesus lived the transcendental call to question, love, and hope, showing us at once what it means to be human and to encounter the Mystery whom we Christians call God.

Conclusion

Our starting point for discussing the Mystery of God has changed since I was child. In that former time, we Catholic Christians might have decreed that God exists, and then we would simply set out to "prove" that truth by description. In our times, it is clear that people seek meaning and value in their lives, although the place of organized religion in providing that value may not rank as high as it used to. Our discussion of questioning, loving and hoping does not provide hard and fast proof of God's existence. However, through the efforts of contemporary theologians like Karl Rahner, we may reflect on the mystery of being human as a starting point for our modest yet confident assertions that our lives as humans are related to each other, and ultimately to the One who is the source of life's Mystery.

In our reflecting, we may come to encounter the truth of Jesus the Christ as at once fully human and The Beloved Son, and thereby see with eyes of hope the future for all Christians.

Mystery: Discussion Questions

1.) Recall a time that you found yourself wondering about the future. What kinds of questions did you ask yourself? What do they reveal about you? What do these questions reveal about being human?

2.) Recall a time when you were disappointed. How did you overcome that disappointment? What did you tell yourself? What is your experience of hope?

3.) Spend a few moments observing a scene (a landscape or a crowded mall will do). Notice the horizon in the scene, and notice that you cannot stare at it forever. The horizon gives meaning to the scene. What does it tell you about the Mystery of God in your life?

4.) Respond to the statement: We Christians can only understand the mystery of Christ's divinity if we understand the fact of Jesus' humanity.

5.) If you were to tell a friend about this reading, what three insights would you need to share with him or her?

Mystery: For Further Reading

Readers who want to consider the thought of Karl Rahner will find an effective introduction to his ideas in *A World of Grace: An Introduction to the Theology and Themes of Karl Rahner*, Leo O'Donovan, ed. (New York: Seabury, 1980). This work is a collection of essays by Rahner experts, some of whom studied with Rahner.

The spirituality of Rahner and his ideas about God as Mystery are shared with readers in many of the brief essays contained in Karl Rahner, *The Practice of Faith*, edited by Karl Lehmann and Albert Raffelt (New York: Crossroad, 1992). Those ideas are developed throughout his many works, spanning the course of a long and remarkable theological career. One text which locates Rahner's ideas on the subject of Mystery in a larger discussion of faith can be found in Karl Rahner, *Foundations of Christian Faith: An Introduction to the Idea of Christianity*, translated by William V. Dych (New York: Crossroad, 1984).

Poems
(1876-1889)

Gerard Manley Hopkins

Pied Beauty

Glory be to God for dappled things-
  For skies of couple-colour as a brinded cow;
    For rose-moles all in stipple upon trout that swim
Fresh-firecoal chestnut-falls; finches' wings;
    Landscape plotted and pieced-fold, fallow and plough
    And all trades, their gear and tackle and trim
All things counter, original, spare, strange;
    Whatever is fickle, freckled (who knows how?)
    With swift, slow; sweet, sour; adazzle, dim;
He fathers-forth whose beauty is past change:
          Praise him.

God's Grandeur

The world is charged with the grandeur of God
  It will flame out, like shining from shook foil;
    It gathers to a greatness, like the ooze of oil
Crushed. Why do men then now not reck his rod?
Generations have trod, have trod, have trod;
  And all is seared with trade; bleared, smeared with toil;
  And wears man's smudge and shares man's smell; the soil
Is bare now, nor can foot feel, being shod.

And for all this, nature is never spent;
  There lives the dearest freshness deep down things;
And though the last lights off the black West went
  Oh, morning, at the brown brink eastward, springs-
Because the Holy Ghost over the bent
  World broods with warm breast and with ah! bright wings.

Get a Grip, Man

Charlene Holden

"Lights, camera, action." Uttering these tinsel town words instantaneously endows any producer or director with poetic license. "Patton," "D Day," "Escape from Sobibor," and "Schindler's List" all had their historical content enhanced and embellished this Hollywood Technique. Is it any wonder that God who created man and women intimately knew what would appeal to man's cognitive process would employ this clever style? After all, God is the ultimate director.

The Hebrew Bible covers prehistory events. There was no "Hebrew Times" events were based solely on man's interpretation of the Word of God. It has only been recently that scholars have approached the Bible as a docu-drama rather than as an actual historical event.

Producer Arnold Kopelson states that his goal in the thriller "Outbreak" is to wake up the world to the threats of some deadly viruses. What was God's intention in the Bible? Clearly, God wanted to give a wake up call to humanity. The Bible does not seek to tell how the world was created, rather it stresses the religious truth that God created the world. The story of Abraham and Isaac teaches us that we must be willing to give up all for the love of God. The parting of the Red Sea points to God's unlimited power. The result of human's sinfulness is explored in the stories of Adam and Eve and Noah's Ark. While some historians continue to search for remnants of the ark, they would be wiser to follow the sage words of Fr. William Graham: "Get a grip, man!"

When viewed in this new light, it is easy to see that our faith is greatly influenced by studying the Bible more for its religious significance than for its historical accuracy. Thus the faithful are able to devote more time to the true meaning of God's religious message without being encumbered by historical inconsistencies.

That's Hollywood, folks!

Biblical Study: A Brief Introduction

Mark McVann, F.S.C.

The Bible, many would argue, is the single most significant book in the history of the West, and perhaps even in world civilization, because Christianity claims the largest number of adherents among the world's great religions and is spread virtually throughout the whole world. And the Bible is the library of Christianity's most sacred texts, which Christians believe is the Word of God.

The English word Bible comes from the Greek, *ta biblia*, which means "the books." So, the Bible really is a library, a compilation of literary works of many different genres, or types, which were composed, edited, and collected together over many centuries by many different authors, editors, and custodians of tradition. Within its pages are found at least the following kinds of writing: prayers, sermons, letters, poetry, songs, historical and biographical narratives, prophecies, myths, legends, folktales, allegories, proverbs and wise sayings, miracle stories, reports of visions and revelations, and laws.

The Bible is divided into two principal parts, the Old Testament (OT) and the New Testament (NT). These divisions are sometimes referred to in modern scholarship as the Hebrew Bible and Christian Scriptures. This is so because the first and much longer half was written in Hebrew (almost completely–there are a couple of small sections in Aramaic) by Jewish authors for Jewish audiences.

Christianity's roots are wholly Jewish since Jesus, the apostles, and the first generation of Christians were all Jews. Christianity was originally a reform movement within Judaism, but failed to win many adherents in its earliest years. It was met with hostility by Jews who rejected Jewish-Christian claims about Jesus' identity as the messiah and their unorthodox views of Jewish tradition and practice. Within its second generation, then, Christianity moved out of the Jewish environment of its birth and early infancy and into the Greco-Roman world. There it met with great success, and spreading throughout the Roman Empire, Christianity grew to maturity. The Christian Scriptures reflect the world in which the new religion was taking hold as they are written not in Hebrew, but Greek, the common language of the eastern portion of the Roman empire, which succeeded the Greek empire built originally by Alexander the Great.

Nevertheless, the great debt to Judaism was not cancelled. Everywhere it went, Christianity carried with it its first book, the Hebrew Bible. But Christians themselves were also producing literature, and some of it came to be venerated as having been inspired by God in the same manner as the holy books of the Jews. This literature became attached to the revered Jewish books to form the second volume of Holy Writ. The Hebrew Bible is thus for Christians the book which prophesies the coming of the Messiah, and the Christian Scriptures interprets for Christians how the Hebrew Bible is to be read: the grand historical and spiritual introduction to the appearance of Jesus, the Son of God and God's fullest revelation to humanity. Thus, both Testaments are indissolubly linked together: the New Testament reflects the influence of the Old on every page, indeed, in almost every line.

The Old Testament

It is impossible in the limited space we have here to describe with even slender justice the immense variety of literatures, historical events, cultural traditions, and theological insights and truths disclosed in the Old Testament. There are, however, several broad categories under which large parts of the book may be classified.

The First Five Books

The first five books of the Old Testament are either called "Torah" (its Hebrew designation, which means "teaching" or "law") or "The Pentateuch" (from the Greek, meaning "five scrolls"). These five books are the bedrock foundation of the entire Bible, both Old and New Testaments. They tell the stories of the creation of the world, the beginnings of the Hebrew people with the patriarch Abraham (the period from 1850-1250 B.C.), and the people's earliest history. They had been forced into slavery in Egypt where they sought relief from famine in Palestine. Eventually they escaped under the leadership of the prophet Moses, the greatest figure in Jewish history. This event, the Exodus (about 1250 B.C.) is the single most significant episode in the Hebrew Bible (and figures prominently throughout the NT as well, see Luke 9:30, and the Last Supper stories). Shortly after the Exodus, Moses mediates God's laws to the people, the Ten Commandments. In addition, then, to narratives about the patriarchs and matriarchs of the first Israelites, the time of slavery, the Exodus and desert wandering, and the emergence of the Twelve Tribes, a vast collection of laws is found in the Pentateuch. These laws grew up as commentary on, and amplification of, the first great Ten Laws or Commandments, and regulate all aspects of Israel's life as a nation of holy people. These laws include everything from rules for the conduct of warfare to dietary regulations to legislation concerning the performance of sacrifices and liturgical rites (especially the book of Leviticus).

The Historical Books

The next large body of material can be called the Historical Books because they chart the evolution of the Israelites from their early conquering days to their establishment as a nation through their growth in time to a small empire (about 1130-587 B.C.). They describe Israel's development from a relatively loose confederation of tribes with no king into a rigidly hierarchical society with a powerful monarchy. The principal figures in these narratives are the great judges and prophets like Joshua, Samson, Deborah, Elijah, Samuel, and the famous kings, David, and his son, Solomon.

The historical books also tell the sad tale of the division of the Israel after Solomon's death into two independent kingdoms. They narrate the total destruction of the northern kingdom (Israel) by the Assyrians, and the painful decline and ultimate collapse of the southern kingdom (Judah) under the Babylonians who succeeded the Assyrians as conquerors.

The Prophets

The next great body of literature in the OT is the writings is the Prophets. The prophets were mostly men (although prophetesses were known, they played a smaller role in the people's affairs), who were in most cases vehement and uncompromising in their denunciations of hypocrisy in Israel's religious, social, and political life, while staunchly defending the ancient traditions of fidelity to the covenant (i.e., the Ten Commandments) and social justice. Prophets appeared throughout Israel's long history, but most especially in times of crisis. They called the people and their leaders to conversion, to return to the authentic worship of God by faithful observance of God's demands for justice and compassion. Although scholars believe that the book that bears his name is actually the work of at least three different writers, the greatest of the historical prophets, Isaiah (active from about 742 B.C. until 687 B.C.), was a key figure when Judah–the southern kingdom–faced the disaster of an Assyrian invasion in 701 B.C. (see Is 36-37).

Wisdom Literature

The last great category of OT literature is called "Wisdom Literature" because it contains the reflections of Israel's sages on God's action in the world; on life's troubles and trials; the importance of family life and child rearing; proper standards of social conduct; right political order; and the meaning of life in general. The great prayer book, the Book of Psalms, is included under this broad heading, as is the collection of the sayings of the wise, the Book of Proverbs. The Book of Job (probably composed sometime between the seventh and fifth centuries B.C.), a justly famous and deeply moving meditation on the meaning of human suffering, also belongs to category of Wisdom Literature.

An Example of Interpretation:
The First Creation Story–Genesis 1:1-2:4a

There are two stories of creation in the opening chapters of Genesis. The first one we read (Gen. 1:1-2:4a) is the work of a "school" called the Priestly writer, usually simply identified as "P." Although it appears first, it was actually the later of the two stories. The second (2:4b-25) was written perhaps as much as five hundred years before P's account. The first is the story of creation occurring in a series of six days, with God resting on the seventh. The second is the story of Adam and Eve, but unfortunately, we will not be able to discuss that story here.

The Priestly author was interested in ideas like order, purity, careful observance of boundaries, and in precision and exactitude in observing religious rituals, customs and laws. These concerns are obvious in his creation story.

P is first of all concerned to show that there is but one God, and that this God is the source and origin of all that is. Presented like an emperor of immeasurable power, God has only to speak and the commands are immediately and fully effected.

Second, P is concerned to show that God created the world to exist in a certain pattern, and that all created things have their proper place and relation to one another. He uses the scheme of six days to show this divine ordering of creation:

DAY 1	DAY 4
Light	Luminaries for the
Day and *night*	*day* and *night*
DAY 2	DAY 5
Firmament (*sky*)	Birds in the *sky*
Waters above and below	Fishes in the *water*
DAY 3	DAY 6
Dry earth separated from *sea*	Animals & human beings
Vegetation	on *earth*

DAY 7
Day of rest[2]

It should be fairly obvious that this poetic and sophisticated scheme is intended to show that the chaos we see at the opening of the story has been set into a specific order: things are placed by God where they belong.

On five occasions during the telling of the story, God sees how good are the things he has created. God blesses the human beings he has created and endows them with a special status as masters of creation. But the author also tells us that God has blessed and made holy the seventh day. So, both human beings and the seventh day receive blessings. This seems to indicate that there is some special relationship between the seventh day and human beings. What is that special relationship?

The answer lies in P's concern for order. We read that God made human beings in God's image, and that God rested on the seventh day. One of the ways P's audience manifests its special status in creation, then, would be to emulate God and rest from work on the seventh day. Indeed, things are created in ascending order of importance, with the creation of humanity and the day of rest coming last, and hence, being most important.

With his creation story, therefore, the P stresses for his Jewish audience that their observance of the sabbath–the seventh day of rest–is so important a responsibility that all of creation runs the risk of falling back into primeval chaos if the sabbath is not observed. God's purpose in creating the world was, according to P, precisely in order to have the sabbath observed. If observed, creation maintains its divinely ordained order and remains humanity's richly blessed home.

It can seen clearly, I hope, that reading the Priest's creation story in a naively literal fashion–that is, thinking it describes the actual way the world came into being–is to do serious damage to the intention of the author, and to miss the message to his intended and first audience about its responsibility to be faithful to its religious obligations. The story reflects the Babylonian catastrophe (587 B.C.) when the Jewish people were threatened with extinction. In such a time of crisis, maintaining customs and traditions is extremely urgent, and careful observance of the sabbath was one measure which could help to ensure the survival of the Jewish people's religious and ethnic identity.

We are not reading science here in Genesis, but rather Israel's profound religious conviction that God created the world, despite the evil often found in it, to be a good place filled with purpose and beauty. Additionally, P wanted to impress on his audience that God's Chosen People must acknowledge his Lordship by following the order he set out at the beginning and rest from work on the seventh day.

There is, of course, a great deal more that could be said about this story and the Adam and Even story which follows it, not to mention the rest of the OT! But we leave our all too brief discussion with the comment that the serious study of the great literature of ancient Israel, the Hebrew Bible, is a life's work. Here we have begun only with the most basic of orientations.

The New Testament

The twenty-seven books of the NT were produced by various writers over some seventy-five years (or even more, some think) between roughly A.D. 50 and A.D. 125. The earliest, Paul's Letter to the Thessalonians, was probably written in A.D. 50, about twenty years after Jesus died. The earliest of the literature collected into the NT was letters from Christian preachers and missionaries (principally the Apostle Paul) which, copied and recopied, circulated among the first communities and came to be especially beloved by them for their clear teaching about the meaning of Jesus Christ and the advice about how to live an authentically Christian life.

Soon, however, the need arose among the communities for a written narrative of the story of Jesus since the first generation of witnesses, the apostles and disciples, was passing from the scene. A number of such stories, called gospels, were written, but only four have been universally acknowledged by Christians as having been divinely inspired: **Matthew** (probably written between A.D. 80 and 90; where exactly is not known, perhaps in southern Syria); **Mark** (the first of the gospels, it was written perhaps in Rome, perhaps in Palestine, depending on how the internal evidence is read; the date is generally thought to be either the late 60s or early 70s of the first century), **Luke** (A.D. 80-85; composed perhaps in Antioch), and **John** (written perhaps at Ephesus in Asia Minor, about A.D. 90).

In addition to the letters and gospels, there are other kinds of literature: in the Acts of the Apostles, Luke's sequel to his gospel, we have the account of the earliest growth of the church under the leadership of Peter, the original apostles, and Paul. And, of course, there is the famous and controversial Book of Revelation (also called the Apocalypse), filled with strange visions and symbols. Thus, the NT, like the OT, is a collection of highly varied kinds of literature, including, among others: hymns, sermons, miracle stories, biographical narratives, letters, mystical discourses, and parables.

The Gospels

It has been known and commented on for centuries that Matthew, Mark, and Luke–the Synoptic gospels–bear close resemblance to one another, while at the same time each maintains a distinct character and tone. Their similarities and differences form an important issue in NT studies, and is called the Synoptic Problem. The Synoptic Problem has received various solutions, but the most generally accepted one runs like this: it seems most probable that Matthew and Luke each had copies of Mark which they used independent of each other as the basis upon which to compose their own gospels. The similarities of material common to Matthew and Luke which are common also to Mark are so striking that Markan priority is fairly firmly established. Mark was written first, and came into the hands of the two other Evangelists.

But this is only a partial solution to the problem because Matthew and Luke share other material which is not found in Mark. Scholars have accounted for this by the hypothesis that Matthew and Luke must have had in common a second document, which scholars call Q (the first letter of the German word *quelle*, "source"). The story of Jesus' temptation in the desert, which receives only passing mention in Mark, is a developed episode in Matthew and Luke and probably was known to them from Q.

The Synoptic Problem is further complicated by the fact that both Matthew and Luke have material found in each of them alone (called M and L, respectively). For example, stories of the birth of Jesus in Matthew and Luke (the Infancy Narratives) are very different. So, it seems that in addition to the commonly known Mark and Q, Matthew and Luke had sources or traditions about Jesus known perhaps only to the communities for which they wrote their gospels. Diagrammed, the solution to the Synoptic Problem looks like this:

Q

(The lines to Matthew and Luke are broken because Q is a hypothetical document; the same with M and L, they are hypothetical sources [oral, written, or both]; Mark, on the other hand, is a document we actually possess.)

The gospel of John is treated separately by scholars because of its unique qualities. Whereas Matthew, Mark, and Luke are interested in the Kingdom of God, miracles, and parables, John often presents Jesus delivering symbolically rich, mystical discourses, many of which focus on his relationship with the Father. John was also probably the last composed of the four gospels. All these characteristics require that John, as well as the letters which bear his name and the Apocalypse (also attributed to him), be studied pretty much on his own terms.

<h3 style="text-align:center">An Example of Interpretation:
The Calming of the Storm, Mark 4:35-41
(Mt 8:23-27; Lk 8:22-25)</h3>

This is a fascinating story in which something of Jesus' power is revealed to his terrified disciples. Let us consider briefly what message for readers may be found in it.

Assuming the crossing of the Sea of Galilee (a large lake) was made in a small fishing boat, how is it possible for Jesus to be sleeping through a violent storm with the boat filling up with water? Why would the disciples wake Jesus to ask him, in effect, to save them, and then be amazed when he actually does it? Additionally, how is it that he can calm a storm on the lake, but can't work a mighty deed a chapter later when he is back home in Nazareth? Both on the lake (4:40) and at home (6:5-6) he encounters a lack of faith, but in one place it does not matter, yet, in another it almost cripples him.

Clearly, the story of Jesus' mighty work on the lake needs an interpretation which calls for something other than an insistence that this is a report of an historical incident. What, then, might Mark want us to understand from this story?

First, we know that from the earliest days of Christianity the boat is a symbol of the church (the barque of Peter; images of boats are still common in Christian churches). Second, we know that persecution was a dangerous feature of life for the first Christians (Mark mentions it twice: 4:17; 10:30). Third, we know that the first Christians looked forward with great anticipation to the return of Jesus in power and glory (13:28-37; 14:62) but in the interim they mourned his absence (2:19-20). But even though Jesus was gone, had he abandoned them? This is the question Mark addresses in this story.

We are now in a position to see that in the "Calming of the Storm,"

Mark is telling a story in which the disciples, fearful because Jesus is "absent" (that is, asleep) started to panic in the storm, a symbolic reference to persecution. Jesus awakes and calms the storm: despite his absence, he has not abandoned them, and he calms the "storm" of their fears of persecution. They should have known all along that they had not been abandoned, and this is why Jesus scolds them in v. 40. Then the disciples are afraid again, filled with great awe, but this time their fear is justified, because they have experienced the *mysterium tremdendum*, the tremendous mystery of an encounter with the divine. They have seen revealed the power of God to save life from death, which will be revealed fully in Jesus' resurrection, which this story points anticipates: Jesus, asleep (sleep is a Christian symbol of death), wakes up (rises from the dead) and is revealed as the Lord of divine power and majesty.

The apparently simple episode of the calming of the storm bristles with symbolic references to Jesus' death and resurrection, faith and lack of faith, the presence and absence of Jesus, to the church and persecution, and to God's power to rescue life from destruction. Most modern readers find such symbolic interpretations more satisfying than literal readings because they speak more meaningfully to the mysteries, challenges, and rewards which inevitably form part of the life of faith.

As was the case in our reading of P's creation story, there is much more that could be added to fill out the interpretation of this story, Mark's gospel and the NT as a whole, but space does not allow us to amplify. However, what was said above about the study of the Hebrew Bible bears repeating here: the serious study of the New Testament is also a life's work, and here we have only barely begun.

Biblical Study: Discussion Questions

1.) The OT contains many kinds of literatures. Among the types mentioned to which genre or kind of literature would you assign the first creation story, and for what reasons?
2.) How would the story of the calming of the storm be classified? It is a miracle story, an allegory, both? How do you know?
3.) Take another biblical narrative, for instance, the story of Jesus walking on the water (Matthew 14:22-33; Mark 6:45-52; John 6:15-21), and compare it with Jesus' calming the storm. What are the similarities and differences? Could this story be interpreted along the same lines as the calming of the storm? Why or why not?

4.) Compare and contrast the first and second creation stories, especially the way God is portrayed. Are the concerns and themes in the second story similar to the first? Why or why not? Do you think these two stories were written by the same hand? Why or why not?

5.) How would you describe the fear and silence of the women to whom the announcement of the resurrection is made in Mark 16? Might this be another example of the *mysterium tremendum*? Why or why not? Can you find other biblical examples of such encounters with the *mysterium tremendum*?

6.) There is an obvious tension between literal and symbolic approaches to biblical interpretation. Which approach do you think offers the possibility of a better understanding of the Bible, and what are your reasons?

Biblical Study: For Further Reading

The Catholic Study Bible. Donald Senior, ed. (New York: Oxford University Press, 1990). The articles in the Readers Guide are excellent and highly recommended for introductions to the Bible as a whole, as well as its individual books.

Norman K. Gottwald, *The Hebrew Bible: A Socio-Literary Introduction* (Philadelphia: Fortress Press, 1985). Although difficult for beginners, this is an excellent book which takes readers into the complex and fascinating process which produced the Hebrew Bible.

Denis C. Duling and Norman Perrin. *The New Testament: Proclamation and Paranesis, Myth and History*, 3rd ed. (New York: Harcourt Brace, 1994). This book places the documents of the NT in broad historical, social, and cultural contexts, and is very well done.

Notes:

[1] Scholars believe that these books represent a composite of the work of at lest four groups or "schools' of writers, called J, E, D, and P. "J" is the earliest and so called because his name for God of Israel is Yahweh (Jahweh in German––German scholars were the first to identify this writer). He–or they, most likely–were probably scribes and historians at the court of the great king, Solomon. The date of 950 B.C. is often given as an approximation of the time when his work–representing the traditions of southern Israel–was composed. The second school, "E", is also names after its designation for the God of Israel,

Elohim. E's work seems to represent the traditions of northern Israel. The general date widely accepted for his work is about 850 B.D., or roughly a hundred years after J. Scholars do not think that the distinctions between J and E are all that easily made, and some question if there really are two independent sources which represent southern and northern traditions. The Deuteronomist, or "D", the third writer or school, is assigned a general date of about 650 B.C. His work emphasizes the law or the great covenant of Moses. The Book of Deuteronomy is believed to be his work. The deuteronomic tradition is an important one in the early parts of the OT, and its influence is felt throughout all the books form Deuteronomy through II Kings. The Last writer "P," is th Priestly Writer. And his work is thought to have been composed roughly around 450 B.C.

² This chart is taken from Conrad E. L'Heureux, *In and Out of Paradise: The Book of Genesis from Adam and Eve to the Tower of Babel* (New York: Paulist, 1983), p. 9.

Nicene Creed

We believe in one God,
The Father, the Almighty
maker of heaven and earth,
of all that is seen and unseen.
We believe in one Lord, Jesus Christ
 the only Son of God,
eternally begotten of the Father,
God from God, Light from Light,
true God from true God
begotten, not made, one in Being with the Father
Through him all things were made.
For us men and for our salvation
        he came down from heaven:

(On Christmas and its vigil, we kneel for the following two lines.)

(Bow:)   By the power of the Holy Spirit
        he was born of the Virgin Mary, and became man.

For our sake he was crucified under Pontius Pilate;
he suffered, died and was buried.
On the third day he rose again
in fulfillment of the Scriptures;
he ascended into heaven
and is seated at the right hand of the Father.
He will come again in glory
to judge the living and the dead,
and his kingdom will have no end.
We believe in the Holy Spirit, the Lord,
        the giver of life,
who proceeds from the Father and the Son
With the Father and the Son he is worshiped
        and glorified.
He has spoken through the prophets.
We believe in one holy catholic and apostolic Church.
We acknowledge one baptism for the
        forgiveness of sins.
We look for the resurrection of the dead,
and the life of the world to come. Amen.

The Trinity and Salvation

Dominic Colonna

Introduction

A simple, basic belief that there is a God is, perhaps, among the easiest religious ideas to accept. Many people find it possible to acknowledge, for example, that there is some transcendent Being or ultimate force which creates, sustains, and gives meaning to human existence. Many people, however, find it more difficult to agree upon the particular features of such a Being. For example, people might disagree as to whether God is a person, a force of nature, or some other phenomenon. Further, even if people agree that God is either a person or a force of nature, they might disagree about the particular features of this person or force. The teaching or doctrine of the Trinity represents the attempt by Christians to describe some of the particular features of God. It is a fundamental teaching of Christianity. The doctrine states that there is only one God and that this God is *triune,* that is, in some way *three* and *one.* The doctrine states, furthermore, that God's *triunity* is revealed or made known to humanity through the history of God's salvation of humanity.

These particular understandings of the triune character of God presuppose two fundamental ideas. First, they presuppose the idea that the human person is a being which is in need of salvation. Second, they presuppose the idea that salvation is brought about by God the Father through the historical person Jesus Christ by the power of the Holy Spirit. In the following pages I will attempt to describe how Christians explain that God is triune. Furthermore, I will attempt to explain how this description of God is related to the Christian doctrine of salvation.

Triunity

To say that God is triune is not to say that there are three distinct Gods. Christian tradition teaches that the Trinity is a single "substance" made up of three "persons:" God the Father, Jesus Christ, and the Holy Spirit. Terms such as "substance" and "person" have been confusing since they were first used to formulate the doctrine of the Trinity in the early church. They are unique theological terms used to develop precise teachings regarding the relationship between Jesus of Nazareth, God, and the reality experienced as the "spirit" of God. Using the terms "substance" and "person" to describe the Trinity, although somewhat confusing today, is not without value. The terms indicate the belief that we experience God in multiple ways. This is not to say that the doctrine of the Trinity describes one God and two other possible manifestations of the one God, that is, Jesus Christ and the Holy Spirit. The doctrine describes God, rather, as revealed to us in three unique ways in the history of human salvation.

Salvation and the human person

Salvation is, according to Christian tradition, a salvation from an eternal death and damnation. Popularly, such salvation is considered to be an avoiding of a "hell" (characterized as a place of unbearable punishment located somewhere "below" us) and a moving toward a "heaven" (characterized as a place of unimaginable reward located somewhere "above" things). For modern Christians, such images, although meaningful at a certain simple level, are less meaningful on another, more sophisticated level; modern physics and geology make it hard to understand how there might be a heaven "above" and a hell "below." Salvation might be more meaningful to modern Christians if it were characterized as the intellectual, moral, and spiritual developmental process by which we become more like God. Such a process may be called human self-transcendence. In this understanding, salvation can be characterized as a closer union with God. This is not to say that we become physically closer to God. This understanding of salvation suggests, rather, that at each stage of our lives we have the capacity to become more aware of God's loving personal presence, a presence which we experience as always already close to us when we direct ourselves toward it.

Our awareness of God's loving presence tells us something important about ourselves and our relationship with God. In traditional Christian language, our awareness of God tells us that we are "sinful" or "fallen" and in need of God's assistance to be "saved." The concept of "fallenness" might be characterized as an experience of ourselves as finite or somehow limited, incomplete, or immature. In our consciousness of God, God is "known" as the infinite reality which provides meaning, order, and value to the world. God is known as that reality (or standard) which allows us to recognize things as valuable, meaningful, good, true, and real in the world around us. Such knowledge enables us to think and act, and, thereby, grow intellectually, morally, and spiritually. This awareness of God's "infinitude" makes us aware of our own finitude, that is, our ability as limited beings to become something more and something greater than what we are. Our experience that we are finite is not merely an experience of the idea that "we could be better." It is also the experience that we, as human beings, have a tendency to be evil and selfish. It is the experience that we tend toward sinful acts, "in our thoughts and in our words, in what we have done and in what we have failed to do."

As already indicated above, our awareness of God's loving presence tells us something positive about ourselves and our relationship with God. This awareness tells us not only that we are finite and flawed ("sinful") but also that we have the ability (with God's help) to grow intellectually, morally, and, especially, spiritually. In other words, we have the ability to help bring about our own salvation by developing a more loving relationship with God. God, by being present to us in a personal, loving way, makes us able to love God freely and thereby contribute to our own salvation. The doctrine of the Trinity provides a description of how Christians believe God acts in our lives to help us help ourselves. Such activity might be characterized as human growth. For Christians, however, two things must be kept in mind. First, our ability to love God and thereby grow as human beings is a responsibility. We have an obligation to pursue goodness and beauty and truth. Such an obligation is not a limitation of our freedom. It is, rather, the fulfillment of our freedom as beings with the potential to grow intellectually, morally, and spiritually. Our obligation can be likened to the responsibility we have toward someone whom we love. A second thing to keep in mind is the Christian belief that human growth (salvation) is possible only because of God who acts through Christ by the power of the Holy Spirit.

God the Father

The term "Father" is used in the doctrine of the Trinity in order to describe the personal relationship which God has with those who share in the "covenant" with God. According to the Bible, God established a covenant or an agreement with Abraham and his descendants, the Hebrew people known as "Israel." The essence of this pact is the agreement that God will protect and preserve Abraham's descendants and they, in turn, will acknowledge that God is the God of all gods. This idea of a covenantal relationship between God and the descendants of Abraham is a fundamental teaching of Judaism and Christianity. It is one which is expanded upon by Jesus and his followers. In this covenantal relationship, God is likened to a father in order to describe how this pact is something more than an impersonal business agreement between two unrelated or disinterested parties. The term "Father" helps characterize the covenant as a personal, loving covenant. "Father" refers to God insofar as God is the source of the love by which we are saved. God acts as a loving parent who gives life, sustenance, and protection which allows Israel to grow. In this understanding, God is the Father and the people of the covenant are the "children of God."

In the New Testament, Jesus explains the Fatherhood of God by referring to his own special personal relationship with God. Jesus preaches that he has come into the world to announce and establish a new covenant between God and those willing to acknowledge and respond favorably to God's power and love. In this new agreement, God is still understood as that "person" who protects and saves God's covenantal partners. Jesus describes God's Fatherhood and the covenant in very personalistic and universalistic terms. He uses language which suggests that he has a unique relationship with God–he is a true son of God–which allows him to have an intimate knowledge of the will of the Father. He teaches, however, that all people can share in the covenant with God and develop knowing and loving relationships with God which are like the one he has with his father. St. Paul, the source for many of the early church's understanding of who Jesus was, explains that we can become children of God by "adoption." (See Romans 8: 18-25, Galatians 4:1-7.)

What does all this specifically Christian talk mean? How does God, as Father, save us? The term Father suggests that God is that person whom we love. God the Father is that ultimately attractive person who draws us toward God's self. God moves us because God is that person who is ultimately lovable. According to Christianity, our love of God is equivalent to the love of truth, goodness, beauty, and that which is real. Our pursuit of these things is a movement toward a better state of existence. In Christian terms, it is a movement toward salvation. In this understanding, God is a passive cause of our salvation. Christianity, however, also teaches that God is an active cause of our salvation. God actively causes our salvation by loving us. Descriptions of the other persons of the Trinity–Jesus Christ and the Holy Spirit–both expressions of God's love for us, help explain how God is an active cause of our salvation.

Jesus Christ, the Son

The crowning demonstration of God's fatherly love for us is God's willingness to sacrifice a part of himself, that is, Jesus, for our salvation. For Christians, Jesus' life, ministry, and death point to the era of salvation. Jesus is the archetypal human being. In other words, Jesus is the model of how we are to live in the world as beings with the potential for unlimited spiritual growth. One way to understand how Jesus is such an example is to look at St. Paul's description of (the nature and function of) Jesus. St. Paul likens Jesus to Adam, the first and representative human being whom we read about in the book of Genesis. Like Adam, Jesus was faced with a decision to accept or reject the love which enables us to live and to grow. Unlike Adam, Jesus made the right choice. On the one hand, Adam attempted to grow more like God in a way which did not acknowledge his need for God. Jesus, on the other hand, chose a different path toward growth. Jesus chose to empty himself, that is, to yield to the power and love of God. Through such a yielding or a defeat, Jesus was paradoxically victorious. By yielding to the power and love of God, he realized his potential, that is, he became that which he was capable of becoming, as a spiritual being. (See Philippians 2: 1-11, Romans 5: 12-19.)

According to Christians, Jesus not only announces the era of salvation he also ushers it in through his death and resurrection. In other words, Jesus is not only a sign which points to God's salvation but he also embodies the reality of that toward which he points. In this way, Jesus is understood to be an active cause of our salvation. Christians understand Jesus to be a God-man, that is, a true human person and true God. He is a unique union of spirit and the human person. Jesus is not merely one of other possible historical examples of how we should act. Christians believe that he is something more. Jesus is understood to be a unique historical person, one whose knowledge and love of God enabled him to express God's love for us through his death and resurrection in way which had not been done before and will not be done again. The understanding that Jesus is a unique savior is one based on a faith which may be characterized as a trust. Early Christians observed the life of Jesus and listened to his words and believed that they were meaningful and valuable. They trusted what he said because his words provided answers to many of life's most important questions. Later Christians trust the words of those who have written about Jesus. Furthermore, later Christians trust their own experience that the resurrected Jesus somehow affects their lives. Christians experience the resurrected Jesus as "Emmanuel," a name which means that God is with us. (See Matthew 1:22-23. Cf. Matthew 28:19-20.) Being with us, the risen Jesus causes our salvation by helping us help ourselves participate in our salvation.

The Holy Spirit

In addition to Jesus, God sends the Holy Spirit as an expression of love for us. The Holy Spirit represents the personal, loving presence of God to humanity. For Christians, it is the gift of God's self to humanity. It is God's grace-as offered-by which we can be saved. It is a presence to which we can respond either negatively or positively. In other words, we can either reject or accept God's personal offer of grace and salvation. Salvation by the power of the Holy Spirit is an event which involves the positive human response to God's loving offer of grace. The grace by which we are saved is completed only in its being accepted. By responding positively to God's offer of grace, by accepting the presence of the Holy Spirit, we become children of God like Jesus. Unlike Jesus, however, we become adopted children of God.

Again the question arises, what does all this Christian talk mean? One way to answer this question is to refer back to what was said above about how Jesus is an active cause of our salvation. The presence of God which is in the God-man, Jesus Christ, is the same presence of God which is in the human person. In the human person, however, there is a different result. The personal presence of God as the Holy Spirit does not cause instances of additional "God-people." It causes, rather, worldly instances of individual spiritual persons with capacities similar to (but not the same as) those of Jesus. Our spiritual growth and salvation, as adopted children of God, can be characterized as an awareness of God's loving presence along with a positive response to that presence. The grace which causes our salvation is simultaneously God's offer and our response to that offer. As was said above in the discussion of salvation, we are able to "know" or be aware of God (the Holy Spirit) as the "horizon" in each and every conscious thought or action. Such an awareness is characterized as a transcendental awareness or experience. We can figure out how to translate this transcendental knowledge into everyday thoughts and actions through the use of our conscience. Conscience is that capacity by which we determine how to grow as moral and spiritual persons. Through conscience, we can determine how to love God through the love of our neighbors. We are able to know what the shape of a positive response to God's offer of salvation looks like through our transcendental experience of the Spirit and through conscience. In this way, the Holy Spirit causes our salvation, helping us to direct our desire to grow intellectually, morally, and spiritually and thereby participate in our own salvation.

Conclusion

The doctrine of the Trinity is a Christian teaching which helps explain particular features of God's relationship with us. The doctrine does not describe three distinct and separate Gods. Furthermore, it's primary value is not to describe the private relationships between the Father, Son, and Holy Spirit. The real value of the doctrine of the Trinity is that it helps us to understand how God acts in history to cause our salvation. Moreover, it helps us to understand the necessary role that we play in our salvation. The doctrine of the Trinity teaches us that God the Father causes our salvation by being that which we desire above all things. As such, God moves us, that is, attracts us toward God. God the Father is that toward which we move in our quest for intellectual, moral, and spiritual development. In this sense, God is a somewhat passive cause of our salvation. Jesus Christ and the Holy Spirit represent our experience of how God is the active cause of our salvation. The two are expressions of God's love for us. They are expressions of love which call for a response from us. At the same time that they call for a response from us, they are also the source for our answer to the call.

The Trinity: Discussion Questions

1.) Do you believe that humanity is need of some sort of salvation? If so, why? Saved from what? Do you believe that you, personally, are in need of some sort of salvation? Why?

2.) Some Christians teach that our ability to participate in our own salvation is limited simply to "accepting Jesus Christ as our personal Lord and Savior." Do you agree with this idea? Why or why not? Is this idea inconsistent with the description of our participation in our own salvation offered in this essay?

3.) Are your own moral and spiritual actions affected by the presence of God?

4.) What is the value in distinguishing the three "persons" of the Trinity?

5.) Does the idea of the Trinity challenge a certain understanding of the first commandment ("You shall have no other Gods before me")?

6.) What, in your understanding, is the relationship between the Father, Son, and Holy Spirit?

The Trinity: For Further Reading

Karl Rahner is a theologian whose ideas about the Trinity have influenced much Roman Catholic reflection on the doctrine. Very advanced students might look at Rahner's *The Trinity* (New York: Crossroad, 1997). Although his writings are often very difficult, he offers a simpler discussion of the nature and function of Jesus Christ in his essay "Can We Still Believe?" in *Do You Believe in God?* (New York: Newman, 1969).

Peter Fransen, *The New Life of Grace* (London: Geoffrey Chapman, 1971), is an older, advanced text. It provides, however, clear, well-written, and still valuable discussions of the Trinity and salvation in terms similar to those used in this essay. See, in particular, the sections "Grace, A Likeness to Christ," and "Our Unity with the Father and with the Holy Spirit."

Catherine Mowry LaCugna has developed Rahner's study of the Trinity and demonstrated its implications for other theological concerns in her book *God for Us: The Trinity and Christian Life* (San Francisco: HarperSanFrancisco, 1991). LaCugna's basic ideas can be found in "The Trinitarian Mystery of God," an essay in *Systematic Theology: Roman Catholic Perspectives*, edited by Francis Schuessler Fiorenza and John P. Galvin (Minneapolis: Fortress, 1991), and "The Trinity: Why it Takes Three Persons to Save One Soul," an interview which appeared in *U.S. Catholic* (November 1993).

Jesus and the Reign of God

Blest are your eyes because they see
and blest are your ears because they hear.
I assure you, many a prophet and many a saint
longed to see what you see but did not see it,
to hear what you hear but did not hear it.
– Matthew 13:17

William C. Graham

Has any other figure been the object of so many queries and studies and opinions and articles and books as has Jesus the Christ? He lived before there was a daily newspaper, before the term "media" was coined, before MTV, before the cult of personality created *People* magazine. Yet no other character in modern times or in any other era has occasioned the comment and the study, no one else has inspired the countless number of imitators and admirers as did the one known as Son of God, love's saving presence among humankind.

An old Christian maxim suggests *lex orandi, lex credendi.* That is to say that the law of prayer establishes the law of belief. Wonder what the church teaches about something or someone? Look in the Church's official prayer, and see there the reflection of what the Church believes. The church's belief is revealed in the words of the Church's prayer. Consider the Christmas I preface to the eucharistic prayer below. What words does it use to identify Jesus as the Savior of humankind, the focus of human hope?

Father, all powerful and ever living God,
we do well always and everywhere to give you thanks
through Jesus Christ our Lord.
In the wonder of the incarnation
your eternal Word has brought to the eyes of faith
a new and radiant vision of your glory.
In him we see our God made visible
and so are caught up in love of the God we cannot see.
And so, with all the choirs of angels in heaven
we proclaim your glory and join
in their unending hymn of praise.

Jesus of Nazareth was born into common people, and lived 33 years among them. He preferred always the company and causes of the poor and oppressed. The gospels assert that Jesus was born of the House of David. Oddly, the genealogy of Jesus found in the beginning of Matthew's gospel traces the lineage of Joseph, who was the husband of Mary, the mother of Jesus. Thus the lineage is not really that of Jesus himself. Remember that Luke tells the story of Mary having been overshadowed by the Holy Spirit. She conceived while still a virgin. Jesus was conceived without sexual intercourse having taken place. The point of Matthew's genealogy, then, is not that Jesus is Joseph's son, but that he was born of a royal line, the House of David. Out of David's house was to come the Messiah, the savior of all humankind.

This savior loved humanity enough to come and dwell on earth. He came with a radical vision of life in and for the human community. His vision found roots in the great Hebrew prophets. He proposed a reversal of values and of fortunes so that the first would be last and the last would be first. He lived this vision on earth, and he challenged others to live as he did. Jesus called for a new humanity and a new earth. This challenge was at the heart of his preaching about the Reign or the Kingdom of God.

Jesus knew that not all would heed or live by his message. He said, "'Let those who have ears to hear me, hear!'" (Mark 4:9). His call was to begin living differently, living morally, living righteously. Following him would be a guarantee that life would not remain an empty riddle, nor would life end on the day of death.

The secret was found in his life of compassion, in hearing others, attending to their distress. Jesus intimately knew God the Father, with whom he was one. His highest duty, like the prophets, was to preach about God's Reign, and to share that Reign and that goodness with all people. In his own love and unwearying compassion, he taught and still teaches others to live, insisting that selfishness and hate destroy, while love will build a new and lasting earth. For Jesus, this kind of religion made life real.

John the Baptist prepared the way for Jesus. John was much like the Hebrew prophets of the Old Testament, the Jewish Scriptures. John demanded obedience to God's commands, preached repentance, called people to abandon sin and death, and cling to what is good and upright. The baptism John offered was a pledge of repentance, a promise of a world to be renewed. How were these faithful people to prepare for the coming of the Messiah? There was just one way: begin a new kind of life in which love rules. Social inequality and oppression must end. He said, "'Let the one with two coats give to the one who has none. The one who has food should do the same'" (Luke 3:11).

Luke the Gospel writer saw John as the fulfillment of Isaiah's prophecy (see 3:10-14). The Kingdom of God was close. Justice would triumph.

Jesus saw John as his forerunner. At his baptism by John, the voice of God is heard, proclaiming, "'This is my beloved Son. My favor rests on him'" (Matthew 3:17). Jesus, too, called people to repentance. Matthew writes that "Jesus began to proclaim this theme: 'Reform your lives! The Kingdom of heaven is at hand'" (4:17). His message was a clear and simple invitation to transform a weary world by a strong and consistent application of the vision of love. Like John and the prophets before him, Jesus also was on the side of society's poor and oppressed. His faith and his hope, his model for life in the human community, was not simply the vision of a Utopia. His life and love would inaugurate God's Reign.

The Reign of God

Christians have often misunderstood the notion of God's Kingdom, thinking that it refers simply to heaven, a place or a state which is entered when life on earth is complete and one's body lies in the grave. Careful attention to the Gospels suggest that this was not what Jesus preached. Salvation is not an individual's call, but a social hope that involves all the community. God's radical intervention in the human community means that the earth is good, as is the human community that dwells there. Radical, remember, refers to the roots, the original or fundamental meaning. Why is it that the earth and humankind are both good? "God looked at everything he had made, and he found it very good" (Genesis 2:31).

Jesus came to a confused earth, one steeped in sin and evil, and offered the promise of redemption. Consequently, when Jesus speaks of the Kingdom of God, he speaks of developing society and of popular hope. He does not speak of conquering by violence and war. In fact, after the vast crowd was fed with the multiplied loaves and fish, they were so impressed with the wisdom, ability and compassion of Jesus that they wanted to make him their King. He withdrew. God's Kingdom is not an earthly empire, and it will not be established by the methods which appeals first to the crowds. (See Matthew 14:22-23, John 6:14-15.)

In the desert, confronted by the tempter, Jesus would not call angels to deliver bread when he fasted. This was not how the Messiah's Reign was to begin. John the Baptizer thought that the Messiah's Reign would begin with judgment (see Matthew 3:10-12). Jesus said judgment would come at the end, the wheat with weeds (see the story in Matthew 13:24-30).

"'The soil produces of itself first the blade, then the ear, finally the ripe wheat in the ear'" (Mark 4:28). You may have seen this Scripture quotation on the front page of *The Christian Science Monitor*. This fine newspaper points to much of what is good in human society. Looking for advancement in human ability to live together, it reports good news. Jesus was the best preacher of good news. He promised the final judgment in the future. But what was important in the present moment was the sowing of seed. How then would the Kingdom come? Like a blast out of the blue? Asked by one of the Pharisees when God's Reign would come, Jesus said: "'You cannot tell by careful watching when the Reign of God will come. Neither is it a matter of reporting that it is "here" or "there." The Reign of God is already in your midst'" (Luke 17:20-21). "Let anyone with ears to hear listen!" (Luke 14:35).

The parables, the stories told by Jesus, provoke reflection and insight. The work of God is seen in beginnings. God is a crafter and lover of promise, but the finished product is a distant reality. The journey of life points to and promises future glory, but God is the pilgrim's guide, and it is in and on the journey that God's promise is revealed.

Jesus makes room at the table for all those who would come. Dining in the house of a leading Pharisee, Jesus sketched his vision of God's Reign where all are welcome at the table. Another guest at the party delighted in this insight and exclaimed, "'Happy is the one who feasts in the Kingdom of God'" (Luke 15:14). This insight is forever enshrined and celebrated in the Christian eucharist. Before the faithful receive the eucharist, the presider shows the consecrated bread and wine, and says, "This is the Lamb of God / who takes away the sins of the world. Happy are those who are called to his supper." Jesus makes it clear that old divisions between Jew and Gentile are beginning to fade. The new dividing line is that between good and evil, between those with open hearts and good will and those with closed hands and selfish interests. Paul reflects this intent and dream of Jesus when he writes that "All of you who have been baptized into Christ have clothed yourselves with him. There does not exist among you Jew or Greek, slave or freeman, male or female. All are one in Christ Jesus" (Galatians 3:27-28). What kinds of changes might be in store if the Church rereads and reconsiders this expression of Jesus's hopes as we look toward the coming years and the turn of a new century and the third Christian millennium? How do the lofty conceptions of the Savior challenge those who read them and try to follow today?

Remember that John, the forerunner of Jesus, boldly claimed that the Kingdom of God was near. Jesus, on the other hand, taught that "'the Reign of God is already in your midst'" (Luke 17:21). Who can enter? Those who experience *metanoia*, a change of mind, of heart, of attitude. Jesus warned that "'I assure you, unless you change and become like little children, you will not enter the Kingdom of God.'" These will be "'of greatest importance in that heavenly Reign'" (Matthew 18:3-4).

The Vision of Jesus: A Radical Call

This vision of Jesus was that of transforming society, of honoring the earth and its human inhabitants. The point is not so much to get individuals to heaven, but to change the disharmony of earth into the peace of God's Reign. Jesus, human himself, knew and understood human nature, the social bent of humankind, the needs that call all people into community. His mission then was to prepare men and women to live together, promoting harmony and goodness. The fundamental virtue, of course, is love, for only love will build a better earth, will stimulate commitment to the common good.

All of this insight made Jesus a profoundly sociable companion. He would often engage others in conversation, and those he chose to converse with or as companions often shocked those with a conventional sense of decency. He spoke with the Samaritan woman at the well, and even she was surprised: "'You are a Jew. How can you ask me, a Samaritan and a woman, for a drink?'" (John 4:8). Tax collectors, too, whom polite society regarded as no more than robbers, also came into the company of Jesus. He visited their homes and they ate together. Jesus made the meal a true social occasion, and those who would understand Jesus and his ways and the sacraments that evolved among his followers must seek to understand the Jewish significance of table fellowship.

When contemporary preachers and theologians refer to the preferential option for the poor, they point back to Jesus's own preference for the poor. Here was the beginning of the fulfillment of his mother's song: "He has deposed the mighty from their thrones / and raised the lowly to high places. / The hungry he has given every good thing, / while the rich he has sent empty away" (Luke 1:52-53).

Jesus saw riches as a point of division in society. Those who are rich do not feel the same dependence on others as do the poor, nor do they need to feel the same kind of responsibility towards others as often the poor do. Such is both the blessing and the curse of riches. This is the dilemma of the rich young man who approaches Jesus. "'What must I do to share in everlasting life?'" he asks. Jesus answers that he ought to obey the commandments, and the youth answers, "'I have kept all these since my childhood.'" Jesus looked at him with love and said, "'There is one thing more that you must do. Go and sell what you have and give to the poor; you will then have treasure in heaven. After that, come and follow me.'" The young man went away sad, the Gospel reports, because he had many possessions (Mark 10:17-22).

Jesus then observes that it is difficult for the rich to enter God's Reign. In fact, "'it is easier for a camel to pass through a needle's eye than for a rich man to enter the Kingdom of God'" (Mark 10:25). Some scholars or preachers will suggest an allegorization of what Jesus says, asserting that he referred to a rocky place which a camel could pass through with difficulty. They seek to make a hard saying less hard. That does not seem to be the meaning in this Gospel story, as Jesus asserts a bit later that "'with God all things are possible'" (Mark 10:27). There is a radicalism here that some try to spiritualize or soften, but it remains clear that the fundamental sympathies of Jesus were with the poor and oppressed. He helped them with his healing power, with heroic generosity and authentic compassion.

A Reversal of Fortunes: An Explosive Message

The Messiah's message was about reversal of fortunes: the poor would be fed, the rich sent away. Those to be blessed were those upon whom the world had not smiled. The bold Jesus suggested that each serve the other. Tyranny must be abandoned in favor of community. Greatness would be found when rank and honor, envy and anger were renounced. Who then is the greatest? Even the apostles quarreled about this, and at the Last Supper no less! Jesus reminded them that earthly kings lord their authority over their people. "'Yet it cannot be that way with you'" (Luke 22:26). Here is the revolutionary Jesus pointing to a new world order, a new way of living together.

There is great power in the words of Jesus. If those who consider themselves his followers were to live in conformity to his words for a full day, the world as we know it would be launched into a new orbit. Even on the cross, Jesus did not abandon this vision, and his followers came to know that the suffering of the cross which seemed utter folly had beyond it resurrection, new life, a transformed earth, and the promise of the fullness of God's Reign.

The faith of Jesus and the possibility of God's Kingdom continue to quicken humanity's hope on the developing earth, in the promise of peace, in the transformation of culture. Jesus was not merely a social reformer, not just a man who would have the earth be better. Instead, his vision was of a completely new order, and religion was at the heart. The new humanity which he envisioned and to which he called those who would follow is the promise of redemption that still beckons to humanity even today. Imagine an earth where people would dare live the fullness of the message of Jesus!

Jesus knew that his message was explosive, and that those who would hear and follow would not be silent. In fact, he was told during his entry into Jerusalem that he should rebuke his disciples. Apparently they were too loud, and embarrassed the sedate and orderly city. The entire crowd of disciples was shouting "'Blessed is he who comes / in the name of the Lord! / Peace in heaven and glory in the highest'" (Luke 19:38-39). The complainers did not associate this cry with the very similar message of the angels to the shepherds earlier in Luke after the birth of the infant (2:14). Jesus, of course, made the connection, and he told the Pharisees who would have the disciples be still that "'If they were to keep silence, I tell you the very stones would cry out'" (19:40). Their cry would be in joy at the presence of the One in whom all the earth will find salvation.

Jesus: Discussion Questions

1.) Why has Jesus been the object of so many queries and studies and opinions and articles and books? Why has he occasioned so much comment and study, inspired countless number of imitators and admirers ?

2.) What does the official, public prayer of the Church tell about who Jesus was and is?

3.) Explain the challenge that is at the heart of Jesus's preaching about the Reign or the Kingdom of God.

4.) How have Christians often misunderstood the notion of God's Kingdom? Does it refer simply to heaven, or a state which is entered when life on earth is complete and one's body lies in the grave?

5.) What is metanoia? Why and how is it important for the follower of Jesus? How does the call to metanoia challenge not just individuals, but society and its structures?

6.) What is meant by the preferential option for the poor? How does this reference point back to the personality of Jesus? How does this idea challenge those who would follow Jesus today?

Jesus: For Further Reading

Johnson, Elizabeth A. *Consider Jesus: Waves of Renewal in Christology.* New York: Crossroad, 1990.

Lunny, William J. *The Jesus Option.* New York: Paulist Press, 1994.

Neusner, Jacob. *A Rabbi Talks with Jesus: An Intermillennial Interfaith Exchange.* New York: Doubleday, 1993.

Meier, John P. *A Marginal Jew: Rethinking the Historical Jesus.* New York: Doubleday, 1991.

Rauschenbusch, Walter. *Christianity and the Social Crisis.* Louisville, KY: Westminster / John Knox, 1991; originally published in 1907. Chapter II, *The Social Aims of Jesus,* provided an outline and inspiration for this essay, *Jesus and the Reign of God.* Rauschenbusch's study of the prophets and early Christianity may also be of interest.

Freedom in the Cross:
Our Limits and Our Hope

Alan Revering

In his poem "The Second Coming," William Butler Yeats reflects on the devastating experience of World War I in Europe:

> The falcon cannot hear the falconer;
> Things fall apart; the centre cannot hold;
> Mere anarchy is loosed upon the world ...

Although these lines were written about the destruction of war, they express a sense of brokenness that is universal in human experience. In any society, in each of our own personal lives, we all face the threat of things falling apart, the centre not holding. When meaning disappears from my life and my direction is confused, when failure or frustration overwhelm my best efforts, when sickness and death remind me of my own ultimate helplessness, then I know the brokenness of life. Theology of the cross is our reflection on this experience.

As Christians, we look to the cross for healing of the brokenness both in our personal lives and in our societies and cultures. The death of Jesus on the cross does not stand outside of culture, for it happened in history, in a particular cultural and political context. It is also grasped, interpreted and handed on within a particular communal tradition of faith. Yet this symbol of our faith is not limited to one culture alone: it has a peculiar power to address the brokenness and ambiguity that characterize our lives. To it we can relate our own experiences of personal suffering, and in it we find a still-valid critique of broader cultural, political and social realities.

Two aspects of the cross

Reflection on the cross will not provide simple answers, however:

> The theology of the cross can never be a brilliant statement about the brokenness of life; it has to be a broken statement about life's brokenness, because it participates in what it seeks to describe. Apart from that participation, it would be empty chatter.[1]

My own thoughts about the cross will fall into two pieces. The first I will call the negative aspect, since it involves limits on our abilities in several different but related ways. I will argue that human knowledge and language are limited in the cross; our words cannot express the meaning of this event adequately, and our reason cannot explain it in a straightforward way. I will also try to show that these limits on knowledge should be related to political limits on force. Since the theology of the cross already has this relation to political life, Christianity is itself a call to work for freedom and justice.

More about this negative aspect in the next section–but there is also a positive aspect, which depends on our belief in the incarnation. We see Jesus as fully human, one like us. In this respect we have knowledge of him, for his possibilities as well as his plight could also be our own. At the same time, we also speak of his life as the incarnation of God, and in this way, even in our limitations, we have a kind of knowledge about God. The positive aspect of the cross forms an ideal toward which we can strive, and a hope to which we can cling. We could speak of this aspect of the cross as the freedom *for* something positive, a good to which we devote our lives and around which we shape our communities, just as the negative aspect is related to freedom *from* forces that threaten and oppress.

The relationship between these two aspects is not easy to state. They are not really in conflict, nor are they simply juxtaposed. Rather, each is like the secret heart of the other, the midpoint around which the other is constructed. The shape of a cross may be a visual image of this: the vertical bar can signify a barrier or limit, negating our attempts to reach through to knowledge of God and regulating our relationships with other persons, while the horizontal bar expresses the real connections and continuities that nonetheless exist among people, and between us and God. Despite their apparent opposition, each really depends upon the other, and only when they are taken together–only when the centre holds!–do we see the shape of the cross. The question for a theology of the cross is not which of these aspects to choose, but how to hold them together amid the brokenness of life.

The Cross as Limit: The Passion of Jesus
Martin Luther's central insight about theology of the cross was this: instead of calling the bad good and the good bad, a true theology of the cross calls things as they are; only in this way can we catch a glimpse of the "backside" of God.[2] This is a warning that our theology must not move too quickly and easily to expressions of victory and hope in the cross. Otherwise we neglect the reality of the cross, the helpless suffering and cruel death of Jesus.

The disciples had to face this reality themselves, and had to find a way to speak of it theologically. How could Christians proclaim as savior a man who had undergone such rejection and suffering? Dramatic accounts of the resurrection grew like valuable pearls around this painful irritant, but they cannot conceal the negative reality of the cross, a scandal that required some explanation. In the New Testament, many different models of interpretation are suggested, but especially in the gospel of Mark and the letters of Paul, the negativity of the cross is freely admitted and even brought to the very center of the Christian proclamation. Paul refers to Jesus on the cross as "cursed" (Gal 3:13) and even says that "God made him who did not know sin, to be sin" (2 Cor 5:21). Mark portrays him as a helpless, suffering man, seemingly abandoned by God in spite of his innocence.

This tradition of acknowledging the negative aspect of the cross has continued in different formulations throughout the history of Christian theology. In the eleventh century, for example, Anselm suggested a theology of "substitutionary atonement." We deserve to be punished by God, but Christ substitutes for us and takes all the suffering upon himself. In this view, the suffering is precisely the means of our salvation, while the resurrection seems to be a mere afterthought. We would now criticize this theology for its one-sided emphasis on sacrifice, and for its legalistic image of a cruel God who demands restitution, but there is some enduring value in its insistence that we confront the negativity of the cross as such, without too quickly passing into more pleasant and comfortable thoughts about resurrection.

Suffering and Limitation

What do we see when we look at the suffering of the cross? It does not look like a sign of glory: it is instead a sign of limitation, pain, and brokenness. Jesus is passive, stripped of his power, silently undergoing suffering and death. He has stood in implicit opposition to the powers and structures of his society, but they have overpowered him: Jesus has reached the limits of his abilities, and he is broken. Contemporary Lutheran theologian Jurgen Moltmann, drawing especially from the gospel of Mark, depicts Jesus as a rebel and blasphemer, and one entirely forsaken by God.[3] If we were to interpret the cross purely in terms of these oppositions, then it would be nothing but tragedy, the final exclusion of Jesus from human society and history.

I have suggested, however, that the theology of the cross must also include a positive element at its core, so that the "centre can hold" and we can see the cross more fully. We must remember, therefore, that Jesus is human like us, so that we can imagine ourselves trapped in an oppressive, deadly situation as he is. Moreover, if these thoughts are to be a *theology* of the cross, then the life of Jesus must also be seen in light of God's presence in the world, and even his death must have some relation to God's action.

But identifying ourselves with Jesus does not explain his passion: on the contrary, it only reveals the impotence of words to touch the real existential question of suffering. Intense suffering takes us to the very edge of language and thought, for pain is of the body; it is what humans have in common with the animals. It deprives people (including philosophers and theologians!) of their ability to understand and to explain. No theories or explanations, no philosophies or theodicies can truly justify the suffering of an innocent person. The inexplicable and unjustifiable suffering that we see in the cross thus brings us to acknowledge limits of our understanding. Perhaps the best theoretical response that we could make would be compassionate silence, not easy explanation.

This silence has theological consequences: none of our concepts, no words, no affirmations can succeed in describing, explaining, or reaching God. We reach the boundaries of our ability to understand and to explain, and so we enter the darkness of the divine mystery. Theology of the cross does not back away from this limitation, but simply calls it what it is.

Social Consequences

The theology of the cross has led us to consider the limitations of our knowledge, but this in turn has some further consequences in regard to our societies. Religious justifications for coercion have been used far too often in the course of history, through an appeal to some superior religious knowledge. Our admission of limits to our knowledge means that we must also accept limits on our use of political or economic force against one another. We simply don't know enough, and can never be certain enough of ourselves, to justify the coercion of others for our own ends. Here we see the critical connection between the theology of the cross and the western political idea of freedom: recognizing our own limits, we seek guarantees of freedom from oppression, for ourselves as well as those who might disagree with us, by limiting the use of coercive force.

I do not mean to fashion a theoretical justification for western-style democratic governments out of the theology of the cross. My concern is not with constructing a positive theory or system at all, but with an attitude, a motivation, that applies in the arena of politics. The fruit of this theology of the cross is simply compassion, identifying ourselves with those who suffer helplessly today. This is not another idea about suffering–it is an attempt to see suffering in the lives of real people. The cross does not direct political action along any predetermined lines, but it does direct our attention to the poor and forgotten, those whom we easily overlook if we think we already understand the world perfectly. The cross calls for a compassion that allows us to see and respond to the suffering of others.

It is true, nonetheless, that this compassion can motivate us to take action and to work for great changes. European and American cultures have attempted to embody a limitation of power in their political structures. Constitutional guarantees of human rights, the rule of law, and opportunities for peaceful transitions of power are genuine achievements in the past two centuries. These arrangements are far from perfect in U.S. society, however, for many people have been left out: only gradually has our nation admitted that African-Americans, American Indians, and all women were unjustly excluded from equal protection of the law. The struggle to make equal rights truly universal still continues today in the U.S.; the international struggle–establishing some equity between rich and powerful nations and those that have fewer resources and less power–is even greater. I offer no solutions here. My argument is that the cross should open our eyes to see the inequities that remain, and should cause us to admit that we cannot impose suffering and oppression on anyone on the basis of our own limited and imperfect theories about God.

The same applies even more urgently in the realm of economic power. While the use of political force has been somewhat restrained in western democracies, economic power has grown enormously. The ability of some people in our societies to wield great power over others is all the more insidious because of the illusion that such power is not coercive.[4] The theology of the cross does not directly point the way to more equitable economic relations, but it calls us to be concerned about those people and nations that are made victims in the present systems.

The environmental crisis is another example of our need to abide within limits. In our confidence that modern science and technology have given us a good theoretical grasp of nature, we have come to consider ourselves as the masters of nature. The consequences for the environment have been disastrous. New and better technology may have some role to play in cleaning up the effects of old technology, but the solution ultimately lies in a change of attitude. Mastery of nature is seen as a temptation in the biblical tradition; for modern society it is instead a vocation.[5] The theology of the cross denies that we can ever be masters of nature, and calls for a more humble and respectful approach to our environment.

The Cross and the Church

The church itself cannot escape this critical aspect of the theology of the cross. "The Church is the Cross on which Christ was crucified; one could not separate Christ from His Cross, and one must live in a state of permanent dissatisfaction with the Church."[6] Of all human institutions it is religion that most often believes itself to have the key to all reality. I have tried to show that taking the cross as this key does not lead us to a clear understanding of all things, but rather forces us to accept limitations on our knowledge and our use of power.

The limits sketched above in regard to political society can also be applied to church governance. It is true that the church is not a state. Still, the church which confesses faith in the cross of Christ must accept some limits on its power over its own members. A purely monarchical and hierarchical structure of church governance might be appropriate for a group in which the highest officials had a clear grasp of all truth. If we are convinced that the cross has permanently ruled out all such claims, however, then a more limited, egalitarian governance is called for.

Church statements have frequently criticized the idea of unlimited need that is at the root of our consumerist societies. Church practice does not always match this preaching, however, for church organizations have found it difficult to provide just wages and to adopt fair labor practices. The church, like society as a whole, must learn to do without. This is also the best witness that we can give in relation to environmental issues. To learn again how to live at sustainable levels, we must acknowledge our limitations and stay within them.

Our purpose as a church is not just to reproduce ourselves. Instead we carry forward the gospel and the tradition of the cross. When we come face to face with our ultimate limitations, including our individual deaths, these things should be neither a surprise nor a discouragement to us. To hold a theology of the cross is to face limitation every day, in the deepest roots of our life. It is to know that we are not the whole, even if we have no clear vision of what lies beyond the horizon. It is to feel the negation, the otherness, the final mysteriousness of life.

The Cross as Hope: The Action of Jesus

There is, as I have suggested, another side as well: this negative moment itself will reveal to us an affirmation of life and hope, the promise of a new wholeness, and an ideal that can reshape our lives. Difference and negation are central to the theology of the cross, but they are not sufficient in themselves to give knowledge and meaning. We must also be able to find identities, similarities, analogies, which enable us to think and speak about our world. God is present in the dark mystery of the cross, the same God whose activity is also revealed in all of creation. The cross is not only an event of past history, a mystery unrelated to our own experience, for we also find its reflections in our lives.

Sacrament of salvation

In the New Testament, this side of the theology of the cross appears especially in the gospel of John, where Jesus is active and purposeful as he moves toward his death. Jesus is understood throughout the gospel as God's gift to the world (John 3:16), and the cross is nothing other than the culmination of this gift, the depth to which God will go out of love for humankind. A classic formulation of this theological tradition appears in the medieval writings of Peter Abelard. He emphasizes the power of Christ's loving example, which is both our salvation and our call. A commentator summarizes Abelard's thought this way: "The purpose of the cross, therefore, was to bring about a change in sinners, to thaw their frozen hearts with the warmth of the sunshine of divine love. Christ did not die on the cross to change the mind of God ..."[7] Contemporary Catholic theologian Karl Rahner takes up this same point of view: "We must say: because God wills salvation, therefore Jesus died and rose again, and not: because the crucifixion occurred, therefore God wills our salvation."[8]

We believe as Christians that God's love does not hesitate to enter into human history, even to its uttermost depths; the negative moment that must remain central to the cross–the unspeakable death of Jesus–therefore becomes for us the effective sign of the strength of that love. Divine presence even in this cruelest hour assures us that we will never lack for God's presence in our own lives, even in our sufferings. This does not deny the harsh realities of life, but it clings to the hope that the divine power can transform them.

We can specify some of the practical consequences of this hope with the help of sociological theory. Sociologists point out that every human being needs a structure of meaning amid the chaos of life, a "sacred canopy"[9] that can protect us from the disorienting events that threaten on every side. Apart from such a canopy, life collapses into a random series of meaningless occurrences, without pattern or orientation: the centre cannot hold. When I live under this canopy, however, I discover the confidence to move forward, a way to understand my world, the hope of finding some meaning in it. The cross never gives me theoretical clarity, but as this kind of canopy it provides the interpretive key that I need to understand even troubling events and to integrate them into a structured life. If God's presence extends not only to the beautiful and peaceful moments of life, but also to the cross itself, then God is also present even through my own losses. Despite life-shaking changes that may threaten my established identity, and despite the prospect of death, nothing can separate us from the love of God (Rom 8:39).

Living in the Sign of the Cross

We do not simply receive this hope passively. In the actions of Jesus that led him to the cross, and in his willingness to be faithful to the bitter end, we also see an ideal for our own action. The theology of the cross thus cannot be separated from an understanding of Jesus' life and ministry: his preaching of the Kingdom, his invitations to table fellowship, his openness to people who were rejected by religious or social authorities. With this as our ideal, we too are called to devote ourselves to the service of others, to become vulnerable for the sake of others, to shape our lives not around our own needs but around the needs of others. Death itself has a new meaning when it is seen, not as the passive loss of the self, but as an active self-gift that is for the sake of another. In the terminology of political philosophy, the cross gives us an image of "the good life," the proper end of human life, and thus a firm direction and a lasting ethical orientation. For those who hold this ideal, it makes life worth living. It is the portrayal of what it means to be fully human.

I have praised societies that try to establish freedom from oppression. This freedom can have its negative side as well, as we are finding in the U.S. today: there is little that unifies us as a society, and respect for the individual easily turns into a selfish individualism. Just as the cross establishes meaning, orientation, and unity in the lives of individuals, however, so too it can give unity to those communities that gather around the cross. As a shared ideal and hope, it binds together the people who freely accept it as their own. We are freed for a particular vision of the good life, a definite end to which we devote ourselves. The two aspects of the theology of the cross thus address a double attitude toward freedom in our societies. It calls for the liberation of those who are coerced or oppressed, but it simultaneously suggests that we are freed for service to one another. In the theology of the cross, freedom from coercion cannot be separated from freedom for love.

The social and political consequences of the positive aspect of the cross are more difficult to specify, however, than those of the negative aspect. The ideal of perfection that we see in the cross does not carry us beyond the limitations we described in the previous section; rather it is embedded within the fact of limitation. We cannot, we must not use the cross as a means of oppression, as it was used at the time of the Crusades. But we can offer it as a hope and ideal, which can both empower individuals and unify communities in our societies that are so divided. We cannot cease to criticize the political and economic structures that continue to make voiceless victims out of the poor, but we can offer the cross as hope for the poor, in the knowledge that God is present even in the depths of human suffering. We recognize that people everywhere need to be freed from the obstacles that prevent them from reaching their ideals, and yet everywhere they can already dedicate themselves to living in the sign of the cross.

Conclusion

The words of scripture can provide a summary of all these reflections, both negative and positive: "No one has ever seen God. Yet if we love one another, God dwells in us, and his love is brought to perfection in us" (1 John 4:12). Neither of these sentences can stand without the other. It is not that we actually see God even in the cross, for God is always beyond our grasp. Yet we affirm that God dwells in us when we love as Jesus did; this is our image of human perfection and our ultimate hope. All of human reality, our living as well as our dying, is caught up in this symbol of our faith. For this reason we cling to the cross, celebrate its power in our lives, and seek to proclaim it in all our words and actions.

Cross: Discussion Questions

1.) How do you experience the sense of brokenness that is universal in human experience? What does it mean to suggest that theology of the cross is our reflection on this experience?

2.) How does the theology of the cross relate to political life? How does Christianity issue a call to work for freedom and justice?

3.) The life of Jesus must be seen in light of God's presence in the world. Even his death must have some relation to God's action. Explain.

4.) Relate the environmental crisis to the theology of the cross.

5.) How is the cross not only an event of past history, but a mystery related to your own experience? How does it find its reflections in your life?

Cross: For Further Reading

Hall, Douglas John. *Lighten our Darkness: Toward an Indigenous Theology of the Cross*. Philadelphia: Westminster, 1976.

Moltmann, Jergen. *The Crucified God: The Cross of Christ as the Foundation and Criticism of Christian Theology*. New York: Harper & Row, 1974.

O'Collins, Gerald, editor. *The Cross Today*. New York: Paulist Press, 1977.

Rahner, Karl. "The One Christ and the Universality of Salvation," in *Theological Investigations* XVI, pp. 199-224. New York: Seabury Press, 1979.

Rasmussen, Larry. "Returning to our Senses: The Theology of the Cross as a Theology for Eco-Justice," in *After Nature's Revolt: Eco-justice and Theology,* edited by Dieter Hessel. Minneapolis: Fortress Press, 1992.

The Lesson

Then Jesus took his disciples up the mountain
and gathering them around him, he taught they saying:
"Blessed are the poor in spirit,
for theirs is the kingdom of heaven,
Blessed are the meek,
Blessed are they that mourn,
Blessed are the merciful,
Blessed are they who thirst for justice,
Blessed are you when persecuted,
Blessed are you when you suffer,
Be glad and rejoice for your reward is great in heaven."

Then Simon Peter asked,
"Do we have to write this down?"
And Andrew asked,
"Are we supposed to know this?"
And James asked,
"Will we have a test on this?"
And Phillip said,
"I don't have any paper."
And Bartholomew asked,
"Do we have to turn this in?"
And John said,
"The other disciples didn't have to learn this."
And Matthew asked,
"Can I go to the boy's room?"
And Judas asked,
"What does this have to do with real life?"

Then one of the Pharisees who was present asked to see Jesus' lesson
plan and inquired of Jesus,
"Where is your anticipatory set
and your objectives in the cognitive domain?"

And Jesus wept.

-Anonymous

Tracing the Early Church

Andrew Krivak

I am a Catholic and a writer. I am not a theologian in any specific sense of the word, but I have spent a great deal of my life learning about the history and the practice of the Church in which I worship, the Church that I love. So when asked to write about this Church, I replied that I would, on the condition that I be allowed to write about the early Church. Why the early Church? Because I am fascinated by beginnings, by the difficulties of change that rise out of new ventures, and because the memory of where it all began is the continual reminder that what one loves ought never to be taken for granted.

Often when we think of the Church, we fail to realize that there is a history to the institution and the faith it professes which has had to adjust to the world in which it exists. The language in which we worship has not always been the same. The writings that the church believes express its faith have had to go through periods of scrutiny. And the social structure in which we live is certainly different from the time out of which Christianity emerged. At the core of ceaselessly changing history, however, is a foundation that remains immutable, the same from generation to generation, like the center of a wheel that moves forward but remains fixed. This is the belief that God, through Jesus Christ, has established his church in the world. "On this rock I will build my church, and the jaws of death shall not prevail against it" (Matthew 16:18). This is what distinguishes Church History from the study of history in general. Beneath the march of time and the ever-present influences of external society, the Church historian works within the frame-work of faith. So let us begin with the beginning.

The time frame of the history of the Church is relatively short, considering the length of recorded history. Yet, the two thousand years of the history of the Church are in themselves a daunting study. This chapter will examine how the spread of the message of Jesus of Nazareth resulted in numerous communities of believers who came to be known in Greek as *Christianoi*, or Christians, those who believed that the messiah, the Christ, had come. It is not possible to go into every detail, with certainty or speculation, about the early church here. The sources themselves from the first few centuries of Christianity alone are vast. I will simply try to paint in broad brush strokes a picture of how the early church began to take shape. We will begin with the end of the first century C.E. ("Common Era," the term commonly used in theology today to replace A.D. "Anno Domini," the "year of the Lord"), consider the highly formative second century, move through the third century up to the Age of Constantine and the founding of the great city of Constantinople, and conclude with the fourth century C.E.

It is not enough, though, to understand the early history of the Church as events spread out on an historical number line, pointing to who was born when, what documents were written, and why various decisions were made. The early history of the church involves an understanding of the internal development of what the earliest Christians believed, along with the events that occurred simultaneously in the otherwise external history of the world. The impact of world events that surrounded these first Christian communities shaped them just as Christianity would come to influence the shape of the world.

The First Century

The Acts of the Apostles, written by St. Luke the evangelist, is the first historical account of the early church. It is in this work of Scripture that we find the Christians of Jerusalem referring to their congregations as *ecclesia* (Acts 5:11. 8:1), that is, a religious group brought together by their convictions and beliefs (from *ecclesia* we get the word ecclesiology, literally, the study of what is "church").

Although all roads led to Rome in the days when Christianity broke into the world of the powerful Roman Empire, Jerusalem was the birthplace of the first church. Initially, the Christians of Jerusalem lived as Jews who believed that Jesus was the Christ, the Anointed One. They still worshiped and lived as Jews, following the laws of Moses, but they had accepted the baptism of Christianity; they were Jewish Christians. It was St. Paul, however, who first preached Christianity to the Gentiles as well as the Jews. St. Paul was the powerful Pharisee Saul (instrumental in the death of Stephen, the first martyr) who, the Acts of the Apostles tells us, the Lord chose to be an apostle. As a Roman citizen, he had access to all of the Roman empire (much like our ability to travel easily within the United States), around which he journeyed tirelessly, and his exceptional education as a pharisee allowed him to converse with educated pagans, convincing them that Jesus was the Messiah for whom Judaism had been waiting. Consequently, Paul's vision of the church was always one of universality, adhering to faith in Jesus Christ, not in Jewish laws or customs. In his letter to the Romans,

Paul writes: "For there is no distinction between Jew or Greek; the same Lord is Lord of all and is generous to all who call on him" (10:12). And in his letter to the Galatians, Paul reiterates the basis of Christianity that sets it apart from all exclusive religions, and establishes it as a universal faith for all of humanity: "We ourselves are Jews by birth and not Gentile sinners; yet we know that a person is justified not by the works of the law, but through faith in Jesus Christ (2:15-16). Neither circumcision nor uncircumcision is anything; but a new creation is everything" (6:15). This essential, universal foundation of Christianity is why the church later came to be called *catolica,* or catholic; that is, universal.

It was, most scholars believe, around the year 64 when Ss. Peter and Paul were put to death in Rome by the emperor Nero. This is the same period during which Nero began the infamous persecution of all Christians in Rome (pitting them against lions in the coliseum, or burning them as human torches in his gardens). Historically there is no real reason why Nero saw fit to put Christians to death. This was also the time when a great deal of Rome burned. Looking for a scapegoat to explain the damage, Nero, it seems, blamed it on the Christians, and punished them accordingly.

It was in the same year that construction of the Jewish temple in Jerusalem was completed. Rather than celebrating their success, however, the Jewish people revolted for having been put out of work, which was probably only a pretense for already hostile relations between the Jews and Romans in the Holy City. In the year 66 the Jews finally rose up in revolt, and a civil war ensued until the year 70, when Roman troops under the commander Titus entered the city and razed it, temple and all.

Despite their religious ties to Judaism, the early Christians were prepared to leave the city once the revolt had proved to be a disastrous failure. The Jewish Christians also realized that, unlike the Jews, the temple of Jerusalem was not an essential foundation of their faith. So they left the smoldering city of Jerusalem, and began moving out to other cities in which established communities of Christians already existed. For their part, the orthodox Jews remained in Jerusalem. The result was the first definitive separation between Judaism and the early Christians. This was an extremely significant moment in the early church, for it points to the last time Christianity would be seen as merely a sect of Judaism. Over against the exclusive birth-right of the

Jews, Christianity sought to include every person in its promise of salvation.

It is important to point out that, as a result of this decisive separation from Judaism and the continual acceptance of Gentiles into the ranks of Christians, the influence of a strong Hellenistic society (the cultural cities of ancient Greece) began to pervade the early church. We know from the Acts of the Apostles that Paul preached in Athens and Corinth, trying to convince the pantheistic Greeks that they did not need gods of war, love, the sea or the seasons. There is only one God, Paul told them, and "in him we live and move and have our being, as even some of your own (Greek) poets have said" (Acts 17:28). Eventually, Greek culture, or Hellenism, would have a profound effect on the early church. The result, however, would be both helpful and harmful. It was helpful as a means to spread the Gospel, since most of the world at that time spoke Greek. Similarly, it attracted educated people of cities such as Athens to the faith. Many would later become great defenders of Christianity by their ability to articulate the soundness of doctrine, and defuse the arguments of antagonistic pagan philosophers and theologians. But it proved harmful (or at the very least challenging) to the faith by allowing for the possibility of poor interpretation of doctrine because of the fact that the Greeks had been pagans, and not similar monotheists like the Jews. We will see shortly some of the controversies that arose within the church to challenge her orthodoxy, or "straight thinking". But all of these conflicts are to be expected when such a dynamic change is occurring within cultures. These were the growing pains of Christianity.

The Written Word

As the first century of Christianity came to an end, we are able to point to the emergence of the Gospels in written form. The story of Jesus was certainly well known and well preserved during the time of the apostles, but it is a misconception that the four evangelists sat down and wrote out the Gospels immediately after Jesus had left them. Keep in mind that the oral tradition was much stronger then than it is now, and scholars also believe that the sayings of Jesus had been written down and were circulated, perhaps in something not unlike a book of quotations and anecdotes; there may even have been a completed version of the Passion Narrative in existence, which was certainly the most important part of the story. In any case, the message of the Gospels, which Paul refers to so often, was alive and well, though not in the completed form of the New Testament.

St. Mark's Gospel was the first to be written, sometime before the year 70. The Gospel of St. Matthew, which we know relied a great deal on the Gospel of Mark, was written sometime shortly after the year 70. St. Luke's Gospel and the Acts of the Apostles would appear roughly 10 years later, between the years 80 and 90. Luke, a gentile who had traveled with Paul, had access to both Mark's and Matthew's Gospels. The Gospel of St. John, written by a community of believers established by the "beloved" disciple of Jesus, was completed between the years 90 and 95. This community, referred to as the "Johannine" community after their founder St. John, was largely separated from the communities out of which came the "synoptic" Gospels, that is, the Gospels of Mark, Matthew and Luke. For the sake of perspective, keep in mind that the letters of St. Paul were written and circulated before the four Gospels were written down, sometime between the years 50 and 64 C.E.

This burst of writing in the first century is evidence that the Christian communities began to see a need for permanence in their message. The story of the Gospels was reaching a larger number of believers, and the demand for something authoritative on which to base church teachings resulted in the writing down of Scripture. Many other early Christian writings other than the Gospels, Acts, and the letters of Paul, also helped to shape the beliefs and direction of these early Christian communities. A work known as The Shepherd of Hermas played a prominent role in the formation of Christian communities. In the more eastern parts of the empire, a work known as The Didache was a great influence on many of the early Fathers of the church, and remained for a long time in the East an inspired work essential for keeping Christians on the path to God. Some of these works, mostly letters found later and authenticated, would stand and become part of the canon (literally the "stick", the measure or the rule of faith and morals) that makes up the New Testament in our Christian Bible; others would be considered apocryphal ("secret") writings, or books which could be read in private by a Christian, but were not part of the public reading. This is what became of The Shepherd and The Didache, as well as works such as the so-called Gospels of Peter and Thomas, and the Revelation of Peter. These works and others provide some historical insight into the beliefs of the early church, and so are still read. Nevertheless, for the sake of teaching consistent doctrine, they contain information that the church ultimately decided was not authentic or authoritative, thereby excluding them from the Canon of Scripture.

The Second Century Church

As we move into the second century C.E., we must keep in mind that, internally, the early church at this time believed that Jesus would return within the lifetime of the first apostles. The parousia, or the second coming, was expected to happen before the end of the first century. This added to the fervor of apostolic and missionary activity, and the high level of intensity among believers. As time went on, and it became evident that the "now" of the parousia meant a spiritual preparation rather than an actual preparation for a timely event, the early church adjusted and, as we shall see, took another step toward ensuring its steadfastness.

The year 70, in which Jerusalem was destroyed marks the end of what church historians refer to as the Apostolic age of Christianity. This term was used because the apostles established and shaped the first Christian communities. Scholars point to communities in this age influenced by the leadership and writings of the apostles Paul, Peter, John and Matthew, each with its own character and influence on the church universal.[10] It is followed by the post-apostolic age, which is also known as the age of the Apologists. The Apologists were those theologians and thinkers who accepted Christianity and found themselves in the role of defending it after the apostles had passed away. Apology in this sense has nothing to do with regret. Rather, it is an explanation of teaching, a clarification of one's stand, and a means by which leaders of Christian communities made clear their unwavering commitment to the faith, even if that meant risking death. Many of the early Apologists were actually minor characters in the larger scheme of the Church, and their writings have been lost or destroyed. But three names one should keep in mind are Justin Martyr and his pupil Tatian (Apologists of the second century), and Origen, the great theologian of the East in the third century whose influence on the Church is second perhaps only to St. Augustine's.

The second century of Christianity, therefore, would be a proving ground. The ground work of faith had been put in place by those who knew Christ. Now a second generation had to prove that in fact the spirit of Christianity was just as alive in its time as it was before. But the road would be a difficult one, due to the mounting suspicion towards this one-time sect of Judaism that had grown to enormous size. The result was often persecution, behind which often stood the efforts of a still largely pagan world to reduce the size and influence of the Christians.

The Struggles of the Second Century Church

Christianity professes that the Son of God had to be put to death by his accusers in order to achieve our salvation. Thus, Christians ought to expect to be persecuted. This was true from the very first days of the early church, and was supported with passages from Scripture, such as Isaiah 50:6 ("I gave my back to those who struck me, and my cheeks to those who pulled out my beard; I did not hide my face from insult and spitting"), Paul's letter to the Romans ("I consider that the sufferings of this present time are not worth comparing with the glory about to be revealed to us" 8:18), Matthew's sermon on the mount ("Blessed are you when men revile you and persecute you and utter all kinds of evil against you falsely on my account" 5:11), and Jesus' final prayer to the Father in the Gospel of John ("They do not belong to the world just as I do not belong to the world" 17:16).

Persecution of the early Christians came first from the hands of the Jews. Under Roman law, the Jews were generally tolerated and respected by the Roman authorities because of the age of their religious traditions; they were not forced to join in the worship of the emperors. Since the Christians were initially Jews who believed in Christ, it was the Romans who considered the Christians to be just another sect of Judaism, and so left them alone. The Jews, however, knew better, and continually sought to silence the Christians who were preaching that Jesus of Nazareth had risen from the dead and was the long-awaited Messiah (see Acts 4:1-31). This seems largely, however, to have been a dynamic that came with the early separation of the two faiths, and was certainly not an ongoing systematic persecution.

Christians were also persecuted by the Romans, though largely on a town-by-town basis. The emperor Nero's persecution of Christians, as we mentioned earlier, was one of the larger, systematic persecutions, but as the church moved into the second century, few emperors actually took aggressive anti-Christian stands. Rather, it was up to the governors of the various provinces or territories, persuaded by local non-believers, as to whether Christians would be accepted or not. Some, of course, were more accepting than others. Overall it was the Christians' intent on separating themselves from the rulers of the world as they waited for the ruler of all the worlds that got them into so much trouble with the pagan citizens among whom they lived each day.

Ironically, we can point to the persecution of Christians as cause for the spread of Christianity. Under the extreme sufferings of persecution, Christianity was seen as a remarkable religion, for which its believers would rather die horribly (and quietly) than give in to their tormentors. The Patristic writer Tertullian is best known for his bold statement that explains why the threat of death could not weaken the early church. "The blood of Christians is seed," he wrote. Of course, some believers did give in; they were called apostates (those who depart or draw away from), and there were probably as many of those as there were martyrs. But consider the situation. All one had to do, in the face of death, was to deny the name of Christ, and perhaps make a bow or pour some incense on an altar to a Roman god. When the alternative was to be crucified or eaten alive by a lion, apostasy was generally seen as a moment of weakness, not as genuine hatred for the name of Christianity. In the end, however, Christianity not only endured, it prevailed. After periods of penance, most former Christians who renounced the faith under duress repented and were accepted back into the Church. Despite these isolated, but nevertheless damaging, persecutions, it was the commitment Christians gave to their beliefs that caused the early church to continue growing throughout those first one hundred and fifty years.

The Rise of Controversies in the Second Century Church

As the external threat of persecution began to wane within the church of the second century, the early Christian communities had to contend with those followers who expressed a difference of doctrine and belief, yet called themselves Christians. These positions were called heresies, and some of the most powerful during the second century had to do with the emerging understanding of Christianity. Although there are many we can target, in the second century and beyond, the three controversial positions involved in Gnosticism, Marcionism, and Montanism caused significant conflict and threatened the internal cohesiveness of the Church. Yet, they arose out of issues that the church had to settle if she was going to survive.

Around the year 134, the heresy of Gnosticism began to emerge. Gnosticism (from the Greek *nous,* or "mind") believed that a certain "insider knowledge" was held by a relative few, and this knowledge was the only release from a life of the body burdened with weakness and pains. They professed a certain salvation, as Christians did, yet the means to that end, and those to whom it was promised, were different. Gnosticism could be understood as something of an alternative community in the burgeoning population of Christianity. Consider claims today that a certain mystic or cult of believers has been keeping secret a heretofore unknown truth of Christianity. This is Gnosticism.

The truths upon which Christianity rests are all revealed in Scripture. There are no secrets kept only for a few. Thus early Gnosticism stood over against Christianity's claim of salvation for all humankind. Although Gnosticism is recognized as a heretical position in Christianity, the influence of this strong movement is one that the Church still feels to this day.

Marcion, an early theologian and the founder of Marcionism, preached that the loving God who is the father of Jesus Christ and the judging God of the Old Testament were two different Gods, and that Christianity ought not to be associated with the judging God of the Old Testament. Consequently, the Old Testament was rejected as the forerunner of Christianity, and Marcion accepted only Luke's Gospel and the letters of Paul as Scripture. This clearly flew in the face of a Christianity that set itself out as the fulfillment and acceptance of the Jewish law through Jesus Christ, not the abolishment of it. Marcion's teachings were rejected by the church in 144 C.E., and the importance of reading the Old Testament as a herald of Christianity was never questioned again. Perhaps it is best to see Marcionism really as an early form of Judaeo-Christian Gnosis, and not as a specifically separate phenomenon.

In 156 C.E., at a time when the early Christians still anticipated the immediate return of the Son of God, the Montanist controversy (from the self-proclaimed prophet Montanus) proclaimed the same, but added that Montanus himself was the mouth-piece of the Holy Spirit, and that only the aesthetical practices he prescribed (denying all other ecclesiastical authority in the Church) could prepare one's soul for the imminent return of the Lord. Furthermore, it was in Phyrgia where the second coming would appear, not Jerusalem. Although Montanus was himself declared a heretic, it is not entirely proper to call the Montanist sect a :heresy as we know it. They were considered extreme in their belief of charismatic prophecy, and they deviated from traditional community structure and ministry, but they were not heretics in the sense that Gnostics (or later groups) were.

Just as the persecution of Christians in the early church had the opposite effect of creating a movement towards Christianity, the church's struggle with heresy also proved to have its positive influences. We can see in these three predominant instances of what were powerful movements in the second century church, a growing need for the church continually to define its doctrine, assert which writings were canonical and which were not, and find agreement among its bishops and presbyterial leaders as to what would be orthodox, and what would be condemned as heretical. Thus, the shape of the church's thought and beliefs began to emerge in these early centuries of Christianity, often out of necessity rather than desire.

The Structure of a Growing Church

As a second generation of Christians began to rise out of the Apostolic era and the imminent second coming of the Christ had clearly gone beyond what St. Paul, St. Peter, and the writer of Revelation had expected, the early church began to think less about her immediate future in the heavenly kingdom, and more about the present state of that kingdom here on earth. The second century turned the corner into its latter half, and all of the elements of the early church that had served in bringing and keeping it together in the first century–the written Gospels, epistles from the Apostles, the separation from Jewish identity, the confession of faith despite the threat of persecution, and the struggles to define beliefs in the midst of heretical teachings–came together to begin forming the structure of an organized, hierarchical church.

To begin with, the various Christian communities that had experienced fights with heretics began to realize that a more stable authority existed in a hierarchy of governing than in groups or committees. Thus, they turned to what is known as a monarchical episcopate, that is, there was one authority, not unlike a kingdom, to which questions of governance would be directed. Furthermore, the trust that the early church had formerly placed in charismatic pronouncements, such as the gifts of speaking in tongues or interpreting the Spirit, had proved dangerously unpredictable, as the controversy with Montanus had proved. For this reason, the church began to define the specific functions of those who would be making decisions in the communities.

There were three major offices: the presbyters, the bishops, and the deacons. The presbyters, a word that comes from the Greek meaning "elder", or "the place of the best," were exactly that–the elders of the community. Their wisdom and long-standing commitment to Christianity gave them the primary position of decision-making and authority. The bishops, from the Greek *episkopos*, which means literally "to oversee," were those who made sure that specific tasks were carried out, and that the community saw to its needs in an orderly fashion. The deacons, from the Greek *diakonia*, "to serve," carried out the specifics of what needed to get done in order for the community to remain intact. They also played the primary role of serving the community in worship. Now the governing body of the early church gradually shifted from placing its authority in the hands of those "inspired" by the spirit, to those who understood that inspiration required interpretation and practical application as well. These men and women of the church were visionaries, not of the final end, but of the historical long haul to which Christianity needed to adjust.

The final outcome of these second century adjustments within the early church community was the common usage of, and by those standards agreement upon, those works of Scripture that the church would consider authoritative. By the end of the second century, the writings used in public worship would remain remarkably similar to the actual New Testament we use today, which was set down in the year 400 at the Council of Carthage. The canon used by the church at Rome in the year 200 consisted of the following works: The Gospels of Matthew, Mark, Luke and John; the Acts of the Apostles; Paul's letters to the Romans, 1st and 2nd Corinthians, Galatians, Ephesians, Philippians, Colossians, 1st and 2nd Thessalonians, 1st and 2nd Timothy, Titus and Philemon; the letter of James; the 1st and 2nd letter of John; the letter of Jude; the Revelation of John; the Revelation of Peter; and the Wisdom of Solomon. Used in private but not public worship was The Shepherd of Hermas. After 400 and the Council of Carthage, the additions were the 1st and 2nd letters of Peter, a 3rd letter of John, and the letter to the Hebrews. Excluded were The Shepherd of Hermas, the Revelation of Peter, and apocryphal Gospels and letters that had found there way into various communities over the course of three centuries, such as the Gospel of the Hebrews, the Letter of Barnabas, and the Acts of Peter.[11]

The Third Century

If we were to look at a map of Christianity in the first decade of the third century, we would no longer be focusing our attention primarily on Jerusalem and the regions of Asia Minor. Christianity was well established in France, and had even made its way as far north as Great Britain. While missionary activity was pushing further and further west, however, the culture of the eastern half of the Christian world—Greece, Egypt, and the Middle East—flourished. What we see happening is a growing distinction between Christianity of the East and Christianity of the West. Initially we may say that it began as a natural geographical distinction, but the cultures Christianity encountered in East and West shaped them in different ways.

The Greek speaking world was the seat of learning and culture. Certainly the Romans produced some of the greatest poets, philosophers and historians of Western Civilization (Virgil, Lucretius, Tacitus), but the fact is Greek was the predominant language of the educated world and of Christianity. (All of New Testament Scripture was written in Greek, and their understanding of the Old Testament relied on a Greek version called the Septuagint). Although we pointed to difficulties in the second century that the Church had with its integration into Hellenistic society, as time went on Christianity was finding some of its staunchest defenders among the ranks of the Greeks. Greek philosophy and Christian beliefs began to find themselves in a happy marriage.

To the west of Rome, the tribes in Germany and in France kept the church more concerned with keeping new members than with weeding out Gnostic tendencies. The result was a church that grew steadily in terms of square miles, rather than refined doctrine. The western church would finally blossom in the Middle Ages, but for now, Christianity was about to reach its apex in a port city on the eastern edge of the Aegean Sea.

The Age of Constantine

Most of the third century up to the year 284 can be summed up as the time during which the collapse of the Roman Empire was imminent. From the year 193 to the year 284 there were precisely 10 emperors who had come and gone, roughly one per decade, none of whom was able to get a hold on governing the vast outposts of the empire, nor able to stop the social disintegration of Roman life at its center. Enter a man named Diocletian. Formerly a soldier of the Roman army, he literally forced his way into politics with his sword, killing anyone who opposed him. He rose to power in 284 and brought order to the chaotic empire by setting up a tetrarchy. Two Augusti would rule the east and west divisions of the empire, assisted by Caesars under their authority. Augustus Diocletian and Caesar Galerius managed the East, and Augustus Maximinus and Caesar Constantius Chlorus managed the West.

For reasons that no scholars or historians are entirely clear on, Diocletian began one of the worst persecutions of Christians in the history of the Church. Speculation varies, but the continual pressure from a still largely pagan society against Christians (as we pointed to earlier) was again perhaps the main catalyst of the persecutions. They were also said to have been even more mercilessly carried out by Diocletian's Caesar Galerius. In any event, they were brutal and thorough. Entire Christian communities were wiped out. Property was burned along with records and books. Presbyters and bishops were imprisoned, tortured and executed. Diocletian even had anyone in his army who confessed to being a Christian executed. The Caesar of the West, however, Constantius Chlorus, did not follow Diocletian's lead. In fact, Constantius was known to have shown the Christians of France and Great Britain favor in response to the bloodshed their brothers and sisters were experiencing in the East.

But the reign of Augustus Diocletian and his Caesar Galerius was not, fortunately for the Christians, as long as it could have been. Diocletian died in 305 and Galerius, raised to the place of Augustus, died seven years later in 311. Meanwhile, the son of Constantius Chlorus, Constantine, had been watching the dust of the tetrarchy settle. Although his father was Caesar in the West, Constantine grew up in the courts of the East. In the spring of 312 he led an army into Italy with the intent of taking Rome from his counterpart, one Maxentius. Constantine succeeded, and the story goes that, while on the outskirts of Rome, well aware that he was facing a superior enemy, he turned to the Christian God for help. The answer was a cross in the sky, and the words, "In this sign conquer," which is what Constantine proceeded to do. In 324 Constantine had to tie up a few loose ends in the eastern part of the empire by defeating a ruler named Licinius. Now the entire empire was under Constantine's control, and it was becoming a unanimously Christian empire. Constantine decided to create a new capitol for his empire. He moved to a city that stood on the narrow straits of the Bosporous, which connect what is now the Aegean and the Black Sea, called Byzantium. The new city was renamed Constantinople, the city of Constantine (later to become, in 1930, the capital of Turkey, Istanbul). In the end, he emerged as ruler of a newly reunited empire. Let me stress, however, "as the story goes." In reality, Constantine remained a religious syncretist for most of his life. True, he was a defender of Christianity and enthusiastic about the faith (as he was enthusiastic about religion in general) but it would be naive to say that it was entirely for spiritual reasons. It is more likely that Constantine's motivation stemmed from a good leader's understanding of power and political order, and the desire to put an end to religious rivalries. In fact, it was not until he was several weeks away from death that he was baptized in 337.

A balance to the Age of Constantine, however, is necessary in our summation here. Few Christians realize the fact that the Church is one faith with two personalities, as it were: one of the East, and one of the West. I have tried to bring that separation to light within the external history of Christianity. In the Age of Constantine, it becomes deeply embedded into the very worship, spirituality and theology of the faith, as Constantinople and Rome began to pair off as the two centers of Christianity. The character of a Church living in an East and a West can only be appreciated by an ongoing study of, not simply the history of the Church, but of her liturgy, art, and spiritual writers, as well as her controversies and schisms. It is in these latter areas of Church History (most notably, the schism of 1054, when the Roman Catholic Church and the Eastern Orthodox Church officially separated into two churches) where we Christians today have been kept blind to the richness that the traditions of the East and the West each bring to the Church that began back in Jerusalem.

Drawing the Fourth Century to a Close

If the second century church was the shape of things to come, the fourth century church was the shape of a church that had arrived. The Council of Nicea in 325 articulated exactly who Christians believe God is. At a time when a heretical group known as the Arians (after their founder Arius) believed that Jesus could not have been fully God and fully human, the Fathers of the Council asserted that the mystery of the incarnation is one in which the Son of God is "one in being" with God Himself. That is to say, in order for Jesus the man to be the Christ of God, he has to have the same "being" as God. They are from the same divine mold; for this reason, the Nicene Creed explains, the Son is not made, but begotten. The Greek word that holds the entire Nicene Creed together is *homoousios*, which is literally "from one substance or being." Church History is not the place to hammer out exactly what the nature of God is. That would probably find a better place in a class on Christology. The important thing to remember about the Council of Nicea in the fourth century is that the Church was fine-tuning its doctrine as the need arose (and the Arians presented the need to define what it meant to say that Jesus is God). Creeds had been written and recited prior to Nicea, often in a liturgical setting, and the *homoousios* language of the Nicene Creed would be avoided until St. Athanasius (in the 350s) used it in his attack against the heresy of the Arians. Nevertheless, as the size of Councils grew, along with the complexity of language used to express doctrine and what the community of Christians believed, we see the movement of the Church out of its infancy and youth, and into a period of recognizable age.

The fourth century also saw some of the greatest Fathers of the Church. Basil the Great, Gregory of Nyssa, and Gregory Nanzianzus were three Greek-speaking Fathers of the East who were known as the Cappadocians. St. John Chrysostom, the Father of the Eastern Liturgy, also lived and wrote in the middle of the fourth century. In the West, St. Ambrose and St. Jerome were towering figures in the Church. Ambrose was the fearless, outspoken Bishop of Milan; Jerome was the genius father of biblical scholarship. The end of the fourth century would see perhaps one of the greatest Fathers of the Church, and a Christian whose story still inspires people to conversion: St. Augustine. After his conversion to the faith from a life of pagan excess (baptized by St. Ambrose in 386 C.E. See Augustine's *Confessions*), Augustine became a bishop in the North African province of Hippo. His writings on philosophy and theology have had the single-most important influence on Western Christianity to this day.

The fourth century brings the history of the early church to an end. Although bishops and theologians continued for centuries to battle controversies within the church on doctrine and belief, the foundation of the Church in the world was, by this time, firmly laid. After the fourth century, the Church will never find itself entirely whole again, or at peace, which may be a disconcerting realization as one goes on to study the history of the Church. But we must remember to bear in mind what is the work of humanity, and what is the work of God. The study of Church History is, in many ways, an attempt to keep careful watch over the desire and struggle of the former to follow the latter.

Tracing: Discussion Questions

1.) What distinguishes Church History from the study of history in general?

2.) Paul's vision of the church was always one of universality, adhering to faith in Jesus Christ, not in Jewish laws or customs. Explain.

3.) Explain the first definitive separation between Judaism and the early Christians.

4.) The message of the gospels to which Paul often referred was alive and well before there was a completed form of the New Testament.

Explain. Also, the burst of writing in the first century is evidence that the Christian communities began to see a need for permanence in their message. Comment.

5.) The *parousia,* or the second coming, was expected before the end of the first century. How did this expectation influence the shape of the early church?

6.) Why ought Christians expect to be persecuted?

7.) The church's struggle with heresy proved to have its positive influences. What were they?

8.) How did Constantine's success influence the spread of Christianity?

9.) Draw time lines for east and west which show the early Christian writers from Paul to Augustine.

Tracing: For Further Reading

Chadwick, Henry. *The Early Church.* Middlesex: Penguin, 1967.

Frend, W.H.C. *The Rise of Christianity.* Philadelphia: Fortress Press, 1984.

Hall, Stuart G. *Doctrine and Practice in the Early Church.* Grand Rapids: Wm. B. Eerdmans Publishing, 1992.

Ramsey, Boniface. *Beginning to Read the Fathers.* New York: Paulist Press, 1985.

Shelley, Bruce. *Church History in Plain Language.* Waco: Word Books, 1982.

Wagner, Walter H. *After the Apostles.* Philadelphia: Fortress Press, 1994.

The Communion of Saints

Michael Kwatera, O.S.B.

When I was a student in Ascension grade school in north Minneapolis (that was when dinosaurs still roamed the earth), I was no stranger to the term "communion of saints." I heard it from time to time in religion classes and in the priest's sermons. I saw it every Sunday and holy day of obligation in the English translation of the Nicene Creed found in the prayer book I used at Mass (Latin reigned supreme in the Roman Catholic liturgy in those days). The term "communion of saints" brought to my young mind an image of the saints in heaven, variously and gloriously attired, lining up to receive the body of Christ in holy Communion-not kneeling at the altar rail as I did, but standing. I considered this to be more proof of what I already knew: that the saints in heaven were the special, privileged friends of God.

Later, I learned that the "communion of saints" is not about the saints receiving the body of Christ in holy Communion, but rather about our being received *into* the body of Christ and having a permanent place there, both in life and in death. The "communion of saints" is how the Church on earth describes its experience of being in union with the Church in heaven and with the Church still on the way there. For "all are one in Christ Jesus" (Gal. 3:28). His life, death and resurrection as the pattern for their own is what unites all the members of the Church, wherever they are.

We earthly members of the Church come to know and love Jesus Christ most especially in our prayer and worship, particularly in the sacraments. In the words and actions of the liturgy, the saving work of Jesus is most powerfully present. Thus, the term "communion of saints" also refers, in a sense, to a union in "holy things," that is, a sharing in all the helps to holy living that draw their power from Jesus Christ.

"*Moi*? A Saint?"

When the apostle Paul wrote his letters to the young Christian churches, he addressed them to the "holy ones," the "saints," in each locality. For example: "To the saints and faithful brothers and sisters in Christ in Colossae" (Col. 1:2). Today, if someone addressed us as "saints," we would likely protest that there must be some mistake. Roman Catholics usually apply the word "saint" only to those persons of extraordinary holiness whom the Church officially recognizes and honors as such. But "saint" can refer to all those who belong to Jesus Christ, both in heaven and on earth. Surprisingly perhaps, "saints" are as real and close to us as the people who sit next to us in church or on the bus. The "saints" on earth share much with the saints in heaven: joys and sorrows, successes and failures, life and death. And most importantly, they find their salvation in Jesus Christ, the King of saints.

The Church: Three In One

"Gaul is divided into three parts," Julius Caesar reported, and so is the Church. But as in the Trinity, three add up to one. Traditionally these three parts have been called the "Church Triumphant" (that is, the members of the Church now sharing heaven's joy after having lived the Christian life); the "Church Suffering" (those undergoing purification for failures to live the Christian life); and the "Church Militant" (those, like us, still struggling to live the Christian life in this world).

What unites all these believers in Christ is not a long-distance phone service, but a shared life: Christ's life, a life not broken by death. The friends and family of God form one body in Christ. Their union of faith and love endures throughout life and beyond death. Those whom God has placed "upon another shore, and in a greater light," according to a lovely Anglican text, remain our sisters and brothers in Christ. "The walls between heaven and earth are not impregnable. In some mysterious way of Divine Providence there is communication between the life of Eternity and the shadows of that life which we share in this world." [12]

We know something about the Church on earth simply by being part of it. Heaven, though, remains God's best-kept secret. Not even the pope receives picture postcards from the beyond. What is heaven like? Mystics, poets and preachers have tried to paint word-pictures of heaven, more or less effectively. If we are curious as to what season it is in heaven, St. John Damascene (d. ca. 749), answers thus: in heaven it is always *autumn*. Why? Because in heaven, it is always the time of fulfillment, the time of harvest: God's saints are being gathered in. And for that eternal harvest festival of rejoicing, we won't need to be fitted for long white robes or to be enrolled for harp lessons.

Roman Catholics believe, according to ancient tradition, that some persons must undergo a purification after death before they can meet God face to face in heaven. This purifying process has been called "purgatory." Such a belief does not seem unreasonable. For, if we are honest with ourselves, we know that we are life-long sinners while we try to live as life-long saints. And having admitted our sinfulness, can we be sure that we will be completely ready to enter the presence of the all-holy and all-loving God at the moment of our death? Perhaps God, with great love, chooses to purify us so that we can receive God's eternal gift of love. Catholics believe that by their prayers, the living can help in purifying those who are sometimes referred to as the "Poor Souls." Yet really they are "Rich Souls," for they are infinitely rich with the promise of God's salvation. Such is the belief reflected in the prayers for the dead at funeral Masses.

Prayer to Saints

Belief in the communion of saints takes verbal form in the Roman Catholic practice of praying for the dead and of praying to the saints. We ask the saints to "intercede" for us, that is, we ask them to join us in presenting our needs to God in prayer. It is traditional Roman Catholic belief that the saints in heaven are both able and willing to hear our prayers, and to pray to God on our behalf. Thus, John Dietzen explains that "it is only natural and profoundly Christian that we ask their help and prayers for anything important to us, just as we ask the help and prayers of the people who are still with us on earth."[13]

Yet praying to saints should not result from a mistaken notion that we cannot have direct access to God, or that the saints provide welcome leverage in catapulting our prayers to the throne of God. The saints, who are not more powerful than God, are not in the business of wresting favors from God. Their intercession is how they "constantly care for those whom they left on earth ....Their intercession is their most exalted service to God's plan. We can and should ask them to intercede for us and for the whole world." [14]

Whatever good the saints do by their prayers for us, clearly that good comes to us through, with and in Jesus Christ. In 1990, after seven years of studying the role of the Blessed Virgin Mary and the saints in the life of the Church, Lutheran and Roman Catholic scholars affirmed that Jesus Christ is the "sole mediator" between believers and God. Mary and the saints can never replace him. But the two groups diverged on the question of whether the saints in heaven intercede for believers on earth, and whether the saints should be called on in prayer, especially in requests for help and special favors. There is some evidence that prayer to saints does not figure so strongly in Roman Catholic practice as it once did. Yet the popularity of devotion to the saints among Hispanic Catholics, who will number 50 percent of this country's

Catholic population by the year 2000, means that the saints can continue to expect a steady stream of prayers.

Honoring Relics

Belief in the communion of saints becomes visible in the Church's reverence for relics. St. Augustine (354-430) observed that "the bodies of our deceased must not be treated lightly or disregarded, particularly the bodies of the faithful or of the virtuous; for these bodies were used by their souls in a holy manner as instruments and agents for the performance of all their good works." In 1986, after the Challenger space shuttle explosion that claimed the lives of the crew, NASA acting director William Graham commented on the search for the astronauts' remains: "We have plans to treat them with great dignity and great privacy, appropriate to the respect that we have for them." Here, separated by sixteen centuries, we find the same wholesome, human instinct: a desire to venerate the memory of the deceased by honoring their remains.

From earliest times, the Church showed special honor for martyrs, those who gave up their lives rather than give up their Christian faith. The places where the bodies of these saints were buried later became the sites of Christian churches. Eventually every altar became a kind of tomb for the saints, for it was required to contain at least one relic of a saint (usually a particle of bone).

The public veneration of relics abounded after Emperor Constantine legalized the Christian religion in 312 C.E. The Middle Ages witnessed a lively traffic in relics, many of which lacked authenticity. Royalty and nobility vied with each other to amass the largest collection of relics. Often, honoring relics was associated with contributing money to ecclesiastical causes, for example, reducing time to be spent in purgatory. The reformer Martin Luther rightly condemned such abuses.

Today, the Church's true purpose in honoring the relics of the saints is not to highlight wonder-working remains, but rather to remind us of the wonders that God worked in the saints during their earthly lives. Relics are physical testimony of the Church's veneration, respect and regard for its saintly heroes and heroines. The saints were not disembodied fairy-tale characters, but flesh-and-blood people like ourselves. Thus, establishing the authenticity of relics is important. Relics are no longer required in altars, not because the Church doesn't value them, but because the Church insists on having genuine relics in its holy table rather than any relics at all.

To honor relics is to affirm the Christian belief that God can work spiritual good through the material creation, of which our bodies are a noble part. That spiritual good doesn't have to be as astounding miracle; it can be as real and as simple as teaching someone to read. The Church honors the relics of the saints because through their bodies, they brought the Lord's salvation to others, just as Jesus did. Similarly, statues and images of the saints in churches and homes are visual reminders of the communion of saints, as are painted icons, those visible signs of the invisible presence of the saints that are so revered by Eastern rite Christians.

Liturgical Commemoration of the Saints

The Church's belief in the communion of saints becomes visible and audible in its liturgy. On the Solemnity of All Saints (November 1), we find ourselves gazing upon a wide-screen scene through the eyes of John the seer: "I had a vision of a great multitude, which no one could count, from every nation and race, people and tongue" (Rev. 7:9). They wear white robes of joy and carry palm branches of victory. And this great assembly's thunderous cheer proclaims, loud and clear, why they are there: "Salvation comes from our God, who is seated on the throne, and from the Lamb!" (Rev. 7:10). It is the death and resurrection of the Lamb of God, Jesus Christ, that is the source of their salvation and ours.

At the very time when the natural world of vegetation is dying, the Church celebrates the everlasting life and glory of all the saints. This feast day in their honor is the liturgy's fullest expression of the communion of saints. The vast assembly of holy ones before God's throne have come from east and west, north and south, and all points in between; from small farms and big cities; from peaceful estates and high-crime neighborhoods; from tumble-down hovels and magnificent mansions; from cold castles, closed cloisters and cozy condos. They are people who have known hard work and tough play, high finance and low income, sickness and health, the pleasures of life and the anguish of death. But their attire shows that they have much in common. All of them have received garments of glory from the God whom they served in life and in death; they carry the God-given trophies of Christ's victory over sin and death.

These people are not strangers to us. We have known people who lived in the power of Christ's dying and rising. We have met people who wore their baptismal garments of salvation very well indeed. We have found such people in our family, in our parish, in our community. Do we doubt that we will meet them in heaven?

Such are the saints, all the saints, saints from all times and places. All Saints is the great celebration of the Christian family in its final triumph over sin and death. Some of these the Church has declared to be saints by a process called "canonization" (carefully examining a holy person's life and officially enrolling that person's name in the list of saints for public veneration in the liturgy). Some of them (perhaps the greatest ones) the Church does not even know by name (but God does). Some are remembered by the universal Church, some only in the smaller circle of family and friends. Yet we can be sure that among the saints in heaven are some whom we have known on this earth. And even now, they remain one with us in the communion of saints. For on All Saints day, the veil between our earthly world and the heavenly world seems to part a bit; and with the eyes of faith, we get some glimpse of the happiness and glory to which God calls us.

All the Roman Church's Eucharistic Prayers (the prayers by which bread and wine are changed into the body and blood of Christ) ask that we may come to share eternal life with the Blessed Virgin Mary, the apostles and all the saints. The variable introductory sections to these Eucharistic Prayers ("Prefaces") for saints' days celebrate how these holy ones in heaven help us now:

> In their lives on earth
> you give us an example.
> In our communion with them
> you give us their friendship.
> In their prayer for the Church
> you give us strength and protection.
> This great company of witnesses spurs us on to victory,
> to share their prize of everlasting glory,
> through Jesus Christ our Lord.
> (Preface of Holy Men and Women I)

During the Litany of the Saints in the liturgy of baptism, a solemn roll call of heaven's holy ones asks their prayers for those who are about to become fellow members of the Church.

The practice of giving saints' names at baptism is one way that belief in the communion of saints become tangible–as tangible as signing one's name on a check or on a test. Centuries-long use has hallowed the Church's custom of giving Christian and saints' names as it christens its sons and daughters. The names of patron saints, invoked in the liturgy of baptism, testify that their namesakes belong to the communion of saints. "Every baptism," declares Mark Searle, "is the concern of the whole Church in heaven and on earth, for the newly baptized becomes part of that living communion which is bonded and transformed by the Holy Spirit into a single body in Christ."[15]   In the one large family that is the Church, the saints in heaven stand ready to help their baptized sisters and brothers on earth in living the Christian life that begins with baptism. To give or bear a saint's name is to profess one's belonging to a world where a person has a special friend in heaven.

Saints as Exemplars

In this world, holiness wears a human face. The lives of the saints remind us that Christian holiness intersects with human space and time. That is why the present Roman Catholic, Episcopal and Lutheran liturgical calendars have deliberately included holy ones from all Christian centuries and from all parts of the world. Holiness can only become visible, audible and tangible for us in this world, the one that God loved so much that God gave the only Son for its salvation. Here Jesus Christ empowers humans of all times and places to accept God's call to holiness.

This is why, in the liturgy and elsewhere, Christians do not passively remember their saintly ancestors as it merely turning the pages of a family scrapbook. "Catholicism at its best wants people not just to admire saints but to be saints. It is a tradition that holds forth its saints as heroes and heroines because Catholicism is not something to know but a way to live. It is a way to live fully and freely and lovingly, as the saints did."[16]   The lives of the saints help us to learn or re-learn what is at the heart of the Gospel of Jesus, so that we can make that Gospel seen and heard and felt by others, just as the saints did.

How would we ever know what the Gospel of Jesus is really like if we had never seen it lived out by people like ourselves? The saints are the best proof of the truth of the Gospel and our best examples for living that truth.   The saints remind us that what they achieved through the power of Christ, we too can achieve. Together the saints present us with a magnificent array of ways to serve God and others after the pattern of Jesus himself.

The Best is Yet to Come

One of the monks of my monastery, after the death of each of our fellow monks, used to ask: "Don't you wish you knew what so-and-so knows now?" As members of the Church Triumphant, we shall know the riches of living together before God in perfect love. But we won't enjoy these riches in heaven if we haven't discovered them and treasured them while living on earth. For in the communion of saints, how I treat my sisters and brothers who sit next to me in church or on the bus will in some way determine my future life. The saints in heaven knew that very well, and so must we. The French author George Bernanos was correct: "There is only one sadness: not to be a saint," and sainthood starts here and now.

In heaven, the communion of saints will become fully and forever conscious of what God has done for and through God's people in all times and places. That understanding will turn into praise. But even now, God invites us, saints-in-training or saints-in-the-making, to join our voices with those of the saints in heaven: "Amen. Blessing and glory, wisdom and thanksgiving, honor, power and might be to our God forever and ever. Amen" (Rev. 7:12).

Saints: Discussion Questions

1.) How were the saints "just like us" and "not just like us"? How were their lives both ordinary and extraordinary?
2.) Who are the most popular saints in your area and why?
3.) How important in your life is praying to saints?
4.) Do you have a saint whom you consider to be a personal friend? Who and why?
5.) Do you think that any contemporary saintly people will become canonized saints? Who and why?

Saints: For Further Reading

Attwater, Donald, compiler; John Cumming, editor and reviser. *A New Dictionary of Saints*. Collegeville, Minnesota: The Liturgical Press, 1994.

Breig, James. "Saints: guides for the upwardly mobile Christian." U.S. Catholic 45 (November 1980): 6-9.

Chervin, Ronda, and Mary Neill, O.P. *Great Saints, Great Friends*. New York: Alba House, 1990.

Gordon, Anne. *A Book of Saints: True Stories of How They Touch Our Lives*. New York: Bantam Books, 1994.

Guardini, Romano. *The Saints in Daily Christian Life*. Denville, New Jersey: Dimension Books, 1966.

Kwatera, Michael, O.S.B. "The Liturgical Veneration of the Saints." *Liturgy: The Calendar*, Vol. 1, no. 2 (1980): 20-26.

The Key to Prayer

Mark Hollenhorst

Would you like to hear about one of the biggest coincidences of my life? Last Sunday I had not yet read the readings for this week, so I had absolutely no idea of what they were about. I was driving alone in my car, listening to the Twins game, and I was utterly depressed, because they were losing the game against Baltimore 5 to 0. So I turned to God in prayer and said, "Lord, help the Twins come back and win this game." Just then, they scored a run to make it 5 to 1.

All of a sudden the bases were loaded, with two outs, and Kent Hrbek was at bat. I prayed again, "Lord, help Herbie get a two run single!" But he hit a weak pop fly to shallow right center field to end the inning. "Thanks a lot, God!" I said.

But the Twins kept chipping back, and, two innings later, the score was 5-3. Again the bases were loaded, with Kent Hrbek at the plate, with only one out this time. The thought of this Gospel came into my head and I prayed: "Lord, you told us to be persistent in prayer and you would answer us. Well, I'm still begging! Help Hrbek to get a 2-run single!" He hit a foul pop-up, for out number two.

"Thanks a lot, God!" I prayed. "I'm asking for an egg here, and You're giving me a scorpion!" With two outs and the bases still loaded, Chilly Davis came to the plate. "I refuse to give up, God! You said You'd answer my prayers if I begged until You got sick of me! Please help Chilly hit a two-run single!"

Bam! There it went, and the game was tied. "Thank you, God!" I said. Then, with a man on third base, and Brian Harper at bat, in the spirit of Abraham, I prayed, "Lord, dare I presume upon Your good will again? Let not my Lord grow impatient if I go on. Please help Brian Harper get the game-winning hit!" BAM! Twins win 7 to 5.

Well, I was overjoyed, and when I reached home and read the readings for this Sunday, I was grateful to God for giving me some instantaneous homily material. Victory is sweet. I was so elated that my prayer echoed the words of today's psalmist: "Lord, on the day I called for help, You answered me."

But does the Lord always grant exactly what we ask? No way! We all know that he does not. All our prayers are not answered in the way we would like. Last night I prayed just as hard. This time it was the

Boston fans' turn to be heard. The Twins blew a lead to lose 5 to 4, and Oakland came from behind to beat Toronto 6 to 5. So, who knows?

The same psalm continues, "When I called, You answered me. You built up strength within me!" That, in my opinion, is the key to prayer. God will give us the strength we need to handle any situation in our lives, if we trust in His goodness and love.

Does Jesus promise to bring victory to the Twins in today's Gospel, if we pray hard enough? No! But He does promise that God will send the Holy Spirit if we ask. The Spirit gives us courage, insight and the strength to endure. The Spirit gives us the understanding to realize that athletic victories and glory are so transient that they have very little significance in the spiritual life, especially when compared to our eternal salvation. The Holy Spirit is the answer to all our prayers.

Let me put it to you this way: Let's say that God would give you a choice between two things. You could either have one million dollars a year for the rest of your life, or you could have the spiritual gift of being totally contented in any situation, no matter what happens to you in life.

I bet that most people would choose the million bucks, even though the second gift is worth a lot more. We really don't know what is best for us. But God, as a loving Father, has our best interests at heart.

Anthony Padovano writes, "God is not someone who grants our wishes; He is someone who fulfills our hopes."

Oscar Wilde put it another way: "When the gods want to punish us, they give us what we ask for."

To me, the Key to understanding prayer lies in the second line of the Lord's Prayer: "Thy kingdom come; Thy will be done!" It's the same basic prayer that Jesus said in the Garden before His death. He wanted the cup to pass and to let Him go on living. God wanted Him to save the world. Jesus ultimately got his prayer answered when he arose from the dead to eternal life. But his prayers were answered by a difficult course of events that only God, in His wisdom, could understand.

The *Our Father* is a perfect prayer, given to us by the perfect *Prayor,* just after He was engaged in deep prayer Himself. The early fathers of the church said that it should be prayed by every Christian at least three times every day.

God is our Father, the head of the family. It is His kingdom in which we reside. He is in charge. He has everything under control. We must be obedient to His will. He gives all and forgives all.

If we truly believe in those words, then we can be at peace no matter what happens to us in life. True prayer is the humility to surrender to God's providence and to trust in his desire for our welfare. His plan is for all of us to share in His boundless love forever.

The Lord's Prayer teaches us humble reliance and a spirit of acceptance and gratitude for whatever comes our way, even when it seems contrary to our prayers.

I had one of the greatest religious experiences of my life last month when I went to Lourdes. Having untreatable cancer has taught me a special appreciation for God's Gift of Life. Consequently, I don't want it to end. So, I naturally went to Lourdes with a strong desire to be cured.

We arrived in Lourdes by train, and I was immediately captivated by its spectacular mountain setting. It is a beautiful city. As we walked through the pearly gates into a gigantic courtyard full of beautiful flowers and statues, I was floored by a spiritual sense of God's presence everywhere. There was no commercialism. That was kept outside the gates. Inside was only peace and love. The church rose above the surroundings in the distance, hovering over the entire area like a fountain of God's graces. The church looked like the church in Fantasyland. I felt like I was in the Magic Kingdom of the Catholic Church. Mass was celebrated about 20 times every day in different chapels and in many languages. It was nice to understand the homily for a change. The priest talked about accepting our difficulties and remembering that we don't have any more suffering than any of the early martyrs.

There was also a beautiful underground church with 29 colorful stained glass windows, depicting the 14 stations of the cross and each of the 15 mysteries of the rosary. I had just bought 16 rosaries to bring home for the people of our parish who have cancer. (I apologize to those I missed. It's amazing how many people have cancer, and my memory is not perfect.) I took out one of the rosaries and walked around to each window, having a great time praying all fifteen mysteries and seeing them come to life in front of me through the windows.

Then I went out into a huge garden on a high hill that had life-size stations of the cross to walk through. It was wonderful to follow the steps of Christ. My prayer became one with his prayer in the garden: "Your will, not mine, be done!"

I then went down to the grotto and blessed myself and all the rosaries in the waters of Lourdes, and composed this little prayer:

"Thank You, Lord, for this beautiful day, and for getting us safely to Lourdes. I ask You to bless these rosaries. May they be a sign to those who use them of Your love and the love of Your Mother, Mary. If it be Your will, free us from our sicknesses, but, above all, grant us peace and a true acceptance of our sufferings. In any case, help us to love You with all our hearts, through all our difficulties. We make this prayer through Jesus Christ our Lord. Amen."

I left that place with a sense of peace and an awareness of God's love surrounding me. To me, it does not matter whether I live or die, because, either way, as St. Paul says in the second reading, "Christ lives in me through my Baptism, and He will bring me to eternal life in His presence!"

Richard Viladesau suggests that "the proper religious attitude is the acceptance of God's will; the proper kind of prayer is praising God for whatever He wills . . . . For many Christians, the notion of 'prayer' that is unconsciously taken for granted is almost the opposite: not submission to God's will, but the effort to change God's will and to get Him to submit to our will or to fulfill our agenda." The prayer of petition is then "a matter of making ourselves–like Jesus–the means of God's transformation of the world in his Spirit, the spirit of love."17

As I left the Lourdes grotto, I came to a lovely statue of Mary, with outstretched arms, and surrounded by a small field of white roses. It looked like a mystical vision of Heaven come to life. My final prayer was, "Lord, if you want to heal me, I would not object, but, if not, please prepare me to go to Heaven." I walked out of the courtyard with a feeling of total peace, knowing that God has my best interests at heart.

Delivered at the Church of St. John in Grand Marais, Minnesota
on the Seventeenth Sunday of the Church Year
26 July 1992

The Key To Prayer: Reflection Questions

1.) "So I turned to God in prayer and said, 'Lord, help the Twins come back and win this game.' Just then, they scored a run to make it 5 to 1." Is this a good model for prayer? Why or why not?

2.) "'Thanks a lot, God!' I prayed. 'I'm asking for an egg here, and You're giving me a scorpion!'" Using a biblical concordance, find the Scripture verse to which Fr. Hollenhorst refers, and comment on how he uses it.

3.) Does God always grant exactly what we ask? If all our prayers are not answered in the way we would like, what does that suggest about God?

4.) Anthony Padovano suggests that God does not grants our wishes, but fulfills our hopes. What does this mean?

5.) Consider the Lord's Prayer: "thy kingdom come; thy will be done . . ." Explain.

The Key To Prayer: For Further Reading

Bacovcin, Helen, translator. *The Way of the Pilgrim,* and *The Pilgrim Continues His Way.* New York: Doubleday, 1992.

Bloom, Anthony. *Beginning To Pray.* New York: Paulist Press, 1970.

Castelli, Jim, editor. *How I Pray: People of Different Religions Share with Us That Most Sacred and Intimate Act of Faith.* New York: Ballantine Books, 1994.

Rahner, Karl. *On Prayer.* Collegeville, MN: Liturgical Press, 1993; originally published in German, 1958.

Salinger, J.D. *Franny and Zooey.* New York: Grosset & Dunlap, 1955.

Van de Weyer, Robert, editor. *The HarperCollins Book of Prayer: A Treasury of Prayers Through the Ages.* New York: HarperCollins, 1993.

Wiederkehr, Macrina. *A Tree Full of Angels: Seeing the Holy in the Ordinary.* San Francisco: Harper & Row, 1988.

The Spiritual Offering of Prayer

From the treatise On Prayer by Tertullian, priest
(Cap. 28-29: CCL I, 273-274)

Tertullian, who lived about 160 - 230 in Carthage, tells us that what God asks of us we learn from the Gospel. Tertullian suggests that prayer is an offering that belongs to God and to whom such an offering is acceptable.

We must dedicate this offering with our whole heart, we must fatten it on faith, tend it by truth, keep it unblemished through innocence and clean through chastity, and crown it with love. We must escort it to the altar of God in a procession of good works to the sound of psalms and hymns. Then it will gain for us all that we ask of God.

Since God asks for prayer offered in Spirit and in truth, how can he deny anything to this kind of prayer? How great is the evidence of its power, as we read and hear and believe.

Of old, prayer was able to rescue from fire and beasts and hunger, even before it received its perfection from Christ. How much greater then is the power of Christian prayer. No longer does prayer bring an angel of comfort to the heart of a fiery furnace, or close up the mouths of lions, or transport to the hungry food from the fields. No longer does it remove all sense of pain by the grace it wins for others. But it gives the armor of patience to those who suffer, who feel pain, who are distressed. It strengthens the power of grace, so that faith may know what it is gaining from the Lord, and understand what it is suffering for the name of God.

In the past prayer was able to bring down punishment, rout armies, withhold the blessing of rain. Now, however, the prayer of the just turns aside the whole anger of God, keeps vigil for its enemies, pleads for persecutors. It is any wonder that it can call down water from heaven when it could obtain fire from heaven as well? Prayer is the one thing that can conquer God. But Christ has willed that it should work no evil, and has given it all power over good.

Its only art is to call back the souls of the dead from the very journey into death, to give strength to the weak, to heal the sick, to exorcise the possessed, to open prison cells, to free the innocent from their chains. Prayer cleanses from sin, drives away temptations, stamps out persecutions, comforts the fainthearted, gives new strength to the courageous, brings travelers safely home, calms the waves, confounds robbers, feeds the poor, overrules the rich, lifts up the fallen, supports those who are falling, sustains those who stand firm.

All the angels pray. Every creature prays. Cattle and wild beasts pray and bend the knee. As they come from their barns and caves, they look up to heaven and call out, lifting up their spirit in their own fashion. The birds, too, rise and lift themselves up to heaven: they open out their wings, instead of hands, in the form of a cross, and give voice to what seems to be a prayer.

What more need be said on the duty of prayer?

Spiritual Offering: Reflection Questions

1.) Compare and contrast Tertullian's ideas with those in the previous essay.
2.) Tertullian writes that of old, prayer was able to rescue from fire and beasts and hunger, but he sees greater power in Christian prayer. Why? How?
3.) "Prayer is the one thing that can conquer God." Explain.
4.) Why does he see prayer as a duty?

What We Dare to Say!

William C. Graham

If I could call back the first 15 years or so of my preaching for retooling, correction, amplification and modification, and if I could begin again wherever I would wish, I might choose Luke 11 in which the disciples seem either unhappy or perplexed that John's disciples have been taught to pray, but their master has not taught them. They approach Jesus as "He was praying in a certain place, and after he had finished, one of his disciples said to him, 'Lord, teach us to pray, as John taught his disciples'" (Luke 11:1). Jesus neither reproaches nor offers recrimination, but gives them the prayer that seems prophetic with regard to message and mission and method and attitude. Too often, we Christians seem to think that Jesus left the complete handbook for the operation of a Church, including all necessary dogmas as well as the floor plan for Winchester Cathedral. It sometimes comes as a surprise that he who tells us "Do this in remembrance of me" (22:19) did not leave a prayer book, and the New Testament was not yet written as he spoke the command.

The fact that what we call The Lord's Prayer really is unique in all the world is a fact that ought not to be lost on us, and one we ought to remember as we continue the ancient tradition of reciting that prayer three times daily. It truly is the perfect prayer: for morning, noon and night, before and after meals, alone or in good company, whenever and wherever Christians gather. But perhaps we are too blithe in saying these words. Annie Dillard suggests that we worshippers are not very sensible. She asks, "Does anyone have the foggiest idea what sort of power we so blithely invoke?" Perhaps crash helmets ought to be the order of the day. And "Ushers should issue life preservers and signal flares; they should lash us to our pews." Such is the power of the God we invoke who "may draw us out to where we can never return." We ought, indeed, to be very careful in claiming in prayer the words Our Savior gave us.

Jesus said to his disciples, "When you pray, say: Father, hallowed be your name" (11:2). For Jesus to call God Father, or Abba, was daring in its informality. God becomes accessible in a new and personal way, and God's love is revealed as unconditional. When we dare to call God Father, we open ourselves to this relationship which really does extend to us. We embrace the good news that in Jesus we are offered divine life. God is now Father to us; we accept the gift of becoming God's children.

Addressing God as Father

In his nineteenth century paraphrase of Psalm 102 (103), hymn writer Henry F. Lyte wrote, "Father-like he tends and spares us; Well our feeble frame he knows; In his hands he gently bears us, Rescues us from all our foes. Alleluia! Alleluia! Widely yet his mercy flows." This is the God who is "Slow to chide, and swift to bless," and "Glorious is his faithfulness." We may sense an even deeper, more radical claim in Jesus's use, and our own, of Abba, and a broader, more inclusive sense of God. We have to dare to say it, to call on God as if children in the night. We must be "formed by the Word" before we really express this relationship, claim it boldly.

The notion of addressing God as Father is problematic for some modern Christians. Ours is an inclusive age, and to use male titles for God evokes the image of a patriarchal church which is unsettling to many. If Jesus had some other form of address for God, the evangelists seem not to have recorded it. While feminists are helping us learn to read and reread the Scriptures in ways that will help us focus on what may have been lost, overlooked or even suppressed, we have yet to make complete peace with the images of Father and Abba. They are incomplete. God is not a guy. But all images are incomplete, and only the God in whose presence we stand is perfect. All our attempts to imagine this God are flawed, and will be flawed until we come to stand finally before the throne of grace (Hebr. 4:16). Those who have not known a dad's tenderness may also have trouble with the image of God as father. But the richness of the image, though incomplete and imperfect, teaches us that God is not just creator or redeemer or sanctifier or judge, but fatherly in expressing and acting on loving concern.

As the millennium approaches and our language evolves, many struggle with translations that change Father to Creator. That change seems to lose or confuse the dimension of divine identity. The gender problem is part of the issue, reflecting an older understanding of biology which saw the father transmitting genetic identity to the child with the mother as receptor, nurturing the person begotten by the father. Some then call on God as Father and Mother. During his short reign, Pope John Paul I said, "God is Father, yes. But even more, she is Mother."

Some use the title parent because it is inclusive of both genders, but it seems to suffer a certain loss of warmth. To say simply Creator or Holy One invokes awe, but not a familial familiarity. The key is that God extends divine identity to us. The challenge is not to let the very real issues of language and gender keep us from the identity that belongs to us as baptized children of the most high God. We dare to claim the relationship which Jesus models and to which he invites us. To many, this may seem threatening, or even blasphemous. In practice, we run the risk of continuing to ignore the implications of the gift, living our Christian lives as fearful servants on trial, hoping to go to heaven, but seeing earth only as a vestibule and not the theater of God's action and active love that it truly is.

The Once and Future Reign of God

As we move forward in pilgrimage, Jesus tells us to pray, "Your kingdom come" (Luke 11:2). Kingdom, too, is an unsettling word for many in our age. Some see it as another patriarchal reference. That unfortunate connotation is one of the reasons that God's Reign is perhaps a better term for us than God's Kingdom. Another reason is that Kingdoms are bounded by time and space. Queen Elizabeth's Kingdom (and why hers is not a Queendom is a good question) is firmly situated where it can be seen, found and landed upon. God's Reign, on the other hand, is more about a way of living together in peace and unity, justice and love, than it is about geography or real estate. We are to remember that "Once Jesus was asked by the Pharisees when the Reign of God was coming, and he answered, 'The Reign of God is not coming with things that can be observed; nor will they say, 'Look, here it is!' or 'There it is!' For, in fact, the Reign of God is among you'" (Luke 17: 20-21). We were initiated into that Reign when plunged into the saving waters of Baptism. While it will come to fulfillment in Heaven, it is not something unknown or foreign to us now.

Our Jewish brothers and sisters assert that if all of them, for just one day, were to keep the entire Torah, all of the law, the Messiah would come. Similarly, we Christians know that if we could live all of the Gospel invitations and commands for a single day, the earth would be transformed, and we with it, the Messiah would come again in glory, and heaven would be wedded to earth. So each act and thought and word of ours is important, either advancing the coming Reign of God, or impeding its arrival by our sin and selfishness. We flawed keepers of both Old and New Covenants have not yet responded completely to

God's call. We continue to move on, sinning and repenting, hoping one day finally to be perfected "as your heavenly Father is perfect" (Matt. 5:48).

We ask then, "Give us each day our daily bread" (Luke 11:3). Note that we do not ask that our Franklin Funds or the Dow Jones continue to rise that we might accumulate huge piles of interest and retire finally in the style to which we hope to become accustomed. Instead, we pray to have an acute realization of our dependence on God, and that we might submit in faith to that dependency. This is the same notion of Islam, or submission, that Muslims hold. Together, we know that God is the all powerful, and we creatures are dependent. We ask to be sustained with what we truly need, rather than the fullness of all that for which we ask.

Praying for Forgiveness

In praying for forgiveness, we are truly bold. And we put ourselves at risk if we make this prayer carelessly. We say, "And forgive us our sins, for we ourselves forgive everyone indebted to us. And do not bring us to the time of trial" (Luke 11:4.). Imagine that! We ask to be forgiven in the same way we have forgiven others. We will certainly want to enjoy the best tenderness and loving kindness that the forgiving God has to offer. This insight will give new depths of meaning to Luke 6: 30-31: "Give to everyone who begs from you; and if anyone takes away your goods, do not ask for them again. Do to others as you would have them do to you." And to Luke 6: 35-38: "But love your enemies, do good, and lend, expecting nothing in return. Your reward will be great, and you will be children of the Most High; for he is kind to the ungrateful and the wicked. Be merciful, just as your Father is merciful. Do not judge, and you will not be judged; do not condemn, and you will not be condemned. Forgive, and you will be forgiven; give, and it will be given to you. A good measure, pressed down, shaken together, running over, will be put into your lap; for the measure you give will be the measure you get back."

In Conclusion

Scripture does not tell us that the Lord's Prayer concludes with "For the kingdom, the power and the glory are yours," but that line is not the Protestant innovation many assume it to be. In fact, the Didache, or Teaching of the Twelve Apostles, a second century Church document, records the line as early as AD 102 or 112. And even then, it probably was not an innovation, but reflected the practice of the Church.

Many people find much of theology and spirituality difficult to read. Theological words have come unmoored as people lose touch with the systems of thought that fit a previous age. Religious truths require context and coherency. Language needs revitalization. Familiar truths must be expressed in startling ways with an honesty about doubt that will force us to go deeper and farther. We require that kind of originality all the more when the subject is as familiar as the Lord's Prayer. As we reconsider the current and coming Reign of God and our place in it, as we continue to make the Lord's Prayer our own, we might do well to remember and restore the invitation to that prayer from the liturgy before Vatican II: "Taught by Our Savior's command, and formed by the Word of God, we dare to say..." This prayer will draw us into something bigger than ourselves, richer than we can imagine, more terrifying in its demands than at first we knew.

Dare: Reflection Questions

1.) Why is the Lord's Prayer considered unique in all the world? Is it truly the perfect prayer?

2.) What prompts Annie Dillard to suggests that worshippers are not very sensible?

3.) What does it mean to be "formed by the Word"?

4.) Why is addressing God as Father problematic for some modern Christians?

5.) What do you make of the Christian assertion that if we could live all of the Gospel invitations and commands for a single day, the earth would be transformed, and we with it, the Messiah would come again in glory, and heaven would be wedded to earth?

6.) Why is it that some Christians conclude the Lord's Prayer with "For the kingdom, the power and the glory are yours," while others omit it?

7.) "Once Jesus was asked by the Pharisees when the Reign of God was coming, and he answered, 'The Reign of God is not coming with things that can be observed; nor will they say, 'Look, here it is!' or 'There it is!' For, in fact, the Reign of God is among you'" (Luke 17: 20-21).   What do you make of that?

8.) Why are we advised that we ought, indeed, to be very careful in claiming in prayer the words Our Savior gave us?

Dare: For Further Reading

Haring, Bernard. Gwen Griffith-Dickson, translator. *Our Father* (Winona, MN: St. Mary's Press, 1996).

A Modern Day Parable

Dan Conditt

This story is adapted from O'Henry's The Gift of the Magi.

Once upon a time there was a young married couple named Gus and Mona. They had been wedded for two years, but were still madly in love with each other. They were also quite poor. Gus worked in construction but work had been on and off of late and he hadn't worked steadily for three months. Mona worked as a file clerk for the State of Arizona. Her income, along with Gus's part-time income from a paper route bought the groceries, paid the rent, the utilities and the insurance, but not much else. Especially as Christmas was drawing near, Gus's frustration increased at not being able to work steady. Mona knew how awful Gus felt and she too wanted to get him a special gift for Christmas. She regretted that they had both torn up their credit cards. Of course, they had charged to the limit and were still having trouble keeping up with the monthly payments. But still, it would be nice to have one of the those cards now to shop and buy for Gus and herself. Sadly, though, she knew that in the long run they wouldn't be able to afford any extra payments for anything.

Gus and Mona both knew what the other wanted for Christmas. Gus knew that second to him, Mona's love was for her 1964 Malibu SS. It had been the first car she bought with money saved from her first job. In its day, it had been a snazzy red sport sedan. Now, it sat forlorn in the apartment parking lot, two tires flat, the right side bashed in, a pool of oil underneath the engine. The hope and dream of Mona was to restore this car which carried so many fond memories. It reminded her of a happily remembered youth. She and Gus had argued about keeping it around. The apartment manager had given them grief about it too. But Mona dug in her heels and insisted that the car was hers and no one was going to make her get rid of it.

Mona knew that Gus wanted a scope for his hunting rifle. Most recently, when work had been slow, Gus had taken a few opportunities to go deer hunting. His 30.06 rifle had been a gift from his deceased father. In fact, the rifle had been his father's. Whenever Gus took the gun out of its case, the image of his father would reemerge in his thoughts; the shape of his father's hands as he held the weapon and pointed out it's features to the young Gus remained as vivid as that autumn day twelve years ago.

Three months ago, while at a job site, Gus's truck had been broken into and the scope (which was carefully wrapped in his tool box) had been stolen. Gus had been glad that the rifle was not taken but was frustrated that he couldn't go hunting without a scope.

As the day of Christmas drew near, the young couple grew more and more depressed. Oh, they bravely assured each other that they didn't need a gift from the other; that their love and devotion was the greatest gift of all. But each secretly ached and schemed to obtain for their true love the gift that was the perfect expression of gratitude for the gift of the other in their lives. And as Christmas Eve dawned, both Gus and Mona silently resolved to act on the only option that they could see for themselves in the ultimate gift for their beloved.

"Gus," Mona said as she slipped on her coat, "I'll probably get off work early but Gwen said she wants to stop after work to pick up a couple of things at the Mall so I might be a little later than usual."

"Well, that's ok 'cause this part-time delivery job I've got may go a little later than usual. You know, last minute deliveries and all. I'll probably be home around 7:00 p.m."

Both heaved a sigh of relief as they went out to their jobs and began their respective plots for "the perfect gift." So far, they both had the time they needed to bring off the wonderful Christmas gift they would give to one another. The work day itself was rather uneventful for both of them. Gus's deliveries seemed to him to be a blur as he drove fast and hard to make his appointed rounds. He looked at his watch frequently, repeating the time that he knew the Auto Supply store would close. The rifle, sheathed in its leather case, rode in the rack behind his head. Mona's day at the office had been one of minimum of duties and a maximum of talk and nibbling at snack food. Once in a while they would cast a glance over at the supervisor's office in hopes that he would come out and let them go home early. Eventually, he emerged at 2 in the afternoon, gave out a loud ho, ho ho and then said "Merry Christmas, drive safely and see you on Monday." Gwen and Mona were slipping on their coats as they raced up the stairs. "Gwen, are you sure Mack is serious about this?" Mona asked anxiously as they pushed through the glass doors. "Dead serious," said Gwen, "he's been waiting for an opportunity like this for a long time."

Mona was the first one to be home. She and Gwen had driven over to Mack's place where she signed over the title of the Malibu to him and gave him the keys. He gave her $200. and a promise that when he had it restored, she could take it for a drive once in a while. He left then for the apartment complex with his brother Earl so that they could bring the car to his garage. Mona and Gwen had then driven to the sporting goods store where she had seen the perfect scope for a 30.06. The dark blue metal case was etched with a fine filigree work. The knurled knob which adjusted the lens moved smoothly and silently. It was a wonderful piece of craftsmanship. Mona hugged it to herself as a smile from within her lighted up her face. "Oh," she thought, "Gus is going to love this so."

Gwen then drove Mona home and, after wishing her a Merry Christmas and giving her a hug, went on her way. Mona stared long at the now-empty parking spot where the Malibu had sat. But, giving another squeeze on the scope in her hand, she marched into the apartment to await her beloved Gus.

He arrived a little past 7. She could tell his step on the stairs. Since she had arrived home she had tied a bow on the scope, opened the two Christmas cards that arrived in that day's mail and began to prepare the ground beef for the evening's meal of hamburgers and beans. Before he opened the door, she picked up the scope and held it behind her back as she turned to face the door when he entered. A slow, shy smile lighted up his face when he saw her but in the wrinkle of the brow of his forehead she could see that something was bothering him. She nearly overlooked the fact that he was carrying a bulky, round parcel wrapped loosely in white tissue paper. As he shifted the weight of the package in his hands, it gave off a muffled clank.

"Mona," Gus asked quietly, "what happened to the Malibu?"

In one long breath Mona gushed "Oh Gus, don't worry about that. I still have the memories even if I don't have the car anymore. No one can take those from me. Besides, Mack said I could take it for a drive now and then when he gets it restored. But listen, I just want to say that I love you and ... Merry Christmas, darling."

On the last word, she brought the scope from behind her and presented it to him with both hands; as a loving offering to her beloved. Gus gave a choked gasp, set down his package and gently took the scope from her. His mouth formed a soundless O as he admired the feel, the shape and the weight of the gift. Yet, Mona could see in his eyes confusion and sadness.

"Oh Mona, Mona, Mona. It's so beautiful. Gosh, it's just perfect."

He then stopped, looked at the floor and cleared his throat. Mona held her clasped hands under her chin and looked at him intently.

"Mona," Gus gently asked. "Did you sell the Malibu so that I could have this?"

Mona blushed and nodded. She felt a warm glow. Her sacrifice had been perfect. She had given Gus the reassurance of her total love. A smile played across her lips with the happiness she knew at that moment.

Gus cleared his throat again and leaned over to pick up the package he had set down in order to admire the scope. He offered the gift to her wile saying "Mona, honey, you are the greatest. You are the most wonderful gift I could ever have. I'm one lucky dude, believe me. I want you to have these ..." His voice trailed off as Mona took the package and, sitting on the arm of the worn, sagging sofa, unwrapped the contents therein. When she spied what was inside she gave a squeal of delight followed by a wail of disappointment. In the loosely wrapped tissue lay four custom Chevrolet Malibu Super Sport hub caps–the kind that were the rage in the days when her Malibu was running. She feverishly admired each of them, noting the racing flags embossed in the hub, the intricate spokes, the shiny chrome. Gus sat down on the sofa next to her, staring fondly at the scope. Mona looked down at him from her perch on the arm and began "Gus, where did you get ...." and then she stopped. From the way he gazed at the scope and fondled it in his hands, she suddenly knew where he had acquired the money for the hub caps. As if reading her thoughts he said softly, "Yeah, I sold the gun."

Mona slid off the arm of the sofa and snuggled next to him on the cushion. For a long time they sat there and held one another. The only sound was their gentle breathing and the occasional whoosh of a car driving by outside.

At the birth of the Christ-Child, wise men or Magi came bearing gifts. The gift-bearers were held in esteem because they recognized the preciousness of the child in a manger and so their gifts were thought to be precious and esteemed as well. On the surface, the gifts we give today may seem to be foolish; however Gus and Mona truly gave the best gift possible to each other. They sacrificed what they had in order that they could have more, not less. It's a wise person indeed who can sacrifice the most precious items one has in order to come out ahead. Gus and Mona had truly given each other the most precious gift of all: they gave one another the gift of the magi.

Parable: Discussion Questions

1.) At the birth of the Christ-Child, wise men or Magi came bearing gifts. Why and how are these gift-givers the models for all who give Christmas gifts?
2.) Why were Gus and Mona's gifts the best possible?
3.) Tell your own story of love conquering obstacles.
4.) Find a copy of O'Henry's *The Gift of the Magi* and compare and contrast it with this story.

Why So Many Christian Churches?

Curtiss De Mars-Johnson

While growing up, I attended different churches. I couldn't understand why some people said the same prayers every week, why some groups worship standing up, sitting down, and kneeling, why some people shout in worship, why some people remain silent and never even move during their worship, why in some churches there are people who pass out every Sunday, why some people handle snakes as an act of worshiping God, why some people dance in church, why others think it is the work of the devil to dance anyplace. People act so differently! When I began talking to people about what they believe I couldn't understand how there could be so many differences within the same faith. Some people were sure that others outside their own church or denomination would go to Hell, others didn't believe in a Hell, some persons were not sure there is a Heaven but they were sure that we live in a Hell here on earth, some persons pray to persons other than God and Jesus, others don't believe in praying to God, some people believe that Jesus is returning while others believe that he never left in the first place. If there is one God, how did we all wind up so different in our behaviors, beliefs, and religious organizations? Why are there so many churches?

It is deceptively simple to contend that since people are different it follows that there would be different kinds of churches. Three underlying cultural patterns will illustrate causes of change and variance in expressions of faith. I will assume that variance in faith and behaviors results in the diversity of churches.

Many people believe that things are getting more complicated and perhaps out of control today. Many are fearful of cultural ways that are different from their own. In this kind of cultural atmosphere, the diversity of churches may be seen as failure. In these terms, diversity is seen as a breakdown, malaise, confusion, and deviation from a set standard.

One possible answer

One possible answer to the question as to why there are so many churches is that the diversity is a result of failure to retain simpler and normative cultural ways from our past. This focus stems from a concern over the maintenance of the core of the culture. Its emphasis is partially based upon the belief that if all the sub-groupings continue to spin off into their own orbits, then we will lose our core identity as a nation, culture, society, and civilization. An advantage of this orientation is that it remembers and values certain lessons and sources of wisdom of the past.

There are challenges with this emphasis. Whose version of the past will be accepted as being the best interpretive lens? Also, who is to say that the past really was simpler? Is this uplifting an actual or an imagined idealized set of circumstances from the past? Is this a proactive or is it a reactive stance in light of contemporary circumstances? If we say that the past was simpler and normative for the future, aren't we cheating ourselves of seeing the complexities and challenges of the past? Consequently, would we then be able to use the past as an effective interpretive tool for the complexities and challenges of the present? Aren't we also failing to see the richness and opportunities arising from the novel circumstances of the present? One possible answer as to why there are so many churches is to contend that the diversity of churches indicates a more general cultural failure to appreciate and embrace the normative and simpler wisdom of the past.

Another approach

A completely different approach to the topic of why there are so many churches would be to examine the diversity of churches in terms of resilience and evolution of human communities. In our time, heavily marked by secular and materialistic thinking and values, Christian churches continue to thrive in so many varied and emerging manners. This is not to say that all movements, groups, and denominations are growing. It does emphasize that the overall picture is changing significantly and that this is desirable. Given this emphasis, diversity is seen in terms of fresh responses, vitality, creativity of the human spirit, evolving understanding, and proliferating opportunities for the future.

This orientation focuses upon the vitality of sub-groupings of the Christian family that each contribute to the mixture and quality of the overarching culture. Each sub-grouping is free to create its own interpretations of the past. Each is free to emphasize aspects of the past which may have been overlooked or suppressed by the dominant culture. An advantage of this emphasis is that it stresses the present needs of people and it embraces the necessity to venture into our future in a flexible and adaptable manner.

There are challenges with this emphasis. Does it directly and effectively deal with the importance of maintaining the larger whole?

How can the center core be acknowledged and upheld while also nurturing and valuing the emerging voices of creativity from what most would call the periphery and margins of society and culture? Does it ignore the rich resources of wisdom from the past? Is this emphasis on individual freedom creating the kind of complexity that verges on chaos? One answer as to why there are so many churches is to judge that the diversity is a reflection of a failure of the culture to maintain its past wisdom. Another set of responses forms an answer around the issues of diversity being evidence of freshness and vitality.

And yet another approach

There is a third motif that doesn't reflect a primary orientation to the past or the future, but rather emphasizes a series of events that eliminate history and culture. Many movements have come into being because of an underlying message that God is going to wipe out al human history. All we need to do now is to be pure in actions and belief while we wait for God to act. Human history is seen as part of cosmic warfare between the forces of good and evil. These movements are apocalyptic in orientation.

There are challenges with this kind of position. Is there any evidence that apocalyptic groups have developed a sensitivity to human responsibility for the consequences of human values and behaviors? What about significant strands of Biblical tradition that speak of human responsibility, creativity, and freedom to affect outward circumstances by acts of love seeking justice? This third motif of apocalypticism is not so concerned about the past or the future as much as it is focused on events that transcend history. Its presence helps to account for some of the diversity in the kinds of churches.

If we delve into the discipline of the history of religions we soon see that all religious movements, groups, and churches are affected by at least one of these three motifs:

- An orientation to the past allows a group to determine a model and norm for all future developments;
- An emphasis upon the benefits of an ever-evolving present moment enables a group to respond to new dynamics with creativity and freshness; or,
- A disengagement from time and history itself and an embrace of a dualistic drama of cosmic magnitude.

All three motifs are reflected in the organized historical churches of today and they help to explain the diversity we experience in the expressions of faith in the life of the churches. Human expressions of faith do not just start out as churches. Faith expresses itself by human congregating to share similar faith experiences.   Some of these free associations result in movements. Some movements become sustained groups. Some groups with a faith orientation become churches. All three motifs mentioned above are driving creative impulses that initiate the emergence of new contemporary movements, groupings, and churches.

Leaders and Movements

Movements coalesce around a leader or leaders who express images, metaphors, ideas, and feelings that reflect a creative twist to the present dominant religious expressions.   Many of these movements fizzle out because they can't sustain themselves over time. Other movements nurture their creative energies over time and become self-sustaining groups. When these groups have been in existence for a sufficient period of time to allow for reflection upon the initial impulses and vision, then organizational structures and guiding theological principles emerge that distinguish it as a formal church. What are some ways to identify, in our contemporary times, emerging Christian movements, groups, and churches?

With these tools of the three motifs and the changes that relate to movements, groups, and churches we can begin to look more closely at the question of why there are so many churches. Let's first begin with the epoch in which Jesus lived.

In the times of Jesus, the Jewish faith had several movements and groupings within its body of beliefs and behaviors. The Sadducees were associated with the rich and powerful people of the culture. They believed that the Torah from the past was the only valid source of religious authority. They rejected some modern ideas of the Pharisees, including angels, life after death with its rewards and punishments, and resurrection of the dead. The Pharisees had their support from the lower classes of both urban and country folk. This group tended to embrace the emergent oral traditions of the faith and the prophetic writings in addition to the Torah. Such beliefs as those rejected by the Sadducees were embraced in diverse ways within the broad movement and grouping labeled as the Pharisees. Several other movements and groupings within Judaism were associated with removing oneself from the dominant culture's influences, the end purposes of history (eschatology-specifically the coming of the Messiah), and apocalyptic beliefs in the imminent demise of history caused by a cosmic war to be fought on earth.

Each of these three main movements and groupings within Judaism reflect to some degree the three motifs previously mentioned. The three motifs that affect the emergence of different movements, groupings, and churches within Christianity are fully in evidence in the cultural, historical, religious, and social environment in which Christianity was born.

The earliest followers of Jesus were divided in beliefs related to the three motifs. The first motif was played out by those who believed ardently that their faith ought to remain an exclusively Jewish faith. They looked to the past for inspiration, context, and for normative descriptions for their lives. The second motif was evidenced by those who believed that this emerging new faith initiated the dawn of a new day for all humankind. Because of evolving models and interpretations of the resurrection event this group began to spread the gospel to the gentile world. They became involved in history and became what we now call the early Christian group which eventually evolved into the church (basically Catholic and Orthodox). The third motif was characterized by those concerned primarily with the delayed parousia (second coming of Jesus the Messiah) and apocalyptic expectations.

In some sense all of the varied movements, groupings, and churches directly or indirectly are related to the two most ancient of churches. These are the Roman Catholic and Eastern Orthodox Churches. They form the framework from which other movements, groups, and churches emerged. Beginning in a period prior to the Catholic Reformation, there were dynamics at play within that church that caused many reformers to found new movements that became distinctly different from the Catholic church.

The first reformer

The first reformer who helped establish a church that had widespread impact was Martin Luther. He did not intend to establish a new church, but the kind of questions he asked and the issues which subsequently came into play caused a divergence of historical forces that resulted in the new churches of the Augsburg Confession (now called the Lutheran Church by most people). His central discovery that changed his life resulted from having studied the epistles of Paul in light of the central organizing question of how we can find acceptance by our God. Justification by faith became the core of his genius that he had to offer to others. This insight was combined with the final authority of scripture, the priesthood of all believers, and the core importance of the cross as a means of understanding the relation between the law of God (the requirements of God) and the gospel (the freedom to live as the redeemed people of God). What became known as the Protestant Reformation is predicated on these vital areas of concern.

During this period, the general populace was becoming literate as the technological means of mass producing books was just coming into being. People wanted to read general and religious materials in their own language. Luther was open to using these contemporary forces to the advantage of this movement. One of the needs was for people to localize or comprehend religious experiences in their own terms of their own culture. The printed word on paper that was easily mass produced and easily transported played a major role in the Reformation.

Forces were unleashed over Europe that were all related to these core values and insights. In order to understand so many other emergent groups we need to look to England next. The Reformation in Germany was spreading to England. The Reformation literature emerged at Cambridge and Oxford Universities. At Cambridge a group under the leadership of Robert Barnes were ingesting these new materials and disseminating them to others. William Tyndale was attempting to get the Bible translated into English so that the masses of people could have direct access to the scriptures.

When King Henry VIII wanted to remarry, in order to have a son, he essentially rallied all the political and ecclesiastical forces under his power to form a new church called the Church of England. He appointed Thomas Cranmer as his first archbishop of the new church. Cranmer published a series of theological statements that clearly reflected Protestant ideas and ideals. He went to the past and adapted the Roman liturgy, Greek liturgy from St. Basil and St. Chrysostom, and new elements in the emerging Lutheran liturgy to create one of the great classic pieces of literature in the English language The Book of Common Prayer. Through various struggles, the Church of England took root and became the dominant force in that country. There were several movements that later sprang up in relation to the Church of England.

The Reformed movement

On the Continent, the Reformed movement was gaining strength. The Catholic Reformation was also gaining in power, while the

Lutheran movement was showing signs of dwindling during the mid-1500s. During the early 1500s in German-speaking Switzerland, Ulrich Zwingli rose as an early and very influential Protestant reformer. The emphasis was upon following the revelations of scripture as guidelines for living. He was a trained humanist having been a follower of Erasmus. He thus described God as "the being of all things." He believed that church and state should be intimately interrelated in the governance of the common lives of people. Another core belief, the election of God, means that God has selected certain folk for redemption. This was seen as an expression of justice and mercy. Faith is a sign of being among God's elect.

John Calvin, the greatest of the Reform church leaders, was based in French-speaking Switzerland during the middle part of the 1500s. He believed that the deep knowledge of God takes place in the heart. This is from the pen of a greatly intellectual person. There are two forms of knowledge: knowledge of the self and knowledge of God. As we examine our lives we come to the need to find the knowledge of God. The Word and Spirit reflected in scriptures is alive in the church. The Word of God causes us to know the Spirit of God through the church. Communion is the spiritual presence of Christ. Predestination was definite consequence of this theology, but not a primary antecedent assumption in his thought.

One reason Zwingli and Calvin stand out so much in the Reformed church movements is that people from all over Europe would come and study with them and then take back home their influential insights. These insights were then transformed and used as bases for inspiration for different movements beyond the confines of what became the Reformed church. Another very famous Reformed church leader in Scotland was John Knox. He greatly influenced the Presbyterian traditions around the world. In our country the Presbyterian church has played an important role. This group has been prominent and influential in most sections of our country.

During this period, a more radical Reformation movement came into being. This movement, comprised of many different groups, sprang up in different locals for different reasons. They can loosely be referred to as being the Anabaptists. They emphasized purity of the redeemed community and the necessity of keeping the faith community's values and behaviors distinct from the dominant culture. There is a great emphasis on moral transformation. The Mennonites, Quakers, Amish, and Hutterites directly descend from these movements.

In England, the radical Reformers were called the Puritans and Separatists. The Puritans ultimately wanted to reform the Church of England and bring it back to its apostolic purity. Many of these reformers wanted to stay in the church. Many of them subscribed to a form of church governance and theology that can be called Presbyterian. The Separatists wanted to separate from the Church of England. They eventually became the Congregationalists. Both reform groups stemmed from the influence of John Calvin. They shared in common a belief that Christ is the head of the church and that all people share in the call to ministry. This has been called the priesthood of all believers. They differed in the way local churches were organized. The Presbyterians organized their local churches in groupings call the presbytery. This group holds legal and financial power and authority over the local churches. The presbytery also holds religious power and authority in the form of being able to remove and transfer ministers. The Congregational way vests power and authority in the local church. The relationship between the local Congregational church and the wider denomination is founded in a covenant relationship that recognizes both the autonomy of the local church and the responsibility to the wider faith community.

The Separatists wanted to separate from the Church of England. Robert Brown was their leader, who was centered at Cambridge University. These folk became known as the Pilgrims, and they later settled at Plymouth Colony in America. From these people stemmed the Congregationalists in North America. Most of these Congregational churches joined a union with a group called the Evangelical and Reformed Church in 1957 to become the United Church of Christ.

A church group that also stemmed from the left wing separatist movement came to be known as the Baptists. They, like the Anabaptists, believed in rebaptizing people converted from others groups and churches. An outward sign of their belief in the rejuvenation and restoration to life of the believer is their belief in total immersion during baptism. Their believe in the separation of church and state, although not different in kind from other Reformers, did differ in emphasis in that they sought to remove themselves from any and all secular influences of the culture.

In Germany, Pietism arose as a movement originating from with the Protestant Reformation. A personal and individual faith experience was stressed. Official and denominational church doctrine was de-emphasized so their influence ran across denominational lines. The Moravians are one such German Pietistic group.

Pietism surfaced in England. John Wesley initiated a movement that was deeply evangelical in nature. Like German Pietism, Methodism emphasized personal conversion and saving souls. John Wesley's enthusiasm earned him the derision of the Anglican clergy. It is said that he preached between 40,000 to 50,000 sermons. His brother Charles Wesley is best remembered for writing a massive number of hymns. The Methodist church has become firmly rooted in our American culture.

Other churches

So far all the church groups mentioned have taken root in America. They all have had their direct roots in Europe. There are many other churches with their roots in the East. These are called the Orthodox churches. You may have noticed some churches with onion-domed church towers. According to Jaroslav Pelikan, in his book entitled *World Religions in America*, "Depending on how one elects to count them and on how seriously one takes their recurrent schisms, past and present, there are as many as twenty-five or more jurisdictions of Orthodox Christians in the United States." Along with their heavy emphasis on tradition their liturgy reflects an Eastern heritage.

Other churches evident in our land do not trace their history directly back to Europe or the East. When movements become churches there may arise within their body of gathered people subsequent movements that continue to evolve in new ways seeking purity in life behaviors and truth in doctrine. One such example is that of the Holiness churches. These are groups that sought to purify the people within Methodism. This is carrying forth John Wesley's idea of the perfectibility of human beings. Dozens of churches sprang from this holiness movement late in the 1800s. At the turn of the century there was a movement that sought to purify the holiness groups by baptism in the Holy Spirit. Scores of churches sprang from this movement. Their emphasis is on the gifts of the Holy Spirit. These are interpreted to mean speaking in tongues, healing, and other effects. Movements within churches are always emerging. Some of them sustain themselves over time by capturing the attention and hearts of converts while other movement play themselves out and cease to be influential.

Fundamentalism and Evangelicalism

In the early years of our century, another movement arose that shook many of the established churches. It is called Fundamentalism. It is a part of a larger movement and resurgence called Evangelicalism.

Its roots are in the Pietism in Germany, Methodism in England, and two related but different phenomena called the Great Awakenings in the United States. The shared emphases are on personal faith experiences that completely changes one's life. Fundamentalism, in the early part of our century, stemmed from a series of volumes published as The Fundamentals: A Testimony to the Truth, by Reuben Archer Torrey. In these publications, he related five basic points that he considered to be absolutely fundamental to all true faith. These are: the inerrancy of the Bible (literal truth that is perfectly and plainly revealed), the virgin birth of Jesus, his atonement (humankind being reconciled to God), his bodily resurrection, and his imminent and visible return to earth. Groups identifying themselves as Fundamentalist arose by the scores and are still a potent religious and political force in our culture today.

Groups identifying themselves as Evangelicals emerged after World War Two. They stress the reliability of the Bible in issues of faith and practice, the Bible as the inspired word of God, and the importance of a personal faith conversion and experience. The Evangelicals do not stress the literal interpretation of the scriptures to the same degree as the Fundamentalists emphasize it. Some Evangelicals interpret the role of language in general and the place of imagery in the Bible specifically as being metaphorical in certain instances.

The Roman Catholic Church in the United States is going through tremendous changes. There are new configurations of movements and groupings within that church body. All three of the motifs are in evidence in this church that continues to play such a vital role in our American culture. The Roman Catholic Church has been and is one of the most potent forces in our culture.

Many people assume that personal expressions of faith are the sole domain of the conservative wing of the Christian church. The liberal wing of American Christianity has been largely marked by an emphasis on social action. The foremost church leader in this area at the turn of our century was Walter Rauschenbusch. There are also a host of other church leaders in the Liberal camp who emphasize the depths of personal transformation, for example Rudolf Otto, Søren Kierkegaard, or Friedrich Schleiermacher. The Christian feminist writers consistently stress the need for transformation of self and society. The Liberation theologians all stress the importance of personal growth of wisdom and social transformation. In this view social transformation can not happen without the personal growth of wisdom.

You may have noticed that the names mentioned thus far are those of men. In our century, one of the greatest and most influential movements is that of the rise of feminist awareness within and beyond the churches. Women throughout history have played a role in the evolution of movements, groups, and churches. Anne Hutchinson in the early 1600s criticized the Puritans for the power of the clergy and their narrow basis for morality. She spoke from the experience of being a woman who emphasized direct intuition as the means of sensing God rather than church beliefs. In our century, Dorothy Day was the organizer of the Catholic Worker's Movement. With power and grace, she forged a place for women on the forefront of social change. Countless lay and ordained women in churches are rising up to take leadership roles and give voice to their issues. There are scores of renowned Christian Feminists writers and theologians today who are shaping the future of our culture.

One of the most vibrant and creative sparks of vitality in the United States is the appearance of the African-American Christian movements, groups, and churches. As American middle-class folk flee the inner city, there has been a major resurgence of new Christian groups that are thriving and meeting the needs of people in the core of our urban centers. Dr. Martin Luther King to this day is one of the most influential persons in the African-American Christian Community. Howard Thurman is one of the most influential African-American preachers of all time. James Cone, a member of the African Methodist Episcopal Church, is another of the best known African-American theologians. In the 1960s he was a leader in the Black Power movement. He has gone on to write extensively about liberation struggles of African-Americans. One of his great accomplishments has to do with his interpretation and importance of spirituals.

There are churches that have sprung from the Christian heritage that have theologies that significantly different than what most people would call orthodox Christianity. These churches are evolving with the same three motifs at play. Examples of these churches are the Church of Jesus Christ of the Later Day Saints (Mormons), Christian Scientists, and Jehovah Witnesses.

And more groups yet

There are many more groups springing from the Christian historical faith. It is a time of ferment and change for all Christian churches. Whether there will be more of them or fewer of them in the future is uncertain. What is clear is that dynamic movements and new groupings will continually evolve. For some this will be problematic. For others this will be a note of grace. All three motifs of the orientation toward the past, the future, and beyond history continually express themselves. Peer below the surface details and behold some of the impelling energies of change. When we combine the tools of the three orientations to time (past, future, beyond time and history) with the insights transformation related to movements, groups, and churches we possess significant resources with which to analyze why there are so many churches. These tools do not entirely explain the existence of diverse churches but they are important explanatory notes that get to the heart and core of the issue.

Diversity is not a new thing. It is not an aberrant phenomenon. Diversity of faith expression is sewn into the life core of the Christian faith. Understanding its significance will lead us to a deeper understanding of our human condition.

Churches: Discussion Questions

1.) What are the sub-groupings that each contribute to the mixture and quality of the overarching culture? What does it mean to suggest that each sub-grouping is free to create its own interpretations of the past?

2.) Why do some people dance, others handle snakes, others pass out, while others sit in silence during worship? What human needs are being met by these diverse expressions of faith?

3.) The three motifs or orientations to time affect different movements, groupings, and churches within Christianity. What is your primary orientation? Do you look to the past and recoil form change? Do you look to the future and welcome transformation? Do you look beyond time and history and hope that God is going to take care of everything?

4.) How did literacy and technology fuel the Protestant Reformation?

5.) What are the five basic points that Reuben Archer Torrey considered to be absolutely fundamental to all true faith?

6.) Why are there so many Christian churches?

7.) Do you most basically believe that some churches are more right in their beliefs and that others are wrong? How do you deal with contradictory beliefs?

8.) What is your responsibility in making this world a better place? What is God's responsibility in improving our human situation?

9.) Do you sense that we are evolving toward one united church? Are we splintering into smaller groups that are having increasing challenges with communicating with each other?

10.) Do individuals change history? Do historical moments and challenges call forth great leaders?

Churches: For Further Reading

Ahlstrom, Sydney, E. *A Religious History of the American People.* New Haven: Yale University Press, 1972.

Neusner, Jacob (ed.), *World Religions in America.* Louisville: Westminster / John Knox, 1994.

Piepkorn, Arthur C. *Profiles in Belief.* Volumes I - III. New York: Harper & Row, 1977-79.

Zaretsky, Irving, I. and Mark P. Leone, *Religious Movements in Contemporary America.* Princeton: Princeton University Press, 1974.

The Welcoming Spirit

Molly K. Stein

Mainline, borderline and on-line churches all over America have invested countless thousands of dollars in analyzing how to recruit new souls while hanging on to the ones they already have. Prudent pastors will bypass the surveys, the consultants and the marketing experts. Instead of relying on high-tech research, they will treat themselves to breakfast at the Coney Island on Superior Street in downtown Duluth every day for a week or so. There they will witness a spirit of hospitality that works on many levels.

For starters, the Coney's doors are opened early every morning to whomever cares to stop in. The owner and his able young assistant are ready to serve all who enter with the best they have to offer. The Coney has no dress code, implied or otherwise. Some visitors wear hard hats, tool belts and a pack of Camels tucked into the rolled-up sleeve of a T-shirt. Other early birds are dressed in coat and tie, skirt and blazer or sweatshirt and leggings. I feel immediately welcomed even when my body—and my hair—are still half asleep.

Every order is a special order. Whole wheat toast, dry, to go, for the tall, willowy young woman who works across the street. Another customer asks for a Number 6 with modifications: no yolks in the fried eggs, no fat on the steak and don't leave the hash browns on too long. All of these specifications are cheerfully relayed by the server, and just as cheerfully prepared by the cook. My order varies, but regardless of what else I order, I always want a cup of hot tea, extra hot water and a glass of ice. All of this appears magically on the table as soon as I sit down. Then the angel of the morning asks if I'm having breakfast. And if so, when I want it served. Doesn't that sound like heaven on earth?

But it gets better. The server always protects my morning quiet time. I often camp out with a stack of papers to sort or a story to edit, which I can do only at the Coney Island without interruption. Other visitors sit and read the paper, nurse a hangover or trade banter with the cook. Not everyone comes to stay. Sometimes the door is opened by a teenager in search of quarters for the bus, an executive who needs a pack of matches or a thirsty tourist who just wants a quick glass of water.

In July, I mentioned to my server that I wouldn't be in for two weeks because we were going on vacation. Since I started the conversation, she asked about our destination, mode of travel, summer weather on the east coast, all sorts of details. As I left, she wished me safe journey and added, "We'll miss you." What a wonderful thing to hear!

What impresses me most about my morning hideaway is not the texture of the French toast or the promptness of the service, but the fact that kindness and respect are extended to everyone who walks in the door. As a result, customers approach their hosts and each other with the same friendly courtesy. I like to think that we're all more cheerful and patient toward our families and co-workers after we've had breakfast with a smile. I realize that the Coney Island workers are paid to provide hospitality to the public, but what they give goes beyond what they receive from the profit on a cup of coffee and a cherry Danish. My trips to Coney began with a simple need for a caffeine kick-start on early summer mornings. Now I find myself nourished in many ways, which is what keeps me coming back.

As summer winds down and fall programs are getting back into full swing, we should take time to reflect on how effective we are at nourishing our communities through our churches. How strong is the spirit of hospitality? How sensitive are we to the needs of a diverse population? How gentle are we with those who don't fit the profile of the average parishioner? Take time to talk about it with fellow church leaders. And if you do come into Coney some morning, stop by my pew and say hello!

Welcoming Spirit: Discussion Questions

1.) What do the author's insights suggest about what church ought to be for the people who belong?

2.) What ought those who look at a church from outside be able to know by observing the members and their activities?

3.) Why is faith an important component of the church at work in the world?

The Basic Teaching of Vatican II

Avery Dulles, S.J.

The Conflict of Interpretations

Vatican II has become, for many Catholics, a center of controversy. Some voices from the extreme right and the extreme left frankly reject the council. Reactionaries of the traditionalist variety censure it for having yielded to Protestant and modernist tendencies. Radicals of the far left, conversely, complain that the council, while making some progress, failed to do away with the church's absolutistic claims and its antiquated class structures. The vast majority of Catholics, expressing satisfaction with the results of the council, are still divided because they interpret it in contrary ways. The conservatives, insisting on continuity with the past, give primary emphasis to the council's reaffirmation of settled Catholic doctrines, including papal primacy and infallibility. The progressives, however, hold that the true meaning of the council is to be found rather in its innovations. For them Vatican II made a decisive break with the juridicism, clericalism, and triumphalism of recent centuries and laid the foundations for a more liberal and healthier Catholicism.

Like most other councils, Vatican II issued a number of compromise statements. It intentionally spoke ambiguously on certain points, leaving to the future the achievement of greater clarity. Many commentators, accenting these problematic features, give the impression that the council left nothing but doubt and confusion in its wake. It may, therefore, be time to acknowledge that, while leaving many open questions, the council did present a solid core of unequivocal teaching on matters of great importance.

Vatican II addressed an extraordinary variety of issues ranging from highly technical questions about the theology of revelation to eminently practical questions about marriage and family life. But its central focus was undoubtedly the self-understanding of the church, and this is the theme highlighted by the Extraordinary Synod of 1985. I shall here set forth, with a minimum of personal interpretation, the basic vision of the church as understood by Vatican II. I shall concentrate on practical and pastoral matters that have a direct impact on the lives of rank-and-file Catholics. For the sake of clarity I shall arrange my observations under the rubric of ten principles that I regard as unquestionably endorsed by the council. Whoever does not accept all ten of these principles, I contend, cannot honestly claim to have accepted the results of Vatican II.

Ten Basic Principles

Aggiornamento

This Italian term, which may be translated by English words such as *updating, modernization* or *adaptation,* was popularized by Pope John XXIII, who made the concept fundamental to his own program for the coming council. Accepting this program, the fathers at Vatican II were critical of the hostility and suspicion toward the modern world that had characterized the Catholicism of the nineteenth and early twentieth centuries. Especially in the Pastoral Constitution on the Church in the Modern World, the council declared its great respect for the truth and goodness that had been brought into the world through modernization (*GS* 42). It stated that we are witnesses to the birth of a new humanism in which people are conscious of their responsibility to one another for the future of the world (*GS* 55). The faithful, said the council, must 'live in close union with their contemporaries' (*GS* 62). Catholics must, moreover, 'blend modern science and its theories and the understanding of the most recent discoveries with Christian morality and doctrine' (ibid.), so that the church may keep pace with the times and enter fully into the new age now being born. In so doing, the church can enrich itself and better understand the treasures it has received from Christ. Far from clinging to ancient forms, the church as pilgrim must press forward toward the consummation of history, when God's kingdom will be revealed in its fullness. Neither Pope John nor the council, of course, held the absurd dogma that the new is always better than the old. In fact, they frequently pointed out that modern techniques can easily be abused so as to distract people from the lasting goods of the spirit. But that is no excuse for burying oneself in the past.

The principle of aggiornamento, like all the others we shall consider, is only a principle. To apply it requires prudence and discretion lest the gospel, in being accommodated to the spirit of the age, lose its challenging power. Still, the principle itself is sound and important. The church, glorying in its magnificent heritage, should not allow itself to become a museum piece. It must not become a relic of the Middle Ages or any past period but rather a vital part of the modern world as it presses forward into God's future. Confident that the Lord himself remains with his people down through the centuries, Christians can have the courage to live out the gospel and bear witness to it under the conditions of today's world.

The Reformability of the Church

In recent centuries it has been common to look upon the church as a divine institution without spot or wrinkle. Although Catholics have sometimes admitted the faults of individual believers, they have regarded the church itself as pure and holy. Vatican II, however, depicted the church in terms of the biblical image of the People of God. As we learn from Scripture, this people, though always sealed by its covenant relationship with God, was sometimes unfaithful. The Constitution on the church, therefore, was able to admit, 'The Church holding sinners in its embrace, is at the same time holy and always in need of being purified and incessantly pursues the path of penance and renewal' (LG 8). Furthermore, in the Decree on Ecumenism, the council declared, 'Christ summons the Church, as it goes its pilgrim way, to that continual reformation of which it always has need, insofar as it is a human institution here on earth' (UR 6).

The idea that the church might be reformable caught many Catholics by surprise. In the late Middle Ages several councils had as their express aim the reformation of the whole church 'in the head and in the members,' but after the Protestant Reformation the idea of reform came under suspicion in Catholic circles. Thanks to Vatican II, however, we are relived of the burden of having to defend the whole record of the past. We can freely admit that not only individual Catholics, but the church itself in its official actions has committed errors and sins, such as the burning of heretics, the persecutions of Jews, and the excesses of Holy Wars. We can admit the Catholics had a large share of responsibility in bringing on the divisions among Christians that so weaken the Christian witness in our time.

Like the principle of updating, this second principle must be applied with discretion. Not everything in the church is suspect and fallible. The basic sacramental structures, its Scriptures, and its dogmas are abidingly valid. The grace of Christ, which comes through these channels, is more powerful than human infidelity and sin. The church, therefore, does not have an equal affinity to holiness and to evil. Evil is against its true nature. For this reason Vatican II, while speaking of the church of sinners, avoided the expression 'sinful church.' The difference is a subtle one but has a certain importance.

With regard to past historical events, we should be on guard against a kind of spiritual masochism that would transfer all the blame from the other party to our own. Often it is best to follow the principle of Pope John XXIII: "We do not wish to conduct a trail of the past. We shall not seek to establish who was right and who was wrong. Responsibility is divided."[17]   Still, to set the record straight, it is well to disavow certain errors. An example might be the present investigation to determine whether the papal commission erred by condemning the theories of Galileo in the seventeenth century.

Renewed Attention to the Word of God

In the Middle Ages, and even more since the Reformation, Catholicism tended to become the church of law and sacraments rather than the church of the gospel and the word. Catholics, too, often neglected the spiritual riches contained in the Bible. Emphasizing the precepts of the church, they allowed the proclamation of the good news to fall into some neglect. They celebrated the Mass in Latin–a language not understood by most of the people–and usually without any homily. In Catholic theology, the Bible was viewed as a remote source of doctrine, hardly used except to find proof texts for later church doctrines.

Vatican II, especially in its Constitution on Divine Revelation, *Dei Verbum*, recovered the primacy of Scripture as the word of God consigned to writing under the inspiration of the Holy Spirit *(DV* 9). The teaching office of the church, according to the Constitution, 'is not above the word of God but serves it, listening to it devoutly, guarding it scrupulously, and expelling it faithfully...'*(DV* 10). 'The study of the sacred page,' according to the same Constitution, 'is, so to speak, the soul of sacred theology' (*DV* 24).

The Constitution on Revelation strongly recommended the use of Scripture by all Catholics. 'Easy access to sacred Scripture,' it stated, 'should be provided for all the Christian faithful' (*DV* 22). The Scriptures were here compared to the Eucharist, since each in its own way offers to the faithful the bread of life (*DV* 21). And in the same paragraph we find the following eloquent sentence. 'For in the sacred books, the Father who is in heaven meets His children with great love and speaks with them; and the force and power of the word of God is so great that it remains the support and energy of the Church, the strength of faith for her children, the food of the soul, and a pure and perennial source of spiritual life.'

Besides rehabilitating the Bible, the council sought to renew the ministry of preaching. It called on Catholic preachers to provide the nourishment of the Scriptures to the People of God (*DV* 23) and warned that, as Augustine had said, 'those who do not listen to the word of God inwardly will be empty preachers of the word of God outwardly' (*DV* 25). Thus priests as well as lay people were exhorted to read the Scriptures prayerfully.

Since the council, such directives have produced excellent fruits. Catholics have learned more about the Bible; many of them attend study and prayer groups that concentrate on the Scriptures. But in this respect, as in others, further progress remains necessary. There is as yet no danger that Catholics, in their enthusiasm for the word, will forsake ritual and sacrament or that, in their devotion to the gospel, they will neglect the law of Christ and the church. The more relaxed attitude toward church law at the present time, while regrettable in some respects, can be viewed as a gain insofar as it helps to overcome an almost pharisaical scrupulosity to which Catholics were subject in the years before Vatican II. Ideally, of course, contrasting elements such as law and gospel, word and sacrament, should not be played off against each other but should rather be mutually reinforcing. The effort to achieve the right balance should be high on the agenda of Catholics today.

Collegiality

It is almost a platitude to assert that the Catholic church from the Middle Ages until Vatican II was pyramidal in structure. Truth and holiness were conceived as emanating from the pope as commander-in-chief at the top, and the bishops were depicted as subordinate officers carrying out the orders of the pope. In our own day, many conservative Catholics lean toward this military analogy of the church.

Vatican II did not deny the primacy of the pope as it had been defined a century earlier by Vatican I, but it did put the papacy into a significantly new context. The college of bishops, together with the pope as its head, was seen as having the fullness of power in the church. The individual bishops were portrayed not as mere lieutenants of the pope but as pastors in their own right. They were in fact called 'vicars of Christ' (*LG* 28)–an ancient title that had been given to bishops in the ancient church but that, since about the eighth century, had come to be reserved for the pope.

The principle of collegiality runs through the documents of Vatican II like a golden thread. Just as the pope is surrounded by a college of bishops, so each bishop serves as head of a presbyteral college, called presbytery, and governs his diocese in consultation with presbyters, religious and laity. Thus the principle of collegiality, understood in a wide sense, may be viewed as pervading all levels of the church. Pastors, according to the Constitution on the Church, 'know that they themselves were not meant by Christ to shoulder alone the entire saving mission of the Church toward the world. On the contrary, they understand that it is their noble duty so to shepherd the faithful and recognize their services and charismatic gifts that all according to their proper roles may cooperate in this common undertaking with one heart' (*LG* 30).

Since the council, many new institutions have been erected to implement collegiality on various levels; for example, the worldwide synod of bishops, national and regional episcopal conferences, national and diocesan pastoral councils, parish councils, priests' senates, and the like. If in some cases too many questions have been subjected to prolonged discussion and debate, it has been necessary to go through this stage to arrive at the proper mean. Parliamentariansim or democracy, if carried too far, is likely to provoke a reaction in the opposite direction, toward a revival of the preconciliar form of authoritarianism, which seemed relatively efficient and rapid. Here the council still calls upon us to devise mechanisms of decision making that respect both the traditional principle of pastoral authority and the nature of the church as a Spirit-filled community. Neither an army nor a New England town meeting is a suitable paradigm.

Religious Freedom

Up to the very time when the council opened, it was far from certain whether the Catholic church could subscribe to the principle of religious freedom that had by then prevailed in most Protestant bodies and won approval in the Assembly of the World Council of Churches at New Delhi in 1961. More specifically, it was being asked whether the church could respect the right and duty of each person to follow his or her conscience with regard to the acceptance or nonacceptance of religious belief. For centuries the Christian churches, Protestant as well as Catholic, had striven to gain control of the apparatus of civil power so as to obtain a privileged status. In the 1950's, when John Courtney Murray began to defend the idea of a religiously neutral state, his orthodoxy was questioned by another American theologians and even by some Roman authorities. Over the protests of his opponents, however, he was invited to Vatican II (not indeed to the first session but from the second session on) and he, as much as any individual, was responsible for the Declaration on Religious Freedom. This Declaration clearly taught that there is no need for the state to profess the true religion or give it a legally privileged status. It approved of civil tolerance for all faiths and rejected, on theological grounds, any coercion in the sphere of belief.

For most Americans, the principle of religious freedom offers no difficulties. We almost take it for granted. Our tendency is rather to fall into the opposite extreme, religious indifferentism. We have to remind ourselves that the Declaration itself asserted the unique status of the Catholic faith and the obligation of all believers to profess and defend that faith. Those who sincerely believe and love the truth received from Christ will strive, as did Christ and the apostles, to bear witness to it by their words and deeds and to share their faith with others.

The Active Role of the Laity

In the Catholic church, at least in modern times, priests and religious have borne almost total responsibility for the mission of the church. The apostolic spirit of the clergy and religious orders has been admirable but, generally speaking, the laity have been rather passive. Seeking to remedy this situation, the movement known as Catholic Action, in the period between the two world wars, sought to involve elite members of the laity in the apostolate of the hierarchy. Not satisfied with this, some progressive theologians during the decade before Vatican II held that the laity, besides associating themselves with the apostolate of the hierarchy, should exercise an active apostolate in their own right as baptized believers. The council, endorsing this development, exhorted lay persons to advance the kingdom of God by engaging in temporal affairs and by discharging their familial and vocational obligations in a manner faithful to Christ.

Since the council some have maintained that the clergy have as their proper sphere of operation the inner affairs of the church, whereas lay persons should regard secular matters as their area of competence. The council, however, does not authorize such a sharp division of labor. The Decree on the apostolate of the Laity, *Apostolicam actuositatem*, exhorts lay persons 'to exercise their apostolate both in the Church and in the world, in both the spiritual and the temporal orders' (*AA* 5). In other documents, the council provides for active participation of the laity in divine worship, in pastoral councils, and in the sphere of theology. In this last area, Vatican II calls upon the laity to speak freely and openly. 'In order that such persons may fulfill their proper function,' says the Pastoral Constitution, 'let it be recognized that all the faithful, clerical and lay, possess a lawful freedom of inquiry and of thought, and the freedom to express their minds humbly and courageously about those matters in which they enjoy competence' *GS* 62).

Since the council, we have seen in the church a great increase of lay ministries, not only the canonically erected ministries of reader and acolyte, but also ministries of teaching, music, social action, counseling, and even the distribution of Holy Communion. There has been a great and welcome influx of laymen and laywomen into theology. These new developments, predictably, have raised difficult questions about the specific role of clergy and religious and the responsibilities and powers of the laity. Even if progress in these areas at times has been slow, we may be thankful that much has been accomplished in a relatively short time. In a period of diminishing vocations to the clerical and religious life, it is urgent that lay persons assume greater responsibility than ever for the faith and life of the church.

Regional and Local Variety

From the late Middle Ages until Vatican II, the characteristic emphasis of Catholicism had been on the universal church, commonly depicted as an almost monolithic society. Vatican II, by contrast, emphasized the local churches, each of them under direction of a bishop who is called a 'vicar of Christ.' Many of the council texts portray the universal church as a communion, or collegial union, of particular churches. 'In and from such individual churches,' says the Constitution on the Church, 'the one and only Catholic Church takes its rise' *(LG* 23). The local bishop, on the ground of his ordination and appointment, is given authority to be a true pastor of his own community, making responsible decisions rather than simply carrying out Roman directives.

Vatican II made provision also for regional groupings. Speaking of the differences between Eastern and Western Christianity, the council said, 'Far from being an obstacle to the Church's unity, such diversity of customs and observances only adds to its splendor and contributes greatly to carrying out its mission' *(UR* 16). Vatican II accordingly recognized a legitimate variety among regional churches, even in the formulation of doctrine. Elsewhere it declared, 'The variety of local churches with one common aspiration is particularly splendid evidence of the catholicity of the undivided Church' (*LG* 23). 'The accommodated preaching of the revealed word,' says the Pastoral Constitution, 'ought to remain the law of all evangelization' (*GS* 44). Each nation, we are told, must develop the ability to express Christ's message in its own way and must foster a living exchange between the church and the various human cultures (ibid.).

The differences between the Catholicism of different regions are much more evident today than twenty years ago, when the customs and liturgy of the Roman church, with its Latin language, were universally enforced. This diversification has not yet run its course. John Paul II, addressing the Zairean hierarchy in May of 1980, spoke in favor of Africanization.[18]

Americanization has been and is taking place in our own Catholicism. Because of our distinctive cultural and political tradition, we must expect certain distinctive ways of thinking and acting in the church. We have different views than Europeans on how the church ought to relate to politics and economics. We have different views regarding human rights and due process growing out of our common law tradition. Probably too, we are more prepared than many other countries to see women rise to positions of leadership in the church, as they have in political and economic life.

While seeking a sound inculturation, we must avoid thinking that our own national traditions are above criticism or that Americans are a superior people who have nothing to learn from other nationalities. Even where legitimate differences exist, we must take care that they do not disrupt our communion with the rest of the Catholic church. In this regard we should respect the authority of the Holy See, which has the responsibility before God both to 'protect legitimate differences' and to make sure that 'such differences do not hinder unity but rather contribute to it' (*LG* 13).

Ecumenism

Since the Reformation, Catholics have commonly adopted hostile and defensive attitudes toward other Christian churches and especially toward Protestantism. Such hostility has left traces in official documents of the Holy See, notably between Pius IX and Pius XI. In this regard, Pope John XXIII and Vatican II effected a quiet revolution. The council in its Decree on Ecumenism expressed reverence for the heritage of other Christian churches, called attention to their salvific importance for their own members, and acknowledged that they possess

5</mark>

true elements of the Church of Christ. As a result, anathema has yielded to dialogue. In the ecumenical dialogues since the council, great progress has been achieved in overcoming major differences that have divided the churches for centuries. While formal reunion between the Catholic church and other communions remains only a distant prospect, Christians of different confessional groups have achieved a far greater measure of mutual understanding, respect and solidarity.

The proper implementation of ecumenism, as of the other principles we are here considering, requires realism and good judgment. On the one hand, we must overcome our habitual attitudes of hatred and suspicion and be open to appreciate all the sound values in other forms of Christianity, both Eastern and Western. On the other hand, we cannot act as though all the ecumenical problems had already been solved. Instead of simply wishing away the remaining disagreements, we must work patiently over a long period to achieve, through prayer and dialogue, a consensus based on truth.

Dialogue With Other Religions

Vatican II was not slow in perceiving that the changed attitude of Catholics toward other Christian churches called for a corresponding shift in their attitude toward the other religions and their adherents. The council accordingly drew up a Declaration on Non-Christian Religions, which contained a major section on Jewish-Christian relationships. Since the council important dialogues have taken place between Catholics and Jews, both in this country and abroad.

The principle of interreligious dialogue, like the other principles, challenges us to develop mature and responsible attitudes. Some commentators have introduced an antithesis between mission and dialogue, as if the importance of the one must undercut that of the other. The council, however, kept mission and dialogue in dynamic tension. While recognizing in its Declaration on Non-Christian Religions, *Nostra aetate*, elements of truth and goodness in all the great religions, and hence the desirability of respectful dialogue (*NA* 2), the council in its Decree on Missionary Activity, *Ad gentes*, insisted on the God-given uniqueness of the Church of Christ and consequently on the abiding necessity of missionary labor so that Christ may be acknowledged among all peoples as universal Lord and Savior (*AG* 6-7).

For Americans, the most obvious application of the Declaration on Non-Christian Religions has to do with Judaism. In parts of the country, many Catholics still hold a latent attitude of hostility, deeply rooted in ethnic and cultural factors. We need to make a special effort to rise above these negative attitudes, which are utterly contrary to the gospel precept of love. As mentioned above, the church collectively has much to repent of in its historic dealings with the Jewish people. Let us not add to these crimes.

The Social Mission of the Church

Since the Reformation, the Catholic church has tended to regard its mission as an exclusively religious one, aimed at preparing individuals through faith, worship, and right behavior to attain external life. Gradually, with the social encyclicals of popes such as Leo XIII and Pius XI, the church began to assume responsibility to teach the principles of a just social order, but this order was viewed in terms of conformity to the natural law rather than as an implementation of the gospel.

With John XXIII and Vatican II, the emphasis shifted. The apostolate of peace and social justice came to be seen as a requirement of the church's mission to carry on the work of Christ, who had compassion on the poor and the oppressed. This changed attitude was eloquently expressed in Vatican II's Message to Humanity, released nine days after the opening of the council in 1962. It was more fully elaborated in the Pastoral Constitution on the Church in the Modern World, which described the church as endowed with 'a function, a light, and an energy that can serve to structure and consolidate the human community' (GS 42). Since the council, this trend has gained momentum. It was reflected in the encyclical of Paul VI, Populorum progressio (1967), and even more clearly in the synod document, Justice in the World (1971), which depicted the struggle for justice and the transformation of society as constitutive dimensions of evangelization. Seeking to carry out the council's mandate to discern the signs of the times in the light of the gospel (GS 4), popes and episcopal conferences have given increasingly concrete directives concerning matters of public policy. The theme of the church's special solidarity with the poor, already broached at Vatican II (GS 1), has given rise in Latin America to the idea of a 'preferential option' for the poor. The theology of poverty and development is further explored by John Paul II in his 1987 encyclical Sollicitudo rei socialis.

This tenth principle is no easier to implement than the other nine. It would be irresponsible for the church to avoid all comment on the moral and religious aspects of public policy issues, for the world legitimately looks to religious leaders for advice in reshaping society according to what Bishop James Malone has called 'a God-centered value system.' On the other hand, ecclesiastical authorities must respect the freedom of individuals and groups within the church to reach conscientious decisions about policies on which intelligent and committed Catholics can disagree. The turbulent debates surrounding the collective pastorals of the American bishops on peace and on the economy make it evident that, while real progress is being made, the right approach to sociopolitical issues is only gradually being found through a process of trial and error.

A Point of Departure

In setting forth these ten principles, I have not tried to say anything new or original. On the contrary, my aim has been to articulate what I hope is obvious to anyone seeking an unprejudiced interpretation of the council. The principles are intended not as a point of arrival but as a point of departure; they may serve as premises, not as conclusions.

Because the principles are general and abstract, they leave many open questions, some of which will be addressed in subsequent chapters. These questions can become bitter and divisive, but this need not be the case, provided that the documents are read from within the broad consensus I have described. If the principles outlines here are accepted and internalized by all parties to the discussion, a certain variety of opinion on other points of interpretation and application can be stimulating and instructive. But if the basic principles explained in this chapter are rejected, consensus can hardly be achieved on the more controversial questions.

Vatican II: Discussion Questions

1.) Why has Vatican II has become, for many Catholics, a center of controversy?
2.) Like most other councils, Vatican II issued a number of compromise statements. It intentionally spoke ambiguously on certain points. Why?
3.) What is *aggiornamento*?
4.) Vatican II depicted the church in terms of the biblical image of the People of God. What does this mean and why is it important?
5.) The idea that the church might be reformable caught many Catholics by surprise. What are the issues involved in this surprise?

6.) The council in its Decree on Ecumenism expressed reverence for the heritage of other Christian churches, called attention to their salvific importance for their own members, and acknowledged that they possess true elements of the Church of Christ. Explain.

7.) The apostolate of peace and social justice has come to be seen as a requirement of the church's mission to carry on the work of Christ who had compassion on the poor and the oppressed. Why is this significant?

Vatican II: For Further Reading

Dulles, Avery. *The Reshaping of Catholicism: Current Challenges in the Theology Of Church* (San Francisco, Harper & Row, Publishers, 1988).

Huebsch, Bill. *Vatican II in Plain English: The Collection* (Chicago, Thomas More Press, 1997).

Liturgy's Tension: Memory and Hope

Julia Upton, R.S.M.

"Is there a difference between eating and having a meal?" I always launch our first discussion of Eucharist in my undergraduate Liturgy course with this question. How would you answer it?

The first responses that come are usually quick "no's" which assume that since having a meal involves eating, there is no difference between the two. Inevitably, though, some brave soul ventures into the circle of conversation with an observation that goes something like this: "Eating is just eating, but a meal involves more."

As any professor might, I immediately latch on to the concept of the "more" involved and together we eventually come to the conclusion that grabbing a chicken leg on the run is "eating," but "having a meal" involves setting the table, sitting, relaxing, usually at least one other person, conversation, and often eating a meal of more than one course. We also realize that during a meal we are nourished by more than food. In fact, it is often the company and conversation that feed us better than the food.

Given these distinctions, I next ask the students when they had their last meal. Silence falls. It isn't one of those vacant silences that seems to make everyone feel uncomfortable, but more of a poignant contemplative silence. You see, on our metropolitan commuter campus where over 80 percent of the students also hold down outside jobs, there are very few meals being eaten in the course of a week. Softly, the realization of how much we humans need meals begins to surface and with it a tinge of sadness.

Jesus knew the importance of meals. When we scan the New Testament we find a whole host of meals. In fact, most of the stories involving his greatest teachings took place over a meal. It seems natural, then, that Jesus would want us to remember his message in that context.

Of course, the meal we remember the most was the Last Supper, Jesus last meal with his close friends before his death and resurrection. During the meal, the synoptic writers tell us, Jesus took bread, blessed it, broke it and gave it to those gathered saying 'This is my body which is given up for you. Do this in memory of me.' Then he took a cup of wine and blessed it as well. Passing it among them he said, 'This is the cup of my blood which is poured out for you. DO THIS in memory of me.'

Both times he said "Do this." What do you think he meant?

Traditionally people have taken the words quite literally, repeating the action of blessing, breaking and eating at Mass, but I think that he had something additional in mind.

Let us turn for a minute to the Johannine account of the same meal recorded in John 13:1-15. When you read that passage you will notice that John never even mentions bread or wine. Instead, he alone of the four gospel authors tells us that during supper Jesus "got up from the table, took off his outer robe, and tied a towel around himself. Then he poured water into a basin and began to wash the disciples feet." He was setting for them an example of service, saying "You also should do as I have done to you"–in other words, "Do this!"

Today we hardly ever wash one another's feet, but when you recall the dusty, arid terrain of Jesus' homeland, it seems less strange that a host would wash an arriving guest's feet as naturally as we would take his or her coat. What makes this scene unusual, therefore, is not that Jesus washes their feet, but that he does so in the middle of the meal. That is what leads me to conclude that his purpose was primarily symbolic.

Present, Past and Future

I think the point which Jesus tried to make so graphically was that this act of "remembering and giving thanks" which we call Eucharist is not just about the past; it is also about the present and even more importantly about the future. Jesus did not intend for us simply to remember his oblation, but to be oblations ourselves and to spend our lives in service of one another. It is as if Jesus is still urging us down through the centuries, "Make your eucharistic table a piece of lavish abundance and extravagant service, where the tired, the poor, the hungry and all who, driven by despair and need, may find real food, real rest, real comfort, real nurture." Do this!

"To participate in the meal is to enact that vision, to surrender oneself to its value, meaning and truth," Nathan Mitchell writes. In coming to the Eucharistic meal we testify to our common belief that it is the Lord Jesus who sustains and nourishes us, and pledge we will likewise sustain and nourish one another with the bread that is our lives. That is our pledge to humanity. In his address to the 41st International Eucharistic Congress in Philadelphia in 1976, Father Pedro Arrupe reminded us that "if there is hunger anywhere in the world, then our celebration of the Eucharist is somehow incomplete everywhere in the world."

Father Eugene LaVerdierre, in his book *Dining in the Kingdom* of God, elaborates on this concept. He approaches Eucharist by examining ten meals Jesus ate with others as described in the Gospel according to Luke, giving us the demands of Eucharist, you could say. LaVerdiere summarizes seven challenges of "table solidarity" that we could each spend a lot of time reflecting on in our own lives. He says that those who dine with Jesus "must be willing to be transformed by his presence . . . to reach out in loving reconciliation . . . be ready for the unexpected . . . must listen attentively to the word of the Lord . . . must attend to interior cleanness . . . must seek the lowest place, and the host must invite the poor and helpless . . . must offer their own lives that others might live."

What is your reaction to those demands? Has that been your experience of Eucharist? Can you ever recall being transformed by the presence of Jesus at Eucharist?

"But it is so boring!" many a student has pleaded, and they certainly have a good point to make. So let us consider "boredom" for a moment. What is the most boring thing you have ever had to do? Remember the whole event as you experienced it, particularly how old you were at the time. Was the event itself boring or were you bored by it?

Consider a seven-year-old child at a retirement dinner. Chances are she would be very bored by the adult conversation about the company's retirement program and benefits, and not even understand the humorous stories they continued to tell about the "good old days." Judging by the adult laughter and camaraderie, however, we could not say that the event itself was boring, but only that the child was bored by it. Why was she bored? If you were her grandparent, how could you have helped her to be less bored by the event?

Expectations

Expectations are an important consideration. Especially in this day of multimedia glitz, if one comes to Eucharist expecting to be entertained one will inevitably be bored. I assure you, there are much better forms of entertainment than worship!

"Then why go?" you ask. Good question! As you age, you will find that your answers to it will change.

The seven-year-old will probably go because her parents take her, and teens will often attend just to keep peace in the family. Some people have social reasons for coming to worship each week, while others think that if they don't go God will get even with them by sending evil things their way.

Why do I go? To keep hope alive. To be changed. To be challenged. As you can see, my answer changes depending on what is going on in my life. In a fundamental way, the altar—the Christian family dinner table—is home to me.

The Table in Focus

Both the latest Catechism of the Catholic Church (CCC) and the church's most ancient tradition repeatedly refer to the "mystery" of faith. That is a term we must all begin to focus on more. Many of our "absent brethren" think that they can't come to the table unless they have all the answers and give complete assent to every papal and episcopal utterance. When we put the accent on "mystery," however, we begin to see the banqueting table in better focus.

The table is a place to bring the questions and to celebrate the mystery–the mystery that death become life–the mystery that "abides and draws everything toward life" (1085). Around the table gather the company of believers, not just of our time, but from two thousand years of believing–during wars and pestilence, floods and droughts, the young and the feeble come dancing or limping to take their place in our circle of faith. This action "makes the Church present and manifests her as the visible sign of the communion in Christ between God and men."
Around that table the faithful are caught up in the new life of the community–a life that "involves the 'conscious, active, and fruitful participation' of everyone" (1071)–accent on "everyone."

It follows then that the table is also a place to bring not just our believing, but also our suffering. Widows and widowers often tell me that one of the most difficult parts of grieving is returning to the table without the spouse with whom they celebrated eucharist in good times and in bad, in sickness and in health. "How can I sing one of Zion's songs in an alien land?" the church echoes the psalmist's lament.

I have a sense of what they mean. During the Vietnam War, a man I was dating was drafted and for a year and a half our relationship existed solely in exchange of letters. Although we wrote almost daily, there were long stretches when no word came and my heart feared the worst. It was at eucharist that I felt the pain most acutely. I couldn't "pray" I thought. I could only cry. Little did I know then how well God hears tears.

There are some days, weeks, months when all one can do is be physically present to place the longings that are beyond words on the altar along with the other gifts, and to receive manna for the day.

Regardless of what we may have done along the way, it is so important to keep on coming back to the table–to keep both memory and hope alive. The CCC reminds us that the entire assembly "should prepare itself to encounter its Lord and to become 'a people well disposed'"(1097). This "preparation of hearts" it recognizes to be the joint work of the Holy Spirit and the assembly.

It might surprise you, but some of the most beautiful Eucharistic celebrations I have recently heard described were not held in a magnificent cathedral with full chorus and brass, but rather in a cramped prison cell where hostages were held. In their recent books, both Terry Anderson and Father Lawrence Jenco describe in detail the way in which they huddled together to keep hope alive. Maybe Terry Anderson's reflections match yours, but remember that this was written by a Christian who spent seven years as a hostage in Lebanon:

It is often hard to take communion and feel anything. Not that I have doubts about my beliefs. It's just that I'm so often angry or frustrated that I can't get my mind calm enough .... Sometimes, though, when I'm able to diminish my frustration, or the anger left over ... I can find a place during this so-simple ceremony where it's close.... There is a clarity, a suspension of things, a sense of being elsewhere, and a feeling of calm power and peace. It's fleeting, but strongly attracting that I reach for it ever mass, as if the reaching prevents me from getting there. It's so difficult to describe, like a Zen trance, but more.

His poem entitled "Eucharist" follows in the text:

Five men huddled close
against the night and our oppressors,
around a bit of stale bread
hoarded from a scanty meal,
and a candle, lit not only as
a symbol but to read the text by.
The priest's as poorly clad,
as drawn with strain as any,
but his voice is calm, his face serene.
This is the core of his existence,

the reason he was born.
Behind him I can see
his predecessors in their generations,
back to the catacombs,
heads nodding in approval,
hands with his tracing
out the stately ritual,
adding the power of their suffering
and faith to his, and ours.
The ancient words shake off
their dust, and come alive.
The voices of their authors
echo clearly from the damp, bare walls.
The familiar prayers come
straight out of our hearts.
Once again Christ's promise
is fulfilled; his presence fills us.
The miracle is real.

Too often we discuss Eucharist almost exclusively in terms of what happens to the bread and wine, how relevant the homily is, whether or not the prayers are inclusive, or the celebrant dynamic. The first Christians focused instead on what happens to the people who share bread and wine in memory of Christ. We have two thousand years of stories about people whose lives have been transformed by their experiences around the Christian family table. Some are celebrated as saints, but others are ordinary citizens who are able to do extraordinary things because their faith in themselves, in God and in the community has been strengthened at Eucharist. Those are the stories we must remember to tell each other.

Liturgy's Tension: Discussion Questions

1.) What was the best eucharistic celebration you ever attended? What qualities made it a fine celebration?

2.) How important are attitude and expectations with regard to any type of celebration? How would you characterize your attitude toward common worship? Over time, has your attitude changed or remained constant?

3.) Even though people may choose not to participate regularly at common worship, they usually choose to celebrate the significant moments of their lives around the family table: weddings; christenings; funerals, etc. Do you think that Christians have a responsibility to support each other in worship in ordinary times as well as in these more extraordinary times? How might such an attitude be fostered?

4.) Suppose if after a typical Sunday Mass in your parish the presider asked you to evaluate your experience of the liturgy. What items would you include in your evaluation and how would you approach the task?

Liturgy's Tension: For Further Reading

Paul Bernier, S.S.S. *Eucharist: Celebrating Its Rhythms in Our Lives*. Ave Maria Press, 1993.

Mary Collins, O.S.B. *Contemplative Participation: Sacrosanctum Concilium Twenty-five Years Later*. Liturgical Press, 1990.

Eugene LaVerdierre. *Dining in the Kingdom of God*. Liturgical Training Publications, 1994.

Monika Hellwig. *Eucharist and the Hungers of the World*.

Margaret Visser. *Rituals of Dinner: The Origins, Evolution, Eccentricities, and Meaning of Table Manners*. Grove Press, 1991.

The Easter Vigil

1994 at All Saints Church in Harlem

Joel Barbara Clarke, F.H.M.

It was a typical March night with the weather seasonably cold and damp. Everything seemed quiet and serene. One of the ushers was guarding the items with which to make the "Easter Fire." At approximately 10:50 p.m. on April 2, 1994, the priest and about 50 members of the parish gathered around the front of the church to witness the liturgical preparation for the start of the fire.

About 100 feet from the church across Madison Avenue, some brothers were standing around in front of a small grocery store. All of a sudden, just as the fire got a good start and the priest began the service, the brothers began talking loud, boom-box blasting and business as usual: selling drugs! I was standing on the top step of about nine or ten steps and I was able to observe the entire scene. The fire caught the momentary attention of the sellers, but once they realized that the fire was intentional and under control, they went back to their nightly activities. One of the ushers motioned to them to please lower their music. They were cooperative.

I felt that even though the men were not involved and concerned about our actions, they had a sense that something special was happening. I was especially aware of God's good presence among all present, as the priest chanted from the great Exultet: "The power of this holy night dispels all evil, washes guilt away, restores lost innocence, brings mourners joy; it casts out hatred, brings us peace, and humbles earthly pride."

The Easter Vigil: Discussion Questions

1.) The author suggests that there is a very certain power in the celebration of liturgy. Have you ever had a similar experience?

2.) The author points to the great Easter proclamation, the Exultet, and zeroes in on a particular verse: "The power of this holy night dispels all evil..." How can a night have such power?

The Celebration of the Eucharist

From *The First Apology in Defense of the Christians*
Saint Justin, martyr
(Cap. 66-67: PG 6, 427-431)

Before reading the selection below, write a description of what happens on Sunday in the church you most recently attended. Then compare and contrast your vision with that of Justin Martyr who was beheaded about 165. His description of the early Christians' Eucharist follows.

No one may share the Eucharist with us unless he believes that what we teach is true, unless he is washed in the regenerating waters of baptism . . . and unless he lives in accordance with . . . Christ.

We do not consume the eucharistic bread and wine as if it were ordinary food and drink, for we have been taught that as Jesus Christ our Savior became a man of flesh and blood by the power of the Word of God, so also the food that our flesh and blood assimilates for its nourishment becomes the flesh and blood of the incarnate Jesus by the power of his own words contained in the prayer of thanksgiving.

The apostles, in their recollections, which are called gospels, handed down to us what Jesus commanded them to do. They tell us that he took bread, gave thanks and said: Do this in memory of me. This is my body. In the same way we took the cup, he gave thanks and said: This is my blood. The Lord gave this command to them alone. Ever since then we have constantly reminded one another of these things. The rich among us help the poor and we are always united. For all that we receive we praise the Creator of the universe through his Son, Jesus Christ and through the Holy Spirit.

On Sunday we have a common assembly of all our members, whether they live in the city or in the outlying districts. The recollections of the apostles or the writings of the prophets are read, as long as there is time. When the reader has finished, the president of the assembly speaks to us; he urges everyone to imitate the examples of virtue we have hard in the readings. Then we all stand up together and pray.

On the conclusion of our prayer, bread and wine and water are brought forward. The president offers prayers and gives thanks to the best of his ability, and the people give their assent by saying, 'Amen.' The Eucharist is distributed, everyone present communicates, and the deacons take it to those who are absent.

The wealthy, if they wish, may make a contribution, and they themselves decide the amount. The collection is placed in the custody of the president, who uses it to help the orphans and widows and all who for any reason are in distress, whether because they are sick, in prison, or away from home. In a word, he takes care of all who are in need.

We hold our common assembly on Sunday because it is the first day of the week, the day on which God put darkness and chaos to flight and created the world, and because on that same day our savior Jesus Christ rose from the dead. For he was crucified on Friday and on Sunday he appeared to his apostles and disciples and taught them the things that we have passed on for your consideration.

The Eucharist

William C. Graham

When Moses wandered in the desert with the Israelites on their long journey to the Promised Land, he told the people to remember that God tested them by affliction. They would discover that in the midst of that affliction, God would not abandon the chosen people. God fed them with manna, with bread from heaven. The connection between manna and the Christian Eucharist ought to be obvious. We, too, are fed with bread from heaven, bread containing within it all sweetness. When Catholics still prayed in Latin, they would chant this truth during Benediction of the Blessed Sacrament. The priest would intone, "you have given us bread from heaven." The people would respond, "containing within it all sweetness." Just as those bowed in prayer remembered and gave thanks, so also are Christians who gather at the eucharistic table today to remember and give thanks for the signs of God's providence, God's guarantee that we will not be abandoned.

The book of Deuteronomy makes an important point in that regard. This fifth book of the Bible first spoke to our older brothers and sisters who share the faith of Abraham and Sarah. Consider the story you see in 8:2-3, 14-16. Together, both Jews and Christians are reminded that God is always faithful. In the body and blood of Christ, Christians are given the new and unending sign of God's never diminishing care. Every celebration of the Eucharist brings all past proof of God's love to the present moment.

The Apostle Paul's first letter to the church at Corinth contains one of the oldest descriptions of the Christian eucharist. It is brief, but powerful. He asks an energetic question which calls for a great **AMEN** from all the church. "Is not the cup of blessing we bless a sharing in the blood of Christ? And is not the bread we break a sharing in the body of Christ? Because the loaf of bread is one, we, many though we are, are one body for we all partake of the one loaf" (1 Cor. 10:16-17).

Paul's summary of what Christians do around book and table suggests that there is a horizontal dimension to the Eucharist. In gathering, offering, blessing, breaking, pouring, eating, drinking, sharing, we are joined to the Christ who assembles us, and whose Spirit lives both within the individual Christian and, importantly, in the gathered community. Thus we are joined in the eucharistic activity one to another. Because we are the Body of Christ, we are united so intimately that loving service one of another is the is the logical consequence of what we have done and what we have become. At the eucharistic table, Christians are incorporated into Christ. Our lives are touched by and embodied into the very life of God.

The celebration of the Eucharist states that those who celebrate have high ideals and are aware of their many blessings. The statement that the community makes in gathering, blessing and sharing is truly profound. We make a statement about who we are, and what we hope to become. This hopeful statement sometimes highlights for us our own imperfection, and the imperfection of both church and world. We come by our imperfection honestly. Though we are children of the light, we have first been touched by original darkness. So had the children of Israel who wandered in the darkness. Though God fed them with bread from heaven, they forgot about the slavery they had endured, and instead remembered fondly the fleshpots of Egypt. They told Moses, they missed "the fish we used to eat without cost in Egypt, and the cucumbers, the melons, the leeks, the onions and the garlic" (Numbers 11:5). God reminded them that manna, that flat and dull food which nourished their bodies, also fed their freedom.

The freedom of Christians in every age and place is fed by the life of Christ whom we are called to imitate. Jesus told us, "if you do not eat the flesh of the Son of Man and drink his blood, you have no life in you" (John 6:53).

Christians come to the eucharistic table wounded and sinful, but hopeful and eager. Just as the manna in the desert strengthened the Israelites for their journey, so too does the eucharistic food and drink strengthen us.

It is then not just a collection of faces who come to the table, but a true assembly of gifted seekers. Each comes to this table with gifts and burdens. Each comes wounded, with memories both of gladness and of sorrow. But at the holy table, we find each other; there we find our true selves. We are given rest and nourishment. We struggle to make sense of the afflictions which burden and threaten to overwhelm us. There we encounter the hope and the promise that is the gift to all who will dine.

Christians believe that we are the Body of Christ. We who are fed at the eucharistic table know that we will live forever.

Oh you who clothe the lilies

   and feed the birds of the sky,

who lead the lambs to the pasture

   and the deer to the waterside,

who has multiplied loves and fishes

   and converted water into wine:

Do come to our table

   as guest and giver to dine.

The Eucharist: Reflection Questions

1.) Lamb of God is perhaps the perfect eucharistic metaphor. Why? Begin with 1 Corinthians 5: 7 ("For our paschal lamb, Christ, has been sacrificed"). Refer to the Passover ritual in Exodus, and to New Testament accounts of the institution of the eucharist as you craft your answer.

This answer may be written from the point of view of a believer, or of one who observes the beliefs and practices of another.

2.) Analyze the table grace in large print on the previous page. What does it tell you about Christian belief and Christian life?

The Eucharist: For Further Reading

Crichton, J.D. *Christian Celebration: The Sacraments*. London: Geoffrey Chapman, 1973.

Durkin, Mary. *The Eucharist: Guidelines for Contemporary Catholics*. Chicago: Thomas More, 1990.

Emminghaus, Johannes H. *The Eucharist*. Translated by Matthew J. O'Connell. Collegeville: Liturgical Press, 1978.

Guzie, Tad. *Jesus and the Eucharist*. New York: Paulist, 1974.

Kiefer, Ralph A. Blessed and Broken. Wilmington, Delaware: Michael Glazier, 1982.

LaVerdiere, Eugene. *Dining in the Kingdom of God: The Origins of the Eucharist According to Luke*. Chicago: Liturgy Training Publications, 1994.

Power, David N. *The Eucharistic Mystery: Revitalizing the Tradition*. New York: Crossroad, 1994.

Power, Joseph. *Eucharistic Theology*. New York: Herder and Herder, 1967.

_____. *The Eucharistic Mystery: Revitalizing the Tradition*. NY: Crossroad, 1994.

Schmemann, Alexander. *For the Life of the World: Sacraments and Orthodoxy*. New York: St. Vladimir's Seminary Press, 1973.

Notes:

[1] Douglas John Hall, *Lighten Our Darkness*, p. 117.
[2] See the Heidelberg Disputation, theses 20-21.

[3] Moltman, *The Crucified God*, Chapter 4.

[4] For example, we pretend that a free-market economy does not restrict an employee's liberty: if one doesn't like the employer's demands, the reasoning goes, one can always quit this job. The reality of needing a job to provide for one's basic need (and for one's family) is ignored in this reasoning, and thus the really coercive nature of economic power is disguised. This false reasoning is also at work in international economic structures: economic theory assumes that poorer nations are equal partners in economic relations, even though they often have no alternative but to accept the terms offered by richer nations or the international monetary organizations (the IMF, the World Bank, etc.).

[5] Larry Rasmussen, "Returning to our Senses," pp. 51-53; also Hall, esp. pp. 46-50, 79-92.

[6] These are Dorothy Day's words, citing a remark of Romano Guardini, quoted in Margaret Farley, *Personal Commitments: Beginning, Keeping, Changing* (San Francisco: HarperCollins, 1986), p. 91.

[7] Jaroslav Pelikan, in his account of Abelard, in *Jesus Through the Centuries* (New Haven: Yale University Press, 1985), p. 106.

[8] "The One Christ and the Universality of Salvation," *Theological Investigations* XVI, p. 207.

[9] See Peter Berger's classic study of the sociology of religion, *The Sacred Canopy: Elements of a Sociological Theory or Religion* (Garden City, N.Y.: Doubleday, 1967).

[10] For an excellent explanation of the place of these communities in the early church, see Raymond E. Brown's book *The Church the Apostles Left Behind* (New York: Paulist, 1984). It will not appear in the final bibliography for further reading because it is rather specific in its approach, but it is well worth investigating if one has more than a passing interest in the early church.

[11] This list of the books of New Testament scripture after 200 C.E. and 400 C.E. comes from Bruce Shelley's *Church History in Plain Language* (p. 82), which will also appear in the bibliography for further reading.

[12] John J. Dietzen, *The New Question Box: Catholic Life for the '90's*, Catholic Bicentennial Edition (Peroria, Illinois: Guildhall Publishers, 1988), 522.

[13] Ibid., 496.

[14] *Catechism of the Catholic Church*, No. 2683 (Collegeville, Minnesota: The Liturgical Press, 1994), 645.

[15] Mark Searle, *Christening: The Making of Christians* (Collegeville: The Liturgical Press, 1980), 56.

[16] Richard Rohr and Joseph Martos, *Why Be Catholic? Understanding Our Experience and Tradition* (Cincinnati, Ohio: St. Anthony messenger press, 1984), 145.

[17] John XXIII, address to Roman pastors at Passionist Retreat house of Saints John and Paul, Jan. 30, 1959. I cite from the quotation given in *Herder-Korrespondenz* 13 (1958-1959): 274-275. This address was never published in full but only summarized in *L'Osservatore Romano*, Jan. 31, 1959.

[18] Text in *Origins* 10 (May 22, 1980), 4-7.

The Social Gospel:
An American Prophetic Tradition

G. Penny Nixon

Discussions began at the turn of the century concerning the phenomenon of the social gospel and continue today. Historians and theologians interpret the social gospel either as a social movement or as a theological movement. To speak in terms of either/or, however, is to dichotomize that which the social gospel seeks to unite. In the eyes of Walter Rauschenbusch, the foremost theologian of the social gospel, and its most articulate advocate, social Christianity has been with us from the beginning. His final and most comprehensive work, *A Theology of the Social Gospel*, contends that the social gospel is the voice of prophecy in modern life. Since the social gospel is both theological and social, and is heralded by the voice of prophecy, it is perhaps best understood when viewed as the prophetic tradition in American religious history.

I have chosen the term *prophetic tradition* because it clarifies the nature of the social gospel. First, *prophetic tradition* provides a distinction that allows the social gospel to be viewed as a voice of prophecy rather than as an "organized" movement within American theology. Secondly, true to the foundation on which the social gospel was built, the term plants it solidly in the tradition of the Hebrew prophets. Thirdly, and most prominently for our purposes, it showcases the role of the prophet as one who evokes a consciousness and perception alternative to that of the dominant theology and culture!

The social gospel is an ongoing prophetic response, seen in different places in different times, often proclaimed when a prophet rose up and lived out the gospel as it addressed social ills and oppression. It was not simply political or social action but a prophet's call to the church and to society for justice at a systemic and structural level. That call was deeply embedded in a God-relationship that gave it strength and passion and made it uniquely the social gospel.

This essay examines two proponents of the social gospel who best represent it as prophetic tradition: Walter Rauschenbusch, who gave the social gospel life, and Martin Luther King, Jr., who brought about its modern day resurrection. A closer look at these two social gospelers and their unparalleled impact on American theology and society will reveal that their self-identity, their relationship with their community, and their consuming vision are those of a prophet.

Walter Rauschenbusch

Prophetic Saint, Chief Apostle of the new order, Prophet of a new Reformation, Founder of the Social Gospel–these are some of the titles historians have used in their endeavor to portray Walter Rauschenbusch. Rauschenbusch, the preacher, professor, social reformer and writer, changed the nature of mainline Protestantism probably more than any single individual of his time. Those who he touched, as a student in Germany, as a pastor in the heart of New York City, or as a professor at Rochester Seminary, were greatly impressed by this compassionate, intelligent man of faith.

From a young age Rauschenbusch had a sense of call. When his mother asked, "Walter, what are you going to be when you grow up?" the reply quickly came, "John the Baptist." The true test always comes at the end of life, however, when the realization of dreams are for others to judge. Sitting by a lake with Dores Sharpe, his friend and personal secretary, Rauschenbusch asked, "How do you think of me and my work?" Sharpe replied, "I think of you as an evangelist and your work as evangelism of the truest sort." Rauschenbusch threw his arms around Sharpe and said, "I have always wanted to be thought of in that way–your testimony gives me new fighting power."

Rauschenbusch's evangelical roots and influences play a significant role throughout his entire life. An astute analysis demands respect for both the continuity and discontinuity found in the experiences that shaped him. His father, August Rauschenbusch, came to America in 1846 as a Lutheran minister. He then became a Baptist, eventually heading the German Department at Rochester Theological Seminary. August Rauschenbusch remained a religious conservative his whole life, unbending in his views, stern and austere. Pietism was the hallmark of the Rauschenbusch family. It was an influence that remained an integral part of Walter's spirituality. He came from a five-generation tradition of university trained Lutheran pastors distinguished by piety and learning.

Even though Rauschenbusch remained rooted in evangelicalism, he was not the typical evangelical of that day. He definitely moved beyond "mainstream" in his thinking. Most of his biographers point to New York City as the breeding place for new ideas in the mind of this budding prophet. In 1886 he accepted a call to a New York City pastorate in a depressing section of West 45th Street surrounded by crowded tenements and noisy factories. In this area infamously known as Hell's Kitchen, he first began to deal with the social question.

Henry George, a crusader for justice through the "single tax," and Richard Ely, a prominent advocate of the social gospel, left an indelible impression on the young minister. Through Ely, Rauschenbusch heard about the social gospel for the first time. As he reflected on the social problems surrounding him in his parish, he struggled to apply the previous religious ideas to the conditions he found. He kept asking himself how it was possible to relate the old evangelical passion with his new passion for social action.

In an attempt to solve this dilemma, Rauschenbusch first turned to the Hebrew prophets to build the foundation of a new theology. He placed great importance on them as sources of the social gospel. His first work, *Christianity and the Social Crisis*, is a book of extraordinary power whose main plea is for Christians to undertake the task of creating a new social order. In it the young preacher contends that the prophets were the heralds of the fundamental truth that religion and ethics are inseparable. Their religious concern was neither with ceremony nor ritual but with the social and political life of their nation. Rauschenbusch constantly points out their sympathies were with the poor and oppressed. Thus, he found great consolation from and identification with the prophets throughout his life.

While Rauschenbusch built his foundation on the prophets, he found the final solution in articulating a social gospel in the doctrine of the Kingdom of God. This became his central theme and consuming vision. Religious historian Martin Marty contends that every pioneer or shaper in American religious history promoted some commanding vision, some conquering idea. Clearly for Rauschenbusch it was this discovery of the centrality of the Kingdom of God.

For Rauschenbusch the Kingdom of God was all encompassing–it embraced the past and looked toward the future and was the literal and symbolic heart of the social gospel. It was the same realm of justice of which the prophets spoke but it was initiated by the prophetic spirit of Jesus Christ. The Kingdom ideal contained the revolutionary force of Christianity. It was the continuous power of the righteousness and love of God. Most importantly, however, was the personal and social union that Rauschenbusch found in this concept for he believed the Kingdom of God was humanity organized according to the will of God. In the final analysis Rauschenbusch proclaimed, "this doctrine is *itself* the social gospel."[5]

Any in-depth understanding of Rauschenbusch reveals that he was a profoundly religious man manifested in his prophetic call to social action. The legacy he would leave American theology was the challenge of relating Christianity to social structures. It was his deep conviction that institutional and social structures should be Christianized. The church was called to undertake the reconstruction of social life.[6] This conviction was born out of his experience of living and working with the poor and oppressed masses in the city in an ever growing industrial society and became the compelling force behind his search for a theology large enough to encompass all people and situations.

Like the Old Testament prophet he was able to discern the signs of the times; he knew that the old evangelicalism was powerless to meet the challenges of the modern world. He understood that this social gospel would have to be embedded in a broad view of evangelism, one that embraced the integrity of social concern and a high standard of morality. He saw his prophetic task as discovering how to restate the Christian message in ways that made God's summons to a social mission plain and inescapable. His greatest desire was for the social gospel to become a permanent addition to Christian theology and life.

The particulars of the social gospel, as realized by its foremost theologian Walter Rauschenbusch, are best replicated and heralded in a new era in the person of Martin Luther King, Jr. He added the needed correctives for a new age by dealing with race relations, a systemic blight the social gospel had sorely neglected. The eloquent preacher, sometimes compared to a jazz musician, employed a prophetic language that called a nation to repentance. While King owes that prophetic language and the shaping of his theology to his black experience of oppression and the liberating message of the black church, his debt to

Walter Rauschenbusch cannot be underestimated. King admits that Rauschenbusch's *Christianity and The Social Crisis* was formative in his thinking by giving him a theological basis for the social concern which had already grown in him as a result of his early experiences.

Rauschenbusch's main emphases were instrumental in King's theological formulations. These emphases included: the prophetic roots of Christianity, the necessary relation of the church to social issues, the Christian faith as an alternative consciousness for society, the Kingdom of God as a christianized social life and a community of righteousness. No truer vision of this was realized than in the life and leadership of the prophet Martin Luther King, Jr.

Martin Luther King, Jr.

In his book, *Parting the Waters: America in the King Years 1954-1963*, Taylor Branch contends that "King's life is the best and most important metaphor for American history in the watershed postwar years."[7] Martin Luther King, Jr. is not only the protagonist in American postwar history, and in the Civil Rights drama in particular, but is also the best and most important metaphor for American theology. King is an amalgam of unique American traditions.

First and foremost he was a preacher who spoke from the wilderness–the *wilderness* of the black experience. He made his own theological way through this wilderness. He synthesized many of the theological and philosophical ideas of Tillich, Bowne, DeWolf, and Thoreau, and while his dream was to teach theology, he found himself doing theology on the segregated streets of the South. His activism in the world, added him to the ranks of great American theologians.

King was catapulted into international fame as a moral and political leader. He was Time's Man of the Year in 1964 and the recipient of the Nobel Peace Prize later that same year. He remained, however, a preacher and a Moses-like leader to his own people. Throughout his tragically preempted life, he represented the best of the American prophetic tradition and he was an American social gospeler *par excellence*.

King's preaching was the touchstone of his leadership. Packed with moral power, his elocution moved massive crowds to lay down their weapons and embrace an ethic of love. Son of a Baptist preacher, King was preaching at an early age. In giving his first sermon at Dexter church he calmed his nerves by reminding himself, "Keep Martin Luther King in the background and God in the foreground and everything will be all right. Remember you are a channel of the gospel and not the source."[8]

He appealed to his vocation as a minister of the gospel of Jesus because it was his primary self-understanding and also because the office of ministry had tremendous respect in the black community. In a statement towards the end of his life King declared: "I am many things to many people: civil rights leader, agitator, troublemaker and orator; but in the quiet recesses of my heart I am fundamentally a clergyman, a Baptist preacher. This is my being and my heritage. The Church is my life and I have given my life to the Church."[9] In his famous *Letter From Birmingham Jail*, King places himself squarely in the prophetic tradition and compares his fight against injustice to that of the eighth century prophets.

King compelled America take black religion seriously. His biblical message, with its theological dynamic, conformed neither to the white conservative agenda nor to the white liberal agenda. Through King's vision, the black church became the prophetic voice in America, calling this "Christian nation" back to the truth of the gospel. King recovered the essence of the Christian message which the white church had distorted by aligning itself with the cultural mainstream and by endorsing and promoting racism in both its overt and insidious forms.

King epitomized the social gospel tradition and brought it modern day resurrection. As a social prophet, he was primarily concerned with the social dimension of life and was interested in changing social structures. He believed it had always been the responsibility of the Church to challenge the status quo. King saw the task of conquering segregation *as a must* for the church of his day. He conceived of the church's role to be the conscience of the state. With the aid of the social gospel and Rauschenbusch, he developed a theological rationale for the Christian church's role as a change agent in society.

From its inception, the civil rights movement, as far as King was concerned, was God's movement. It was a campaign for righteousness and a march for justice. There were larger issues at stake than the rights of the black population; the real issue was justice in the kingdom of God. The movement centered on the love ethic of Jesus. It was not just a political ploy, as the media and government wanted America to believe. And, parenthetically, King was not a communist. Despite the vituperative comments of Hoover, King believed communism was a Christian heresy; it was profoundly and fundamentally evil.

With Rauschenbusch, King believed that the societal structures should be christianized, and that justice should reign. King looked for God's answer to racial injustice. He was careful to point out that Christ furnished the spirit and motivation while Gandhi furnished the method. The demonstrators that marched with him had to sign a statement that impelled them to embrace the Sermon on the Mount and to pray. Every time they were thrown in jail, King would fast and pray for the first two days. At the most tense moments, King and his followers would kneel in prayer. His speeches were filled with Scripture and the meetings during the boycott were like church services. At one point he thundered, "if we are wrong then the Supreme Court is wrong. If we are wrong then God Almighty is wrong!"[10]

King's all consuming vision was of the *beloved community*. This was his "dream." It was the organizing principle of his life and the driving force for his involvement in the civil rights struggle. His famous "I Have A Dream" speech is the *beloved community* in eloquent prose. The well-known imagery of a community and a dream, the only symbolic experiences of hope for black people in America, is found in many of King's writings, sermons, and speeches. Clearly it was his heart and soul.

King's dream was not one grounded in "the hopes of white America but in God. Replete with imagery from the Hebrew prophets of swords into plowshares, and the lion laying down with the lamb, King's conception of the beloved community reflects the prophetic vision of justice, mercy, peace, and righteousness. This was the theological and spiritual basis for his hope of an inclusive human community.

According to King, this was the manifest destiny of America. This was justice, peace, and all people living together in harmony. This dream was the "kingdom of God" through the eyes of Martin Luther King, Jr.

King not only carried on Rauschenbusch's legacy but also helped bring his dream a little closer to earth: "Our chief interest in any millennium is the desire for a social order in which the worth and freedom of every least human being will be honored and protected. We hope for such an order for humanity as we hope for heaven ourselves."[11]

The Social Gospel: Discussion Questions

1.) What is the prophetic tradition?
2.) Why might one refer to the social gospel as an ongoing prophetic response? Response to what?
3.) Why do Walter Rauschenbusch and Martin Luther King, Jr. best represent the Social Gospel as prophetic tradition:
4.) While Rauschenbusch built his foundation on the prophets, he found the final solution in articulating a social gospel in the doctrine of the Kingdom of God. Explain.
5.) Why might it be said that throughout King's tragically preempted life, he represented the best of the American prophetic tradition and he was an American social gospeler par excellence.
6.) From its inception, the civil rights movement, as far as King was concerned, was God's movement. Why?

The Social Gospel: For Further Reading

Baum, Gregory. *Compassion and Solidarity: The Church for Others* (New York: Paulist, 1990).

Graham, William C. *Half Finished Heaven: The Social Gospel in American Literature* (Lanham, MD: University Press of America, 1995).

Handy, Robert T. *The Social Gospel in America*, 1870- 1920 (New York: Oxford University Press, 1966).

Washington, James , ed. *A Testament of Hope: The Essential Writings of Martin Luther King, Jr.* (San Francisco: Harper & Row, 1986).

Zepp, Ira. *The Social Vision of Martin Luther King, Jr.* (New York: Carlson Publishers, 1989).

Liberation Theology:
An Introduction and a Challenge

Martin Carney

Liberation theology originated in Latin America amidst a situation of poverty and oppression. Liberation theology emphasizes the liberating activity of Jesus and explores how the Gospel can be understood and used to build a more just world. This essay will explore some of the major aspects of liberation theology and pose some critical questions concerning what this Latin American-based theology might mean for North American people.

We begin our discussion of liberation theology by examining its perspective. This may seem a strange place to start, but for liberation theology, perspective is absolutely critical. Liberation theology asks very fundamental and unsettling questions concerning perspective: who is doing theology and for what reasons? Liberation theology asserts that the perspective from which one approaches theology will make all the difference in the world about the nature of the theology produced. As mentioned above, liberation theology was born of poor and oppressed people (roughly 80 percent of Latin Americans live in poverty). Liberation theology asserts that poor and oppressed people will see and understand the Gospel in a way different from those who are comfortable and well-fed. Liberation theology also points out frankly that most of the theology of the church has been constructed by those who are comfortable and well-fed (and white, male, and European and North American). This is an important phenomenon: as one of best articulators of liberation theology, Gustavo Gutierrez, states, liberation theology is from the underside of history, formulated by the losers in history, the poor, the ones who normally do not have a voice in such matters. If we are to understand liberation theology, we must understand the context from which it arises. It is spoken, written and lived by people who are attempting to make sense of their lives of oppression and misery in light of God's word and the Christian faith. Yet, liberation theology is about more than trying to make sense of suffering: it is also committed to eliminating this suffering. Indeed, liberation theology propels people to seek liberation from oppression and poverty by interpreting the liberating message of Jesus as both an inspiration and instrument for achieving this liberation. Liberation is an enormously rich word with many meanings. Liberation theology interprets these meanings to include freedom from hunger and disease, freedom from oppressive political and economic structures, and freedom from sin as a prelude to ultimate union with God. But all of these theological insights have come to light because they are from the perspective of poor and downtrodden people.

One of the unique aspects of liberation theology is its method. Methodology is a key feature in any theological discussion–how theology is being done is, many would argue, as important as what theology is being done. Many liberation theologians maintain that liberation theology's major contribution to the area of theology in general is in the area of method. This can be succinctly expressed in one word: praxis. By praxis, liberation theologians mean a concrete commitment to the cause of the poor. Gutierrez goes so far as to state that theology is actually the second step in the theological process: the first step is praxis, tangibly embodied in the commitment to the poor. After this commitment has been made, then one can reflect upon it and "do" theology in the more classic sense. Gutierrez defines liberation theology as the "critical reflection on praxis in light of the word of God."

We arrive now at a central question: what are the theological implications of liberation theology's perspective and methodology? What impact has liberation theology had on theology as a whole? While there are many theological implications from liberation theology, I would like to focus on three specific and critical areas of theological inquiry: Christology, Soteriology and Ecclesiology.

Christology

Let us start with the extremely important area of Christology, the study of Jesus of Nazareth, the one whose followers proclaimed him to be the Christ. How do the perspective and method of liberation theology influence Christology? The Christological emphasis of liberation theology has been on the historical Jesus and his message of liberation for poor, outcast and marginalized people in the Gospel. Here we see how liberation theology's perspective influences its hermeneutics (the science of interpretation). Poor, hungry and oppressed people in Latin America have found great solace and inspiration in Jesus's words and liberating activities. They have read the Gospel in new ways, ways which people who are comfortable, well-fed and powerful might not be able to understand. Poor people in Latin

America have come to understand Jesus's message of the kingdom of God as applicable to them, indeed, as meant for them. The Gospel is understood with new insights and new emphases. People hear that the good news will be preached to the poor, that God will depose the mighty from their thrones and raise the lowly to high places (Mary's Magnificat), that the poor outcast who begs outside the rich person's table will rest in the bosom of Abraham, that the prophets'–Amos, Micah, Jeremiah, Isaiah–messages of social justice will be made real, that Jesus, who associated with the marginalized, the outcast, the sinner, came for poor people. Liberation theology has found new insights into who God is by looking through the eyes of poor people. Liberation theology acknowledges that Jesus came to save all people and that God loves all people. But God and God's son have a special covenant with poor people as clearly evidenced in the Bible. Rich and powerful people may not ever have realized that.

Soteriology

Liberation theology has arrived at some very interesting soteriological conclusions. Soteriology is the science or study of salvation. Liberation theology has boldly asked the question: what does salvation mean to the hungry person, to the unemployed father who cannot feed his children, to the young Latin American boy forcibly conscripted into the army, or to his mother who may never see him again? From the perspective of liberation theology, and from the experience of its praxis, soteriology has taken on a very earthly dimension. Liberation theology has discarded the idea that salvation is purely a phenomenon which happens after death. The Gospel, and the theology it inspires, must have an impact in our lives; salvation must have an earthly component. Indeed, liberation theology advises that we are in the midst of the salvific process now. Liberation theology acknowledges that ultimately, salvation means union with God and the conquering of our sinfulness. But what about the sinful structures of our world–do not they need saving? To what extent are we called to immerse ourselves in and, to whatever extent possible, save history? Liberation theology eschews the dualism that has pervaded so much of Christian theology. It refuses to accept that this life is merely a preparation for the next life. The coming reign of God which Jesus announced is a message to all Christians that this world is to be transformed. This message takes on special urgency in the miserable conditions of so much of Latin America.

It is important to note that liberation theology understands there are different levels of salvation. Jesus came to show humanity the way to ultimate union with God, and the overcoming of personal sin. This, ultimately, is what salvation entails. Yet we also participate in the salvific process when we work to transform the sinful structures which oppress the world and cause immense suffering. To transform the world is to save the world. Thus, liberation theology willingly embraces the social sciences–economics, political science, sociology–and any other types of knowledge which may participate in the saving of this world. The best of liberation theology acknowledges that human efforts to save the world are often times ambiguous and disastrous, and that God will have the final say in these matters. But Jesus intended that human beings be liberated–from sin and suffering. Salvation begins today, and we are God's agents on this planet. While it is correct, in one sense, to call ourselves the children of God, we must also realize that we are the adults of God, with critical responsibilities for building God's world.

Ecclesiology

A third major area in which liberation theology has had a major influence–and has caused a fair amount of controversy–is in the area of *ecclesiology*. Ecclesiology is the study of the church–its mission, history and structures. Liberation theology teaches that the church must be on the side of the poor. This was articulated in two significant Latin American Bishops Conferences, one in Medellin, Colombia in 1968 and the other in Puebla, Mexico in 1979. It was in Puebla that the phrase "preferential option for the poor" was first formally articulated, although the sentiment for this idea was certainly present at Medellin. Liberation theology has interpreted the "preferential option for the poor" to mean that the church must take the side of the poor. Liberation theology believes that this opting for the poor is in contrast to what has been much of the church's history in Latin America, namely, one of siding with the rich and powerful. The preferential option demands that the church not only take the side of the poor but also be of the poor. For too long, according to liberation theology, the church has not spoken out against the poverty and oppression rampant in Latin America. By not protesting against it, by adopting conservative stances toward society and by encouraging the maintenance of the status quo, the church has, in effect, aligned itself with the wealthy and powerful against the poor. This endorsement of the status quo, in which millions suffer poverty and oppression, cannot remain. The church must be a leading force in the establishing of a more just society. This is what the Gospel mandates.

Furthermore, liberation theology has caused–and been the result of –what many Latin Americans are calling a new way of being church: the basic ecclesial communities. These are gatherings of the faithful in which people read Scripture, pray and discuss how God's message can positively impact on their lives. People in base ecclesial communities ask how Gospel values can be implemented in the transformation of society. Liberation theology is, to a large extent, the result of these meetings of thousands of communities throughout Latin America. The base ecclesial communities have called upon the church to challenge the structures of Latin America which oppress and impoverish people. These communities insist that society is fractured by poverty and oppressive systems: the church cannot pretend that there is a unity in the church or in society when so much of the community is broken by political and economic systems which hurt and dehumanize people. These injustices and divisions must be addressed if community is to be formed. In particular, many liberation theologians have some very harsh criticisms of capitalism which they see as creating gross economic inequalities within society, and as being foisted upon them by dominant American, European and Japanese markets.

Criticisms of Liberation Theology

Liberation theology has certainly had its share (some would say more than its share) of criticism, particularly from the Roman Catholic Church. Much of this criticism has to do with the extremes to which liberation theology can be taken. These criticisms can be summarized in four categories:

1.) One of the major criticisms has been that liberation theology is too *Marxist*. This criticism asserts that liberation theology has adopted Marxist ideology uncritically and is, therefore, subject to the pitfalls inherent in Marxism. Many liberation theologians, observing how capitalism has hurt people, have delved deeply into Marxist teachings in pursuit of establishing a more just society. However, the Vatican has accused certain liberation theologians of going too far in their analysis.

2.) Others have said that liberation theology is too *political* and fails to pay enough attention to the interiority and piety of faith. Liberation theology, in these critics' eyes, wants to use the Gospel to establish a new political and economic order, but what about personal prayer, sacraments, devotions to the saints, personal piety? These are critical aspects of faith and religion, but liberation theology neglects them. How, they ask, is liberation theology any different from other political movements with their agendas for social change? A religious movement must account for the higher realm of spirituality.

3.) Others have expressed grave concern that some liberation theologians advocate the use of violence to establish a more just order in society.

4.) Others criticize liberation theology as being too fractional and divisive. Catholic means universal and united: how can we tolerate something so divisive within the church? Liberation theology would argue that the community, the fellowship of which Catholics boast, is already fractured in Latin American society, because of the immense divisions between the rich and poor, the powerful and the non-person (as Gutierrez refers to the poor person in Latin America). Liberation theology is merely identifying what already exists.

Liberation: Discussion Questions

1.) Liberation theology, by its own admission, is a theology born of, and pertinent to, the people of Latin America. The vast majority of these people live in poverty, suffering hunger, disease, marginal housing, unemployment and underemployment. Perhaps liberation theology makes sense in this context from a Latin American perspective. But what does it mean for North America? How does it apply to the United States and Canada, where a significant majority of the people are economically secure, largely as a result of a capitalistic system?

2.) Does God, the creator and universal lover of humankind, really favor poor people? Did Jesus? Discuss.

3.) Can frail sinful human beings truly "build the Kingdom of God?" How can we ever be assured that our sin-wracked institutions have anything to do with God's works? Is not it called "God's Kingdom" because God is the one who will inaugurate and enact it?

4.) Does liberation theology place too much emphasis on perspective? What about the objectivity of truth and God's revelation? How can the objective and the subjective be reconciled here?

Liberation: For Further Reading

Dorr, Donal. *Option for the Poor: A Hundred Years of Vatican Social Teaching.* Maryknoll, NY: Orbis, 1992 (revised and expanded).

Gutierrez, Gustavo. *The Power of the Poor in History.* Maryknoll, NY: Orbis, 1983.

_____. *A Theology of Liberation.* Maryknoll, NY: Orbis, 1988.

Hennelly, Alfred, editor. *Liberation Theology: A Documentary History.* Maryknoll, NY: Orbis, 1990.

Sobrino, Jon. *The True Church and the Poor.* Maryknoll, NY: Orbis, 1984.

Visit To Washington Heights

Mark McVann, F.S.C.

When poverty is more disgraceful than even vice,
is not morality cut to the quick?
— Mary Wollenstonecraft

On a Friday shortly before a recent Christmas, I spent the day in Washington Heights. It's sort of a northern extension of Spanish Harlem, a teeming neighborhood with thousands of people from the Dominican Republic (there were riots there a few summers ago when a cop shot dead a reputed drug dealer). I had taught English to Dominican leather factory workers in the Boston area one summer while I was in college and wanted to visit a Dominican neighborhood again. So, I went with a young Dominican man named Alex whom I met at Manhattan College where I was guest professor for a year.

We passed by his old high school, and there were knots of kids milling around the building–looking defensive and vulnerable. He went up to several that he knew, and encouraged them to finish their studies and to go to college, as he himself was doing. I wasn't introduced, but there were inquisitive glances. They figured, maybe, that I was an undercover cop or something. The cops are always white and never to be trusted. It occurred to me then that Alex might later be quizzed by his friends about what he was doing with me, what I wanted. I wondered what would he say: that I was some college professor who wanted to go slumming with safe conduct through the barrio? That I wanted to practice my Spanish?

As we continued winding through the crowded streets, he bumped into all sorts of people he knew: aunts, cousins, friends. Now there were introductions: I was certified as harmless (at least) and so was immediately accepted. We visited some of his relatives and his mother treated me to saffron rice, boiled plantain, fried pork chops, and polite invitations to return as soon as possible.

The streets of Washington Heights are lively, colorful, interesting and dangerous. There was clear evidence of gangs and there were drugs for sale on any number of corners. I suppose anything else might be available, for a price.

I was immediately and deeply impressed with these Dominican people, like I had been in Boston many years ago. They are astonishingly beautiful and have an immense dignity–despite the very rough neighborhood, despite the tang in the air of anger and frustration. But any such neighborhoods–whether in New York, Chicago, or Los Angeles–always raise hard questions. The first and hardest: why do they exist?

But the answer is hard, too. These neighborhoods exist because the wealthy want an inexhaustible supply of inexpensive labor. They want their burgers flipped and their hallways swept up and they want it cheap, with no responsibilities towards the people who labor for them. This is cheerfully admitted–"Cost is Religion" as posters plastered on walls around New York proclaim–but we hide from ourselves the high human cost of such gross social and economic injustice. (And it is indeed gross: 50 percent of the wealth in the U.S. is controlled by only 20 percent of the population.) But how do we hide this from ourselves?

It's easy: all we have to do is look at the violence in these neighborhoods, the bad schools, the gangs, the drugs. Clearly, we reason, there is something wrong with these brown and black folk whose English ain't so good: they must be inferior to us! Why else would they live like this and tolerate these conditions unless they wanted to? And on and on. So, blaming the victim justifies the exploitation, keeps us from asking hard questions, hearing hard answers, and conceals from us our own violence and bad faith.

Speaking of which, it's fashionable now in another place south of Washington Heights, also called Washington, bad faith capital of the continent, to denounce the hapless poor and the clumsy endowments for the arts and humanities and the too earnest National Public Radio, and anyone or anything else that serves as a social conscience, that reminds us of our responsibilities, that clamors for democracy and justice and the American Dream and that asks hard questions about elitism and meritocracy and the "Contract with America."

But there is also, thank God, an ancient dream and a better contract by far, made years and years ago with other cheap laborers who escaped from intolerable conditions in Egypt. Centuries later, their dream was refashioned and the contract rewritten to extend to all humanity. The dream goes like this, the renewed contract reads: "Blessed are you poor, for the kingdom of God is yours . . . But woe to you who are rich, for you have received your consolation" (Lk. 6:20, 24).

Save us, Lord, from such numbing consolation, and kindle in us a fire for the kingdom of God!

Visit: Discussion Questions

1.) What does Mary Wollenstonecraft mean by "When poverty is more disgraceful than even vice, is not morality cut to the quick?"

2.) Certain neighborhoods, whether in New York, Chicago, or Los Angeles, always raise hard questions. What are some of those questions?

3.) What does it mean to blame the victim? By whom are victims blamed? Why?

4.) What conditions in your own neighborhood might prompt questions about justice?

5.) Explain both the blessing of the poor, and the woe to the rich, which Jesus promises (or threatens) in Luke's Gospel.

Spike and the Diminished Body of Christ

William C. Graham

Three of the well-known delights of being a college professor are June, July and August. I treasure these opportunities to abandon New York City and to return to the See City of my home diocese in the Midwest where I spent both my youth and the early years of my career. This last summer, the high school I attended and where I later taught as a young priest was having an all-school reunion. It was a great opportunity for me to see old friends, my former teachers, colleagues, students and their parents, many of whom were members of the various parishes in which I had served. My graduating class had the biggest group at the reunion. We are just about the age when people enjoy these opportunities, we were the second biggest class ever to go through the school, and all but three of us are still alive.

As the party progressed, classmate Spike suggested that we keep on carrying on, and move the party just down the block to his home. We did. Once there, Spike had one more drink. He didn't have to drive anywhere, so he drank perhaps one more ounce than would otherwise have been prudent. I knew what was coming. For priests, this is an occupational hazard: Spike would want to talk theology or religious practice. What's the deal with inebriates of the lapsed Catholic persuasion anyway?

We should have been talking sports. Even in July, northern Minnesotans talk hockey, the University's Bulldogs. "How 'bout them 'Dogs," we're supposed to say. It's in a northern Minnesotan's contract. "How 'bout them 'Dogs?" "I saw Coach Sertich in the Super Valu and he said to me . . . " we're supposed to say.

Not Spike. It was quiet; an angel must have just passed through the room. Spike announced, after being certain that he had my attention, "I don't go to church anymore. Not ever. Not even Christmas or Easter."

What is the priest classmate supposed to say? "Congratulations, Spike?" Or, "Your mother must be proud?" Or, "I'm not paid on commission anymore?"

The *Didascalia Apostolorum* addresses that problem which has apparently plagued the church in every age. Maybe I should have preached a couple sentences of that third century teaching to Spike: "Let no one diminish the ecclesia by his absence, that the Body of

Christ may not be diminished by one member. Do not tear apart the Body of Christ!"

But Spike continued. "I may not go to church anymore, but I'll tell you this." Pause, two, three, four. "I am a very fine Christian. Very fine."

Well, there is this stuff about pride and humility that he may have overlooked, but I didn't mention it. It really wasn't Spike speaking, after all. It was instead, I think, the voice of our friend Jack Daniels. But because we priests are often much like the family doctor, perhaps I should have said, "Take two aspirin and call me in the morning."

Spike is a good man. He loves his wife, Wanda. He cares about and for his family. He does not, to the best of my knowledge, defraud anyone in his business. He may love Jesus. Jesus, no doubt, loves him. But I don't think that Spike can qualify as good Christian or good Catholic. This religious business is a social affair. It is not about me at home in my Lazy-Boy recliner loving the Lord who (as The Unsinkable Molly Brown sings of her husband, Leadville Johnny Brown) loves "just to look at me."

When we were high school frosh, Father Fred Fox, in Social Problems 101, told Spike that he would be just like his father in about fifteen years. Freddie, rarely wrong, missed this call. Spike is, I think, less a contributor to God's reign than was his father whose strong presence and undying Catholic loyalty made the church a formative presence in Spike's and my formative years.

Spike is neither an envelope holder nor a contributor. There is no way it would be apparent that he is or even was a Catholic were it not for his post-prandial protestations.

The church is smaller and poorer for Spike's absence.

If we who remain choose not to diminish or be diminished, the call to evangelism in this age, it seems, must mean a new mission to the baptized who were not catechized, or imperfectly catechized, or who somehow lost the way or the will.

Instead of waiting for Spike to call me, I'll be in touch with him by morning, inviting him to come home with all his energy and critical insight. "Look homeward, angel," I'll say. And, "you can come home again." We can stand together on the heights, in the valleys, and on the plains where God's breeze is sure to blow. We can transform the face of the earth.

Spike: Discussion Questions

1.) What kind of effect did alcohol have on Spike? The author writes, "It really wasn't Spike speaking, after all. It was instead, I think, the voice of our friend Jack Daniels." Explain and comment.

2.) What problem does the author believe is addressed by the *Didascalia Apostolorum*? Do you think an ancient document can speak to modern people? How, why, or why not?

3.) Is religion a social affair? It is possible to be religious while at home in my Lazy-Boy recliner? Can one pray in the woods? What is different when one prays in the midst of the Church?

4.) The author thinks that "the church is smaller and poorer for Spike's absence." Do you? Explain.

5.) Read the letter below from Fr. John Whitney Evans and draft a response to him in which you comment on each of his concerns:

"Congratulations on the publication of *Spike and the Diminished Body of Christ*. It is interesting that he raised the matter with you at all. If he has resolved his feelings, they should all be gone, and there would be no interest in raising it. Some corner of his psyche must still be a little uneasy.

"I am not familiar enough with *Didasacalia Apostolorum* to recall the passage that you cited. It is surely a telling one. But here is where I think you and I face a real serious pastoral and pedagogical problem

"If a 'modern' North American does not have a sense of community beyond his nuclear existence, the quotation you cite means nothing to him or her. What brought this home to me a few years ago was a lecture I heard at a Newman conference in Canada. It was by a Scripture professor who is now a bishop. I have forgotten his name.

"Anyhow, he noted that Christ spoke to people who were members of a tribal, communitarian society. They heard everything as addressed to 'you-vos' not to 'you-te,' to us and not to me. I heard it in the plural because they were members of the larger social unit. He was Paul of Tarsus, not Paul Smith, Ignatius of Antioch, Jesus of Nazareth, etc.

"Here was the killer: North Americans can read and listen to the Gospel all they want. If they hear it as 'Jesus and Me' and not as 'Jesus and Us', they have missed the entire Gospel message. Indeed, they have never heart it!

"So what would a plea not to diminish the church by one's absence from a liturgy mean to a 20th century individualist? He would probably say, 'I suppose the author of the DA is entitled to his opinion ....'

"I don't know how to get people into a communal mind-set so they can filter all this stuff correctly. Most everything in our culture impresses a mind set antagonistic to communalism.

"Just curious! Keep up the good work."

The Challenge of Feminism

Johann M. Vento

The last thirty years have witnessed a worldwide feminist movement which has criticized the traditional roles of women in society. Such critique is not new; scholars have dated the emergence of feminist consciousness in western culture to the seventh century C.E. However, feminist ideas and practices have never been as widespread as they are today, as a result of the most recent wave of feminist action and thought around the world. Moreover, feminists are sharing ideas and strategies for social change across cultures in unprecedented ways. Feminism has called attention to the fact the a large majority of the world's poor are women and their dependent children, that women are often battered, abused, and raped, denied education, good health care, and the right to make decisions about our own lives–simply because we are women. Feminism exposes the philosophies, theologies, and practices which either state or imply that females are not as fully human as males, and therefore do not have a right to the same level of respect, dignity, health, safety and opportunity as males.

Feminism does not deny that many people are oppressed throughout the world for many different reasons. But the unique role of feminism is to point to the ways in which women are oppressed as women. Of course, many women throughout the world carry the burden of several oppressions: for example, poor women and women of color in western nations suffer not only sexism, but also classism and racism. All of these–isms can sometimes seem like a jungle of terms, confusing and even contradictory. But the problems that these terms attempt to describe are very real and cause a great deal of controversy in almost every society in the world today. Whatever our stand on the many issues surrounding the roles of women, it is necessary to understand some basic distinctions at the heart of many of the controversies about the roles of women. What is needed is a healthy debate at all levels of society about the appropriate roles for males and females in the home, in the public sphere, and within religious bodies.

A Charged Term

The term feminist is a charged one in current debate. For some people, the word represents a philosophy that is liberating and positive. They point to the fact that the feminist movement is responsible for women's right to vote in this country, for our right, at least in principle, to seek higher education and to participate in public life. Beginning only thirty years ago, women fought for the right to be admitted to Roman Catholic theological schools in this country, making my profession as a theologian possible.

For others, the word feminism represents something dangerous and threatening. I have had discussions with women who in large part share my ideas about the value of women, and who enjoy rights gained for them by the feminist movement, but are very hesitant to use the term feminist to describe themselves, because of the negative connotations they feel it carries. In many instances, these concerns are a result, not of how feminists use the term, but of the ways in which those who oppose feminism have used it in a strictly pejorative sense. There has been much discussion about the backlash against the feminist movement in the U.S. This reaction characterizes feminism as a moral evil which seeks to break-up marriages, harm children and, in general, destroy the American family. Further, it characterizes feminists themselves as sick, deviant, or unattractive. These are examples of the ways in which those who oppose feminist values try to define feminism on their own terms, using scare tactics to alarm people and divert their attention from a serious discussion of the issues at hand. It is this kind of characterization of feminism by its opponents which stifles honest debate about how adult men and women should structure public and private life–about who has what rights and how society should ensure those rights.

Feminism and Theology

Many people are surprised to learn that feminism can have anything to do with theology. They question what feminism can have to say about what we believe about God and about how we worship, teach, and preach. This begs the question of the nature of theology itself and the role of perspective in theology. Simply put, theology is God-talk–it is what people say about God. Every theology is profoundly affected by the historical and cultural conditions under which the theologian is operating. Every theologian, whether consciously or not, brings his or her own presuppositions, concerns, and questions to the task of theology. Theology has until very recently been done almost exclusively by men, and at least for Roman Catholicism and Protestantism, by a largely homogeneous group of European, educated men. Several contemporary theologies, newly sensitive to the role of perspective, ask how those particular historical, social, and cultural circumstances have affected the traditional theologies which have predominated in our churches and have determined how we interpret scripture, formulate moral codes, and organize church life. Feminist theology is one of many contemporary theologies which asks these kinds of questions. This has brought us to a new and exciting era for theology, for learning takes place and discourse is furthered only by the asking of new questions.

Feminist theologians bring the question of the value and status of women to theological study. Moreover, feminists bring the experience of oppression under patriarchy to the task of theology. Feminist theology uses women's experience of oppression as a source for theological reflection alongside scripture and tradition. Other theologies which use an experience of oppression as a source in their theological method include Latin American liberation theology and Black theology. Feminist theology itself is not univocal, but encompasses the various perspectives of the women who engage in it. Womanist, mujerista, and Asian-American feminist theology are just a few which operate in the North American context alone. All of these theologies can be considered liberation theologies in as much as they engage in the struggle for justice in the face of oppressive political and social systems. They are called "interested" theologies, for they espouse a specific political interest or agenda. The various forms of feminist theology seek to unearth patriarchal religious beliefs and practices which serve to sustain oppressive systems in society. This forms the basis of their "interest" or theological agenda. This variety of perspectives might be considered by some an unfortunate fragmentation of theology. Moreover, interested theologies are often accused of not being objective. Liberation theologians argue that there is no purely objective theology, since every theology is shaped by the perspective, including the political agenda or interest, of the theologian. For those who engage in liberation theologies, the fact of multiple of perspectives underscores the function of political interest in determining the content of any theology.

The Feminist Theological Critique

I will speak about the the feminist theological critique within the western Christian tradition, but it is important to realize that the feminist question is being raised in every major world religion around the globe. In fact, feminists have often united across religious and confessional lines as they explore feminist issues within their own religious bodies. It is also important to note that some feminists feel that they can no longer remain within their religious traditions, because they believe that the teachings at their very roots are misogynist and therefore cannot offer a saving word to women. Other feminists, myself included, believe that their tradition remains a valid path for sincere people in search of God, and that misogyny and patriarchy, although they have predominated in the history of religions, do not have to win the day. In my specific case, I believe that although the Christian tradition has developed throughout its history with strongly patriarchal values, the domination of men over women, or of any group over another, is not at the heart of the Christian message. This belief allows me to stay within my church, difficult as that may sometimes be, in an effort to challenge the church to live more explicitly according to its fundamental belief in the value and dignity of each human being.

I have already used several terms which may be unfamiliar, but which are essential to understanding the feminist critique. The first is patriarchy, which refers to any societal or church structure which is based on the rule of a few men over all other men, as well as women and children. patriarchy as a structure of society has predominated throughout much of human history, and patriarchal biases have influenced to a very great extent the way that theologians and church leaders have interpreted scripture, formulated moral codes, and structured church government. Patriarchy is a model of domination which places power in the hands of the ruling few. It not only describes the domination of men of women, but also that of men with economic and political power over all other men. The ancient Greek household in which one man, the patriarch of the family, had power of life and death over his wife, his children, and his slaves (men and women of a different class and usually a different ethnic or racial group) is one example of patriarchal domination. This example illustrates that patriarchy is not only a matter of sexism, but also of racism and classism. As a model of both public and private life, it has been very influential throughout the course of human history and survives in varying degrees into our own day. Some people claim that since it has predominated, patriarchy must be natural and inevitable. But much historical and anthropological research has shown otherwise. Feminist historian Gerda Lerner has built a convincing argument in her book, *The Creation of Patriarchy*, that the patriarchal model has specific historical roots, that human communities have not at all times and in all places structured their societies according to the patriarchal model, and that since patriarchy has a historical beginning, it can also have a historical end. It is not, therefore, inevitable.

Sexism and Patriarchy

Sexism is a term which is often confused with patriarchy, but there is an important distinction. Sexism refers to an attitude or action which accords more value or more fully human status to one sex over the other, just as racism accords more value or more fully human status to one race of people over another. While patriarchy is by definition male domination, sexism can in principle favor either males or females over the other. Another important distinction relates to individual versus structural responsibility. Just as a distinction can be made between institutional racism and personal racism, a distinction can be made between institutional patriarchy and personal sexism. The distinction has become an important one in church politics, for while Pope John Paul II as well as the U.S. Catholic bishops have denounced personal sexism as a sin, they continually fail to give attention to the ways in which personal sexism is related to patriarchy at the structural, institutional levels of church and society.

The last term which may be unfamiliar is misogyny, which means the hatred of women. This might seem like a harsh term, but there are many religious teachings as well as civil laws and practices which seem clearly based on a serious disdain for women. The witch craze in Europe in the fifteenth through the seventeenth centuries offers a glaring example of how civil and church authorities tapped into the hatred and suspicion of women. The witch craze took on various forms throughout Europe during this period, but overall significantly more women than men were victimized, and the accusations against the women were often based on an irrational fear of and hatred for women's sexuality. Throughout the history of the church, many theologians have blamed women for the presence of evil and sin in the world, since, according to their interpretation of Genesis, it was Eve who first gave into the temptation of the serpent. Women have been considered to be more prone to sin, especially sexual sin, and to be the cause, paradoxically, of both sexual indiscretion and impotency in men. The *Malleus Maleficarum*, a sort of handbook for church inquisitors written in 1486, is a very clear example of misogynist reasoning. The text argues that more women are found guilty of witchcraft because they are morally and intellectually weaker than men and more prone to evil deeds. This document claims that women are weaker in faith, liars by nature, more carnal thaN men, and sexually insatiable. And for Eve's responsibility in the temptation of Adam, women are to be considered "more bitter than death."[12]   This document is one of the clearest examples of theological misogyny in the Christian tradition.

Feminist theology responds critically to the patriarchal values and outright misogyny which have dominated the history of the church into the present day.   Feminist biblical scholars have pointed to the patriarchal bias of scriptural texts themselves as well as to the ways in which that bias has influenced the translation and interpretation of those texts. They also have studied the many biblical texts which have been largely ignored–those which speak of God using female images, as well as those which describe strong, virtuous women who are active religious subjects.   Feminist biblical scholarship has highlighted the active roles taken by women as disciples of Jesus during his lifetime, and as apostles during the early years of the Christian community.

Feminist church historians have approached the study of the history of Christianity with the question of the status of women in view. They have pointed to the gross examples of misogyny in the theology, teachings, and practices of the church, and they have unearthed the positive, but often hidden or trivialized, role that women have played in various religious movements.

Feminist systematic theologians have critiqued classical theology and uncovered its patriarchal biases. These theologians have brought the feminist question to bear on all areas of systematic theology–revelation, the Trinity, Christology, Anthropology, Theology of Church, the Sacraments, Moral Theology, and Spirituality.

Feminist pastoral theologians have examined the life of the church and the way that the faith is manifested in the lives of the laity. This work is very valuable, because it focuses the attention of theologians on the way that their work is received by the faithful. Some of the most important work of feminist pastoral theologians has been with women who have been the victims of domestic abuse. These theologian relate the pain of women who, when seeking help from their preachers or priests, have been told that since the Bible says that they must be submissive to their husbands, they must do everything to preserve their marriage, including tolerating physical and mental abuse. Feminist theologian Susan Brooks Thistlethwaite describes forming a Bible study group with women who have been battered, inviting women to question the texts and interpretations that devalue them and pointing to scriptural and traditional sources which teach the equal dignity of women.

The Tasks of Feminist Theology

The tasks of feminist theology, in any of these areas, follow a general pattern of critique, retrieval, and reconstruction. The first step is to look at what we have been given, the scriptural texts, the tradition, theological formulations, and church teachings, and to point to the ways in which these data deny the full humanity of women. One excellent example of this critical mode of feminist theology is Phyllis Trible's book, *Texts of Terror*. Trible focuses on texts of the Bible in which women are abused, battered, mutilated, and killed. What is most terrifying about this study is that she finds no moral voice within the texts themselves to condemn the violence against these women. Trible exposes the misogyny of these texts. Her analysis lays bare the attitudes of the writers which objectify women, denying them their status as human subjects.

In its next mode, feminist theology seeks to retrieve the lost history of women, both in scripture and in the history of the church. Since most theology and history have been done until very recently with patriarchal bias, much of what women have accomplished has not been fully documented or has been ignored by biblical interpreters and historians. My own Master's thesis was written about a woman named Anne Askew who was a Protestant reformer in England in the mid–sixteenth century. Askew was put to death for her religious views. For some fifty years after her death, she was considered a martyr and her story was widely known in Protestant circles in England. Her life and work were quickly forgotten, however, because later historians did not deem her significant enough to write about, even though her religious adversaries feared her influence enough to put her to death. Feminist retrieval searches the sources for the stories of women which have not made it through the filter of patriarchal history. Through these efforts women learn of a history which has been denied us. Political historians teach us that the best proven method for enslaving any group of people is to erase the memory of its history. As women's history begins to unfold anew, thanks to the efforts of feminist historians, women gain a new sense of identity, community, and purpose.

The last phase of feminist theology is reconstruction. After the patriarchal bias of the tradition has been exposed and the lost history of women has been recovered, feminist theologians focus their energy on constructing theologies based on the insights of feminist critique and feminist retrieval. In the reconstructive mode of feminist theology, women's experience is considered, along with scripture and tradition, as a source for theological reflection. One example of the way in which feminist theologians have reconstructed or reshaped theology is in re-framing traditional teaching about sin. Theologians have long considered human pride and selfishness as fundamental human sins and encouraged humility and self-sacrifice as virtuous and holy. But feminist theologians have suggested that such an interpretation of sinfulness relies exclusively on the experience of privileged men who, within patriarchy have learned to reserve power for themselves, and might indeed tend to sin out of pride and selfishness. However, once women's historical and contemporary experience are brought to the question, different conclusions suggest themselves. Some feminist theologians have argued that within patriarchal systems many women tend to sin more out of a lack of self love and a distorted sense of their own value as human beings. Self-sacrifice has been a long-cherished Christian value, but for women who have never developed a sense of self, and who learn to locate their value as human beings in their functional capabilities in other people's lives, the preaching of self-sacrifice can be meaningless or even dangerous. Consider again the battered wife who seeks spiritual counsel about what to do about her abusive husband. Does this woman need a lecture on self-sacrifice and the dangers of pride, or rather does she not need to learn, perhaps for the first time, her value and dignity before God? Feminist theologians have not argued that women never sin out of pride or selfishness, but they show how traditional understandings of sinfulness and holiness have largely ignored women's experience.

In this brief chapter, I have tried to give a sense of the contours of the relatively new and burgeoning field of feminist theology. The emergence of feminist theology is related to other crucial questions for theology, for example, the relationship between the cultural perspective of the theologian and theological discourse itself, and the relationship between religious life and political life and their mutual influence on each other. My hope is that this introduction will inspire further reading in feminist theology, and further questioning into the relation of theological study to public and private life.

Feminism: Discussion Questions

1.) Is there open, honest debate about the roles of women on your campus? Is feminist considered a negative term? What are some of the connotations that the word feminist implies?

2.) To what extent are patriarchal values operative in public and private life in our own context? List some examples. How have attitudes about the roles of women and men changed in our culture in recent years? What is your opinion of these changes? How have attitudes remained the same?

3.) What is new about feminist theology? What does it uniquely have to offer theological discussion?

4.) Is it possible to embrace the feminist perceptive and remain within Christianity? What are some of the dangers involved in this? What are some of the possible rewards for feminists? For the Church?

5.) Think of some of the changes that have occurred in church teaching and practice throughout church history, for example the church's position on slavery, or on democracy. How have these evolutions in church teaching come about? Are they legitimate? How might they relate to the debate in the church about women's roles?

6.) Examine some of the church's official statements about the ordination of women. What might be included in a feminist argument against such statements?

Feminism: For Further Reading

Aquino, Maria Pilar. *Our Cry for Life: Feminist Theology from Latin America*. Maryknoll, New York: Orbis Books, 1994.

Carr, Anne. *Transforming Grace: Christian Tradition and Women's Experience*. San Francisco: Harper & Row, 1988.

Daly, Mary. *The Church and the Second Sex*. New York: Harper & Row, 1968.

Virginia Fabella and Mercy Amba Oduyoye, eds. *With Passion and Compassion: Third World Women Doing Theology*. Maryknoll, New York: Orbis Books, 1988.

Fiorenza, Elisabeth Schüssler. *In Memory of Her: A Feminist Theological Reconstruction of Christian Origins*. New York: Crossroad, 1983.

Johnson, Elizabeth. *She Who Is: The Mystery of God in Feminist Theological Discourse*. New York: Crossroad, 1992.

Russell, Letty, ed. *Feminist Interpretation of the Bible.* Philadelphia: Westminster Press, 1985.

Townes, Emilie, ed., *A Troubling in My Soul: Womanist Perspectives on Evil and Suffering.* Maryknoll, New York: Orbis Books, 1993.

Trible, Phyllis. *Texts of Terror: Literary-Feminist Readings of Biblical Narratives.* Philadelphia: Fortress Press, 1984.

This Business of Mary

Lee Stuart

As someone who entered the Catholic Church relatively late in life, I did not receive any catechesis on Mary, no inculturation about Mary as I was growing up, and no rituals surrounding devotion to Mary. In fact, my first contact with Mary was when I was thirteen years old. My Latin teacher arranged a field trip for our beginning class to visit the Trappist monastery near Atlanta. He wanted us to hear Latin actually being used, I guess, and so off we went. I remember looking from above, over the church, through a type of fence. We heard people praying, but as a demonstration of Latin-Alive-Today, it was rather weak. We could hardly hear or see. I was much more intrigued by the gift shop, and purchased my very first jar of raspberry jam (I still prefer it above all others) and, of all things, a rosary and an instruction booklet. I shared the jam with my family, but the rosary I kept secret. I thought Presbyterian parental reaction to such a Catholic thing might be rather drastic. I tried day after day to pray the rosary; I tried to follow the booklet. I attempted long conversations with Mary concerning the mysteries, whatever they were. They didn't seem particularly mysterious to me, and after a while, I gave up.

Nineteen years later, God brought me to the South Bronx and to the parish of St. Augustine. Largely through the welcome and faith of the members of this African-American Catholic Community to me, a white woman alone and far from familiar surroundings, I became Catholic. Seeing the strength and solidarity of the people of St. Augustine, I thought I had encountered what real Christianity was all about. I was embraced, adopted, fed, challenged, and loved; and I in turn, embraced, adopted, fed, challenged and loved. It has been a wonderful 11 years as we at St. Augustine's have laughed and cried together, and done our best to bring Christ present to one another, to those around us, and to a severely broken world.

This Difficult Business of Mary

But this business of Mary–this is very difficult, an obstacle, a presence I have not yet integrated into my faith. As so much of being Catholic is to me, it seems a journey, a never quite getting there, a life unfolding. Catholic faith is a wrestling match for me; I struggle with elements of doctrine, dogma, practice; I struggle with the humanity of the Church; I live in tension within the Church; as a community organizer, I work in the tension between the Church and the world. Mary is very much tied up in this. We are still growing together, and I am hardly sure I know her at all.

The first image of Mary that I encountered was Mary as Perfect Submission to God: the soaring Magnificat, the example of saying yes, no matter what God puts in front of us, a willingness to carry the Holy within us, and to give birth to Christ. This was all very lovely, and had much with which I could identify. But in practice, something seemed confused. Mary submissive to God too often seemed Mary submissive to everything, especially men–the hierarchy within the church, a male–dominated society outside the church with a consequent marginalization of intellectual and spiritual gifts. I experienced a cult of Mary, a cult which stressed only one aspect of womanhood. A cult which appreciated frilly statues of frozen reserve; clothes and crowns which would make ordinary movement impossible, a Mary removed and quiet. Even the songs-gentle woman, gentle dove, peaceful spirit, perfect love-encouraged passivity, withdrawal, and submission. And I saw countless women emulating a submissive Mary which kept them bound in quiet, in submission, saying "let it be done according to your will" when the will was not that of God, but of husbands, fathers, brothers, the Church and the State. Asked to submit to much, these women depended on a full partner in submission; they found relief and encouragement with Mary.

While not to be discounted, this approach took all the fire out of Mary. Mary must have been tough! A very young mother, pregnant out of marriage, poor . . . willing to raise the Son of God as her own son-his is not a woman in a glass case, not a woman with folded hands and downcast eyes, not a woman of silence. But this tougher Mary is not seen in the symbols and airy forms of Mary that adorn our churches. Not hardly. The symbol, rather than enlarging our understanding, reduces it. The Mary in our churches is worse than a mannequin-too perfect to touch, stiff, even cold. I am angered by the cultural translation of Mary as submission not to God, but to everything. I was not trained to submit, not to material poverty, nor to men who wished to dominate my creativity, nor to a role limited by my gender in public or private life. I found I could not accept a Mary who submits to everything; I can embrace a Mary who submits to God and nothing else. But where is she?

The Mother of God

Having failed to be able to meet Mary on the terms of some of her cultic practices, I tried to reach her as the Mother of God. This went much better. Mother was something I could relate to. My mother died about five months before I became a Catholic. If I put all of my love for my mother and all her love for me onto Mary, and thought about how Mary could carry this for the whole world-well, this connected. I began to imagine Mary as the Mighty Mother Force.

I had good experiences with Mary the Mighty Mother. When I visited the monks at Christ in the Desert Monastery in New Mexico, I was struck by their respect and honor for Mary. She provided a feminine, mothering presence for those monks, as they lived and worked in fairly rugged circumstances. But I really felt Mary as Mother last December when I visited Mexico City and went to the Plaza of Guadalupe. Thousands upon thousands of people come to see the shrine every day; the day I visited was no exception. Many came on their knees, and I watched parents carefully teaching their children, some barely old enough to walk, how to approach the shrine on their knees. Crowds of pilgrims waited on the Plaza for their turn into the shrine. The air was full of the endless chorus of La Guadalupana. Masses were said continuously, not just in the shrine, but in the chapels and churches around the central shrine. Everywhere was Mary, Mary, Mary, Mary. There were songs, paintings, key chains, pencils, T-shirts-a madly commercialized Mary that was superficially tacky, but escaped by being so full of energy and love. Everything Mary, Mary, Mary, Mary. Among the huge crowds, the longing to be where the Mother of God and stood was palpable. So many people came to see where the Mother of God had come to see them–500 years ago. It took my breath away. I had to sit down on a bench behind the old shrine, in the shade, and think. I felt the spirit of Mexico wash over me, the spiritual essence of her people. Now this, this was a mystery.

The Virgin of Guadalupe appeared to Juan Diego, an "Indian," just a few short years after the conquest of the Mexican empire by Spain. The Conquistadors brought Catholicism to Mexico, they brought Jesus to the native people, and for this we should be glad. But Spain was in the middle of the Inquisition, and the horrors of the Inquisition came to Mexico, too. In addition to the Inquisition, the Spaniards brought the system of the *encomienda*, a savage system of near slavery, where every soldier in good standing got a certain amount of land and enough Indians to work it for him. The Indians were bound to the land and to the conquistador. The Church, by and large, supported this system, and depended on its own supply of Indians. It was a rare priest who recognized the humanity of the Indians, and some of the writing at the time concerned whether or not the Indians were fully human, and therefore, whether or not they were subject to grace.

As severe as the Catholicism of the Inquisition was, it might have been a relief after the traditional practice of the empire: massive human sacrifices, particularly of young men. A religion that even had a woman and a child involved must have been attractive, particularly to the mothers who had watched their sons marched off to be slaughtered as tribute to the emperors–by the tens of thousands their beating hearts were cut out. No wonder people flocked to a sign of a gentler religion, or at least the manifestation of the possibility of gentleness. The bishops and priests were extremely antagonistic to Guadalupe, finally coming around with the miraculous appearance of roses in winter. The spirit of Guadalupe has continued for 500 years. In the old shrine, thousands upon thousands of hand painted testimonials to the intercession of the Guadalupana are exhibited. For each miracle, an artist has reproduced the circumstance–an accident, surgery, war; a stylized Guadalupana looks down on the scene, and a handwritten sentence expresses gratitude to Mary. I met the force of Mary, the mighty force of Mother Mary, at Guadalupe.

Problematic Aspects

But here at home, I again encounter several aspects of Marian devotion that are extremely problematic. I could be at Guadalupe and be full of joy, feeling Mary's loving presence all around me. But at home, we have twisted and are twisting Mary in to something far less than she is. In many parishes, there are certain types of Marian devotion which are extremely restrictive, even para-military. I have encountered Legions of Mary which are more like Thought Police of Mary. These Thought Police are doing their best to inculturate young girls into a life of submission and quiet piety, following the rules, instead of acculturating young girls to be the Mighty Mothers of us All. Priests, religious or directors of religious education who try to update or bring these restrictive practices back to center, encounter extreme resistance from women who need a submissive and controlling Mary to make sense of their lives.

The saddest part of the state of Marian devotion in the Bronx is what I call the Mary Wars. They are just beginning. Each group of immigrants brings with them a particular devotion to Mary, based on a visit by the Mother of God to their people at the height of their struggles. The Puerto Ricans have Providencia. The Dominicans, Altagracia. The Mexicans, Guadalupana. And in parish after parish, these Mary's are now at war. *Whose* statue shall have prominence? Should we have all three? Which is the *real* Mary? Is there one Mary, or three, and if one, then *whose*? This is a great tragedy and a great heresy. Certainly the retreat to the pale blue and pink will not do. How to be culturally sensitive, yet theologically aware–can you rotate these national Mary's? Multiply them? We are badly in need of a new version of Mary for the plural society we have become. The Mary Wars require great prayer and pastoral understanding.

So for me, I am aghast at Mary the Submissive, and Mary at War. For me, it has to be Mary the Mother. Mothers submit, and mothers fight, but they submit and fight selectively.

In Luke 2:33-35, Simeon pronounces an ominous blessing over the child Jesus: "This child is destined to be the downfall and the rise of many in Israel, a sign that will be opposed–and you yourself shall be pierced with a sword-so that the thoughts of many hearts may be laid bare." What must the Mother of God have thought?

What if we, today, consider this passage not Jesus, but all children? What if we place in Mary's arms, as she listens to Simeon, the little baby I saw yesterday in my neighborhood market? He was eight days old. His mother, a young Mexican woman, was looking for diapers for him. His older brother was as proud as he could be. Or what if we placed in Mary's arms, the new great grand daughter of Mama Taylor, an octogenarian pillar of St. Augustine's? A child born to an addicted mother, and the odds of escaping poverty virtually insurmountable even at the age of five months? Are not the destinies of these children to be the downfall or rise of many in the United States? How we treat the least ones will mark whether we rise or fall. How we treat our children is a sign of who we are.

Simeon said that Jesus was a sign to be opposed. What is the opposition to these, our children? A steady chorus of: get out, go home, you're worthless, you welfare cheats, where's the father, prone to violence, thrown into bad schools, a very rough world. The thoughts of our national hearts are being laid bare in how we oppose these children.

These thoughts are not the thoughts of Mary.

A New Model

We need a new model of Mary–one as connected to the children of today as Mary was to Jesus. One who can extend motherhood to all children, everywhere. Mary's task today is not to be glacially submissive to the opposition her children face. Nor is it to represent one group's children preferentially over another's.

Mary today must claim to be Mother of us All. She is the only one who can make this claim, because she gave birth to Jesus. Anyone who can birth and raise Jesus certainly has the capacity for us. Mary must take dominion like a mother takes dominion. She must offer fierce protection for her children. She must submit to God, the all powerful and the all loving, and to nothing else for the care of her children.

So this is where I am on the walk with Mary. I recognize her as Mighty Mother, and I hear her calling us to speak, not in opposition, but for her new children. This is not the Mary the world sees, and this is not the Mary seen in the Church. The non-Catholic world, the dominant culture, sees Mary as the Church has presented her-quiet, submissive, withdrawn, contemplative, passive. I'd like the other side of the real spirit of Mary to come forth from the Church again–a Mary demanding the care of her children, and a Mary, through whose common motherhood and through the brotherhood of her Son–we can somehow arrive at the right conclusion that we are indeed children of the one God, brother and sister and mother and father to one another.

It is the job of Catholics to teach the world a new model of Mary. No one else can do this. I'd like to unleash this Mary the Mighty Mother of God on all the world. Out of your crown, Mary; dress in something a bit more practical than those robes and frills. Come down and claim your children. We need you. The world won't mess with a mother.

Mary: Discussion Questions

1.) The author finds "this business of Mary" to be very difficult, "an obstacle, a presence I have not yet integrated into my faith." What do you understand as the problem?

2.) Do you think that images of Mary encourage passivity, withdrawal, and submission? Should they? What would be a better image?

3.) What do you understand to be the message of the Virgin of Guadalupe?

4.) Do you agree that the image of Mary as Mother is powerful? As you read Mary's prayer in the first chapter of Luke's Gospel, do you see her as someone with a vision of the world transformed? What does it mean to suggest that her prayer promises the reversal of fortunes (with the mighty deposed)?

5.) The author suggests that "we need a new model of Mary." Do you agree or disagree? What might that model be?

The Key To Prayer: For Further Reading

Cunneen, Sally, edited by Joanne Wyckoff. *In Search of Mary: The Woman and the Symbol.* New York: Ballantine Books, 1996.

Psychology and Religion:
Strange Bedfellows?

Stephen Maret

In the very first chapter of the Old Testament book of Ecclesiastes, the writer observes:

What has been will be again,
what has been done will be done again;
there is nothing new under the sun.
Is there anything of which one can say,
'Look! This is something new'?
It was here already, long ago;
it was here before our time (vv. 8-10).

These words, which may initially strike us as cynical and world-weary, are really quite insightful, particularly as they relate to the relationship between psychology and religion.

The field of psychology as a distinct and separate field of study is relatively young, especially when compared to philosophy and theology. While the ages of these disciplines are measured in millennia, psychology as we know it is just a little over a century old. Of course, psychology just didn't pop into existence in 1879; rather, it has been around since the beginning; since Adam and Eve were first trying to figure each other out (Adam to Eve: "What's wrong?" Eve to Adam: "Nothing!"). Psychology, however, was not considered a distinct discipline, but was simply thought to be a sub-field of theology or philosophy. We psychologists, however, tend to forget this fact and are prone to the fiction that we have discovered "something new under the sun." In fact, much of what modern psychology has discovered has already been thought of, discussed, and written about by theologians and philosophers in centuries past. Some suggest that the greatest and most insightful psychological minds in history weren't Sigmund Freud, Carl Jung or B.F. Skinner, but rather would include Solomon, Jesus, St. Augustine, Theresa of Avila and Soren Kierkegaard.

There are many examples of how theologians have anticipated psychologists. For example, Freud wrote extensively about a defense mechanism he called repression. Simply put, Freud noted that when we are faced with an emotion that we are anxious about, we repress it, and push it down into our unconscious and forget about it. This emotion, however, is not gone, but manifests itself in our behavior. John Chrysostom, a theologian from the fourth century A.D., anticipates Freud's idea of repression, particularly focusing on the emotion of anger:

> There are some, like those dogs that bite secretly, which do not bark at all at those that come near them, nor are angry, but which fawn, and display a gentle aspect; but when they catch us off our guard, will fix their teeth in us. These are the more dangerous than those that take up open enmity . . . . Dost thou not know that these conflagrations are the most destructive of all which are fed within, and appear not to those that are without? And that those wounds are the deadliest which never break out to the surface; and those fevers the worst which burn up the vitals?

When psychology as a distinct discipline did come on the scene in the latter part of the 19th century, it emerged out of philosophy and human physiology. Prior to Freud, much of psychology focused on the mechanics of human functioning, particularly sensation and perception. One characteristic which emerged with Freud was an antipathy toward religion, which religion was glad to return. This is ironic in that many early and seminal figures in psychology came from religious homes, had fathers who were ministers or themselves studied for the ministry. Freud, however, viewed religion as an extension of our infantile dependency on our parents and the source of much neuroses. It is fair to say, that with some exceptions (e.g., Carl Jung, Abraham Maslow and Victor Frankl), psychology tended to see religion as unhealthy, and far from beneficial, but rather a cause of people's psychological and emotional problems. This hostility to religion, initiated early on by Freud and others, has continued until very recently and can be readily seen in the ideas of prominent psychologists such as B.F. Skinner, Carl Rogers and Albert Ellis.

The street of hostility and suspicion was a two-way one. Many religious thinkers and leaders were skeptical and wary of psychology, in part reacting to the negative view that psychology had of religion. I remember telling my grandmother, a Baptist missionary to Africa, that I was going to study psychology. She was quite upset, and sent me a little brochure titled something like "Psychology: The Devil's Science."

This mutual hostility between psychology and religion has gradually subsided, with the initiative coming first from the religious side. Various clergy and theologians realized that psychology has much to offer in understanding the people to whom they ministered. In the 1960s and 1970s, many books were written by religious figures and pastoral counselors which appropriated psychological insights. Among them was the work of British psychiatrist Frank Lake, who saw a large gap in the training of clergy from a psychological viewpoint. Some have argued that the embrace of psychology by religious thinkers and clergy went to far, and in the process religion inadvertently imported psychological assumptions into religious practice which were at odds with a rigorous theology.

Psychology has been slower to give up its collective hostility toward religion, but has gradually come to see religion as either psychologically neutral or as even having potentially great benefit. Many studies have found that religious people tend to be happier, more emotionally healthy, less likely to use and abuse drugs, and have higher levels of marital satisfaction than nonreligious persons. For instance, one study found that non-church attenders were four times more likely to kill themselves than were people who attended church frequently. In fact, Stephen Stack at Wayne State University found that church attendance predicted suicide rates more accurately than any other variable. Thus, psychologists have gradually had to face research which, far from showing universally negative results of religious commitment and belief, show numerous psychologically positive results.

One very interesting example of the gradual evolution in the way religion is viewed by psychologists can be seen in Albert Ellis, the founder the Rational-Emotive school of thought and therapy in psychology. In 1962 and again in 1971, Ellis wrote that being religious was antithetical to being mentally healthy and that the more religious a person was, the greater the likelihood the their being emotionally disturbed. After being challenged on this statement, he gradually modified his ideas but continued to affirm that while religion per se was not necessarily problematic, religiosity was. He defined religiosity as "a devout or orthodox belief in some kind of supernatural religion which holds dogmatic, absolutistic convictions."

In 1986, two researchers, Paul Sharkey and H. Newton Maloney, asked Ellis if they could have access to the patient files at the Albert Ellis Institute for Rational-Emotive-Behavioral Therapy in New York City. They studied Ellis' own patients and found that there was no connection between strong religious belief and commitment and emotional problems; in fact, they found that atheists were the most likely to have some sort of psychopathology. While Ellis was not immediately convinced, he has gradually modified his views. In fact, he has co-written a book with a religiously-devout psychologist named Brad Johnson about religion and his therapeutic approach.

The fact that psychology and theology have historically been at odds is not surprising, partly because the scope of their endeavors overlaps to large degree. This turf has been defended on either side and is broad: both fields are concerned with growth and development, with human function and dysfunction, with helping people, with the pursuit of meaning, and ultimately with the pursuit of truth. The fact that these fields can work together and not in opposition is hugely beneficial, because we are both psychological and spiritual beings, in addition to our physical selves. A wise person observed, "all truth is God's truth," whether theological or psychological. The truth of that statement is corroborated in John's Gospel when Jesus says, "I am the way, and the truth, and the life. No one comes to the Father except through me" (14:6).

Psychology: Discussion Questions

1.) Do you think that Adam and Eve really were among the first psychologists? What does the author mean in pointing to them when suggesting that psychology has been around as long as humans?

2.) Do you agree that religious thinkers and theologians can be great psychologists? Why or why not? Can psychologists be great theologians as well? Wy or why not?

3.) Explain how Freud and John Chrysostom shared an insight about repression.

4.) What particular issues in the lives of humans are addressed by BOTH psychology and religion? Give some particular examples beyond those cited in the article.

5.) The author sees a gradual evolution in the way religion is viewed by psychologists. Why do you think that feelings and opinions have changed?

6.) Why do you think that Jesus says, "I am the way, and the truth, and the life. No one comes to the Father except through me"?

Psychology: For Further Reading

Frankl, Victor. *Man's Search for Meaning.* Boston: Beacon Press, 1946.

Jones, Stanton L. & Richard E. Butman. *Modern Psychotherapies: A Comprehensive Christian Appraisal.* Downer's Grove, IL: Intervarsity Press, 1991.

Lake, Frank. *Clinical Theology.* London: Darton, Longman & Todd, 1964.

Maret, Stephen. *The Prenatal Person.* Lanham, MD: University Press of America, 1997.

Peck, M. Scott. *The Road Less Traveled.* NY: Touchstone Books, 1978.

The Sadness of a City

William C. Graham

Though I've lived seven years in New York, I had, until recently, successfully avoided any excursion to Atlantic City. When a recent visitor arrived from the frozen midwest, however, we planned a two day trip to that ocean front hot spot on the Jersey Shore. We stayed but two hours and headed quickly back to NYC and Harlem where the plastic is not so offensive nor the sleaze so repugnant, where even rip-offs seem a bit more respectful, and the poor, while marginalized, are not mocked.

An amazing number of tour buses (10,197,884 in 1996!) filled with eager gamblers speed down the Garden State Parkway where the law suggests 55 miles an hour as the maximum. I saw troopers stop any number of cars along the way, but didn't see any buses pulled over even though I tailed a couple at speeds close to 15 mph above the limit. They are astonishing in number, those speeding buses, and carry cargo important to the economy of the casinos.

Donald Trump's Taj Mahal has a bus depot on the ground floor, just one of many spots in town where buses land, that is bigger and busier than most any bus station in a city many times the size of the relatively small Atlantic City, population 37,000. I checked on an expected bus from Caldwell in north-eastern New Jersey. Three coaches had arrived from that tiny hamlet within minutes of each other. These folks are part of the 37 million annual visitors to Atlantic City who, in 1996, dropped $39,263,075,000 in casino hotel activity. This multitude of visitors makes Atlantic City the most popular tourist destination in the United Sates.

Much is written about the sadness of Atlantic City itself, a depressingly poverty stricken place where the ocean front is given to tee-shirt shops and casinos dotting the boardwalk. I have lived for four years in Harlem and am more accustomed to the face of poverty than I want to be; I found Atlantic City's poverty distressing from another perspective. The ocean and the souvenirs are not the real draw there. The casinos are. And what a distressing and disturbing reality are they. The Taj Mahal is so far removed from any real sense of grandeur or majesty that any right thinking developer should have been embarrassed to propose it. But I can't ask who might find such a place attractive; there seem to be millions of them; in 1996, Atlantic City's hotel occupancy rate was 89.5 percent with 3,368,871 room nights filled.

The Taj Mahal Casino is on the hotel's ground level. With the boardwalk and ocean just yards away, this cavern is free of natural light. Without a watch, one wouldn't know the time, the day or even the season. There seem to be acres of gaming tables and slot machines. These machines can no longer aptly be called one-armed bandits since they are operated by the touch of a button and not a vigorous pull on a lever. The arm is gone, but the machines remain bandits. Isn't this gaming invention a true triumph of business acumen? Watch a steady procession of middle and lower income men and women willingly, fearlessly, happily, tirelessly drop coins into a slot, pushing a button to make their money disappear. Go figure.

I spent just minutes walking through the Sands Casino (looking for a bathroom, if the truth be told, though there seems slim evidence that casino operators much favor the truth). I dropped a quarter in one of the casino's slots and pushed the button. My coin disappeared in a whirl of wheels and was lost to me forever. I spent minutes more in the Taj, as they seem to call it. While there is no maharani buried there, plenty of dreams are deep-sixed daily. I lost another quarter after accidentally horning in on an older woman with dyed-black hair and silver sequins on her polyester top who had been playing two machines simultaneously. Had I won a barrage of silver coins, I would have feared her reaction.

There is an enormous crystal chandelier hanging over the Donald's casino in a mirrored, gilt framed vault. One can only imagine the horrific expense. Standing there, one of the few looking up, I felt suddenly and overwhelmingly sad for the pastors and pastoral committees who, seeking to improve worship and its environs, are greeted with angry and even self-righteous cries of "This money should be spent on the poor." Indeed, more, much more, should be spent on the poor in this post-welfare age. But what of those fortunes lost to greedy entrepreneurs a dollar or five at a time, and social security checks given over freely twenty-five cents at a time? How much of what is lost belongs, in justice, to the poor?

Paul VI, in his 1971 apostolic letter *Octogesima adveniens*, notes that "it is up to the Christian communities to analyze with objectivity the situation which is proper to their own country, to shed on it the light of the Gospel's unalterable words and to draw principles of reflection, norms of judgment and directives for action from the social teaching of the Church." Paul also observes that "If, beyond legal rules, there is really no deeper feeling of respect and service of others, then even equality before the law can serve as an alibi for flagrant discrimination, continued exploitation and actual contempt."

John the Baptist, standing to one side, calls out: "'Let the one with two coats give to the one who has none. The one who has food should do the same'" (Luke 3: 11).

A blighted Atlantic City, sporting 14 glittering casinos with plans for seven more, stands as a judgment on me and my two lost quarters, and on all of us who have dumped cash into hungry machines while the ever present poor stand hungry on the fringes.

Sadness of a City: Discussion Questions

1.) What prompts the author's observation: "I have lived for four years in Harlem and am more accustomed to the face of poverty than I want to be; I found Atlantic City's poverty distressing from another perspective."

2.) Why does the author ask: "Isn't this gaming invention a true triumph of business acumen?"

3.) Paul VI, in his 1971 apostolic letter *Octogesima adveniens*, notes that "it is up to the Christian communities to analyze with objectivity the situation which is proper to their own country, to shed on it the light of the Gospel's unalterable words and to draw principles of reflection, norms of judgment and directives for action from the social teaching of the Church." Explain.

4.) Pope Paul VI also observes that "If, beyond legal rules, there is really no deeper feeling of respect and service of others, then even equality before the law can serve as an alibi for flagrant discrimination, continued exploitation and actual contempt." How does the apply to society as you experience it?

5.) John the Baptist calls out: "'Let the one with two coats give to the one who has none. The one who has food should do the same'" (Luke 3:11). How would such an ethic change the face of the earth and the city in which you live?

6.) Why does the author suggest that a blighted Atlantic City, sporting 14 glittering casinos with plans for seven more, "stands as a judgment on me and my two lost quarters, and on all of us who have dumped cash into hungry machines while the ever present poor stand hungry on the fringes"? Do you agree?

The Last Straw:
The Earth and Religious Concern

Rose Zuzworsky

Several years ago, in his *The New York Times Magazine* article "Not So Fast," Bill McKibben put the lie to much of what "environmental optimists" have been saying. While progress is being made in eliminating some of what we see–smog, river pollution, acid rain and crowded landfills–it's what we don't (or won't) see that might do us in once and for all. What we don't or won't see is simply that "our societies and their appetites have simply grown too large."

Using medical analogies, McKibben claimed that optimists have diagnosed the world's environmental problems as indigestion curable by an antacid, while others diagnosed arteriosclerosis. The latter, McKibben claimed, means that our most basic behaviors must change.

That is both a prescient and disturbing diagnosis indeed. It is also what prompts this reflection. After a recent day spent touring a local landfill, I think I know what Bill McKibben is saying. At the landfill, I saw acres and acres of turned-over top soil covering garbage which had last been dumped there in the 1970s. In spots yet to be covered, I could see some of the remnants of our lives: dark vinyl garbage bags, shoes, some newspapers, glass bottles. I saw the huge trucks and cranes which do the hauling and lifting of the landfill material to and at the site. I saw the air-monitoring pipes and smelled the fumes which linger there.

Wearing rubber boots, I sloshed along with my colleagues–sometimes in ankle-deep mud–to walk on the completed sections of the landfill, now covered with three layers of impermeable materials. I saw workers, men and women, in full work gear, readying another section of the landfill to receive the second or third layer of covering material.

Notwithstanding the all-too-real sights before my eyes, the whole scene was surreal. First, the sheer size of a landfill is a jolt to the uninitiated–which means most of us. After all, we hurry past these sites in our cars, looking the other way as if the garbage and the smells had nothing to do with us. What most impressed me, however, was the thought that kept going through my mind, "All this for garbage! All this for garbage!"

Unable to shake the consequences of that thought, I said later to those whom I made this visit that it certainly doesn't take a great visionary to realize that unless we come to grips with our waste, we are just putting our finger in the dike.

I think this is what Bill McKibben identified so clearly in his article: It's our thinking, and our behavior born out of that thinking, that has to change if we are to make any headway with what has come to be called our environmental problems.

Which brings me to straws–the ordinary, plastic drinking straws most of us use every day. My personal crusade to change my own thinking makes me save one straw and use it over and over again. This habit forces me to think about how much of the earth's resources I use in any given day. It forces me to think about other things too: all those plastic bags we bring home from the stores and the tons of virgin paper we use for our various projects. Mostly, however, it forces me to think about convenience.

All of this was brought home to me recently during a family outing to the New York Aquarium. A sign in the cafeteria noted the non-distribution of straws there, in order to protect the animals. As I was pointing that out to my family, a funny thing happened. Going past us, away from the service counter, was a thirty-something father who had obviously just tried to get straws for his children. He walked past us shaking his head and muttering to no one in particular, "they don't serve straws!" The look on that man's face was one of incredulity. Obviously, straws have become so much a part of our lives that the thought of doing without one was strange, even bizarre.

This slice of like story, I think, depicts the difficulty of the behavior changes build into the questions with which McKibben ends his article, "How much is enough?" and "How much convenience?" How much convenience are we willing to give up if, indeed, our grown-too-large appetites have contributed to planetary arteriosclerosis? These are radical and disturbing questions, and I think about them often.

Now, where did I put that straw?

The Last Straw: Discussion Questions

1.) Explain your understanding of how Jesus's command to love our neighbors might have a bearing on caring for the natural world of God's creation.

2.) If we are to reverence the earth, how far do you think human "domination" of non-human creation–animals, marine life, birds, as well as the atmosphere, trees, bodies of water, and the earth itself–should go?

3.) If, as the American bishops claim, parents, teachers, and scientists are to be involved in furthering attention to concern for the earth, what is the church's own particular role in this endeavor? Does it differ essentially from other groups' roles?

4.) What would you add to this discussion which might convince people that reverence for the earth is a religious issue?

5.) In your own life and in your own situation, how do you show your respect for God's creation?

6.) Have you ever considered that all of creation is meaningful to God, and not just the human creation? How does Genesis' account of God's covenant with Noah as including all creation bear on your response?

7.) How might the question 'how much is enough?' qualify as a religious question?

The Last Straw: For Further Reading

The United States Catholic Conference. "Renewing the Earth: An Invitation to Reflection and Action on Environment in Light of Catholic Social Teaching." *Origins* 21 (December 12, 1991): 425-432.

Pope John Paul II. "The Ecological Crisis: A Common Responsibility." Washington, D.C.: United States Catholic Conferences Publication No. 332-9, 1989.

Flynn, Eileen P. *Cradled in Human Hands: A Textbook on Environmental Responsibility.* Kansas City, Missouri: Sheed & Ward, 1991.

Murphy, Charles M. *At Home on Earth: Foundations for a Catholic Ethic of the Environment.* New York: Crossroad, 1989.

Garascia, Anthony. "Environmental Issues in Catechesis." The Living Light 27 (Winter 1991): 123-130.

Sacred Adventure: A Conclusion

Thoreau had his eye on the rich reward of properly undertaken exploration when he observes in the Conclusion to *Walden* that "It is not worth the while to go round the world to count the cats in Zanzibar."

He writes for those who would learn to speak all languages, and to conform to the customs of all nations: "if you would travel farther than all travellers," and even "cause the Sphinx to dash her head against a stone," then "obey the precept of the old philosopher, and Explore thyself." Archbishop Anthony Bloom assures us that the God who will draw you out to where you can never return will be found in this exploration.

This ongoing study is an invitation to hear God's call, and to pick up the phone. Perhaps the issues of life, of mercy, of wickedness and repentance, of Love which knows no bounds have quickened and challenged you. Good! The point has not been to convert or indoctrinate. A consideration of the discipline of theology is an important part of a liberal education. But having read and studied this text, whether or not as a person of faith, has been an opportunity to see both the interconnectedness and the distinct features of religions in hearing and responding to God's call. If the writers gathered between these covers have intrigued and challenged, then a very good thing has begun, and we can be confident "that the one who began a good work among you will bring it to completion" (Phil. 1:6).

Concluding Discussion Questions

1.) What does Thoreau mean in writing in the Conclusion to *Walden* that "It is not worth the while to go round the world to count the cats in Zanzibar"?

2.) How will "you would travel farther than all travellers," and even "cause the Sphinx to dash her head against a stone," by obeying "the precept of the old philosopher, and Explore thyself"?

3.) Explain Archbishop Anthony Bloom's assurance that the God who will draw you out to where you can never return will be found in this exploration.

4.) Have the issues of life, of mercy, of wickedness and repentance, of Love which knows no bounds which you encountered in this text and through thought and discussion quickened and challenged you? How? So what?

5.) If the point of a theology or religious studies class is not to convert or indoctrinate, what is the point of such study?

Notes:

[1] I am indebted to the creative work of Walter Brueggemann and have adapted his definition of prophetic ministry for our purposes here. See his *The Prophetic Imagination* (Philadelphia: Fortress Press, 1978).

[2] Dores Sharpe, *Walter Rauschenbusch* (New York: Macmillan, 1942), 393.

[3] See Sharpe; also Paul Minus, *Walter Rauschenbusch, The American Reformer* (New York: Macmillan, 1988); and, Klaus Jaehn, *Rauschenbusch: The Formative Years* (Valley Forge: Jusdon Press, 1976).

[4] Minus, *American Reformer*, 50.

[5] *TSG*, 131.

[6] *CSC*, 146.

[7] Taylor Branch, *Parting the Waters: America in the King Years 1954-1963* (New York: Simon & Schuster, 1988), xii.

[8] *Freedom*, 17.

[9] Martin Luther King, Jr., "The Un-Christian Christian," *Ebony* (August 1965), 77.

[10] Branch, *Parting the Waters*, 140-141.

[11] *TSG*, 224.

[12] Elizabeth Clark and Gerbert Richardson, *Women and Religion* (San Francisco: Harper & Row, 1977), 124.

About the Contributors

William C. **Graham** is a priest of the Diocese of Duluth in Minnesota where he served for 10 years as a pastor. He is associate professor at Caldwell College in Caldwell, New Jersey, where he directs the Caldwell Pastoral Ministry Institute. He is a columnist for the *National Catholic Reporter*, and the co-author with Molly K. Stein of Paulist Press's *Catholic Wedding Book.* He is co-editor with Benedictine Fr. Timothy Backous of *Common Good, Uncommon Questions: A Primer in Moral Theology*, published by The Liturgical Press in 1996. His *Half Finished Heaven: The Social Gospel in American Literature* was published by University Press of America in 1995. Also, he has edited *More Urgent Than Usual: The Final Homilies of Mark Hollenhorst*, published by The Liturgical Press in 1995. He holds the Ph.D. from Fordham, the Jesuit University of New York City.

Martin **Carney** is a doctoral candidate at Fordham, the Jesuit University of New York City.

Franciscan Handmaid of the Most Pure Heart of Mary Sr. Joel Barbara **Clarke** is a member of a Congregation of predominantly Afro-American Sisters living and working in Harlem. She most recently worked All Saints Church in Harlem with the RCIA program, and has been a member of her community for over 40 years.

Dominic **Colonna** received his doctoral degree in systematic theology from Fordham University in 1998. He has recently taught introductory theology courses at Fordham University and Manhattan College.

Dan **Conditt** is a writer and social worker living in Long Beach, California.

Curtiss **De Mars-Johnson** is a United Church of Christ pastor in Okemos, Michigan.

Jesuit Fr. Avery **Dulles** is among the most respected theologians in the United States and a prolific author. He holds the McGinley Chair in theology at Fordham University.

Charlene **Holden** is a recent graduate of Caldwell College in Caldwell, New Jersey. She was a freshman when she wrote her essay.

Mark **Hollenhorst** was a priest of the Diocese of Duluth, Minn., until his death from cancer on Dec. 27, 1993.

Michael P. **Horan** is associate professor of Theological Studies at Loyola Marymount University, Los Angeles. His pastoral experience includes youth ministry and catechesis among high school and university students in New York and Washington, D.C.

Andrew **Krivak** is a writer who lives and teaches in Cambridge, Massachusetts.

Benedictine Fr. Michael **Kwatera** is a monk of St. John's Abbey, Collegeville, Minnesota, teaches graduate and undergraduate theology at St. John's University and serves as pastor of St. James Parish, Jacobs Prairie, Minnesota.

Stephen **Maret** is associate professor of psychology at Caldwell College where he also chairs the Psychology Department and teaches in the Pastoral Ministry Institute. He holds the Ph.D. from Drew University.

Christian Brother Mark **McVann** is professor of religious studies at Lewis University in Romeoville, Illinois. He took the Ph.D. in Theology and Literature with a specialization in New Testament from Emory University. Author of a number of articles and reviews, Br. McVann is also executive editor of *Listening: Journal of Religion and Culture*, and has lectured in several Asian countries as well as in Kenya, and has taught as guest professor at Manhattan College in New York City, Loyola University in Chicago, and Caldwell College in New Jersey.

The Rev. G. Penny **Nixon** is Special Assistant to the Dean of Students at San Francisco State University. She is a Presbyterian minister and has been a campus minister for ten years in New York City, South Africa, and San Francisco. She holds the Master of Divinity degree, and is preparing to return from a leave of absence to Fordham University as a Ph.D. candidate with a specialization in American religious history.

Alan **Revering** is a doctoral candidate at Harvard Divinity School.

Molly K. **Stein** is co-author with William C. Graham of Paulist's *The Catholic Wedding Book,* and is the director of development at The Marshall School in Duluth, Minnesota.

Lee **Stuart** is the lead organizer of South Bronx Churches, one of the affiliates of the Industrial Areas Foundation in New York City.

Mercy Sister Julia **Upton** is Professor of Theology at St. John's University in New York. She currently serves as Associate Provost for Teaching and Learning.

Johann **Vento** is a doctoral candidate at Fordham University. She works with the National Conference for Community and Justice as the director of Seminarians Interacting, an inter-religious dialogue program for future religious leaders.

Rose **Zuzworsky** is an adjunct professor at St. John's University in Jamaica, New York.

Index